VANISHED CIVILIZATIONS

© 2001 Assouline Publishing, Inc. for the present edition
First published by Editions Assouline, Paris, France

Assouline Publishing, Inc.
601 West 26th Street
18th floor
New York, NY 10001
USA

www.assouline.com

ISBN: 2 84323 246 5

Translated from the French by Charles Penwarden
Proofreading: David Ross

Printed in Italy by Arte Grafica

VANISHED CIVILIZATIONS

FROM THE ANCIENTS TO EASTER ISLAND

JEAN PAUL BARBIER

Preface
by
Jean-François Revel
of the Académie Française

ASSOULINE

"What madness, to awake ambition in our breast.
This to give us up to the Furies!"
Heinrich von Kleist

CONTENTS

PREFACE

There can be few art lovers in today's world who do not feel a special attachment and admiration for the Musée Barbier-Mueller of Geneva, Switzerland. In fact, the diversity and quality of its collections make it something other than a museum in the administrative, didactic sense of that word. Wherever one looks, one senses that here is the fruit of one, or rather several, private collections: that of its founder, Josef Mueller, in the first place, but also that of his daughter and son-in-law, Monique and Jean Paul Barbier-Mueller. In their own way, and in accordance with their own tastes, they have continued the founder's quest. Not surprisingly, the originality that lies behind the museum's creation is also evident in its exhibits. The Musée Barbier-Mueller is renowned, in particular, for its rich holding in the field of what a recent piece of linguistic contortion has dubbed the "arts premiers"—the "first" or "primary" arts. The concern to remove the pejorative associations of the old adjective "primitive" is laudable, but do we really need an adjective at all? If a Gheonga statuette and a Kavat mask are "primary" art, then what are the "secondary" arts? Praxiteles? Giorgione? Cézanne? In art, classification is always absurd because art is not about quantitative issues; it belongs to a purely qualitative sphere where each artist measures himself against the criteria of beauty that he has himself invented, and that would never have existed without him. A great work of art only satisfies those needs that it has itself inspired in the beholder.

However, if each work of art is a radically individual and unique reality, it is also true that, taken together, works engender what we call civilizations. It is the long procession of these civilizations through the ages that Jean Paul Barbier brings alive here, with a mixture of discreet stylistic mastery and learning lightly worn.

As the author humorously and modestly told me not so long ago, "I should point out that this book is an attempt to answer those same old questions that visitors to our museum are always asking." He does much more than that. In a succession of chapters that are so many limpid and carefully structured monographs, he instructs and dazzles with his disquisitions on Prehistoric Art, Cycladic Art, the Etruscans, the "Greek miracle," the Art of the Celts and of the Iberians, that of "our ancestors the Barbarians", of Egypt and the pre-Columbian civilizations of the Americas. And many more. These chapters are of inestimable value to the reader because they not only offer a synthesis of current knowledge on the subject, but also review the questions raised by the latest historical and archeological discoveries. I would add that the clarity of the discussion is backed up by the pertinence of the illustrations. Pertinence, because they are more than just impressive and relate directly to the text, each explaining and supporting the other. This precise complementarity contrasts with all those "art books" in which the function of images is often merely decorative.

"Lost Civilizations"? Why "lost"? This takes us back to the debate launched in 1918 by Oswald Spengler in his famous and hefty tome, Der Untergang des Abendlandes (The Decline of the West), and compressed by Paul Valéry in his joyous 1931 funeral oration, Regards sur le monde actuel (Considerations on Today's World): "We other civilizations now know that we are mortal." But the ranting of the German prophet and the bantering of the French poet both oversimplify the destiny of civilizations. It is societies that are mortal. Civilizations can be perpetuated and reincarnated in other societies than those that witnessed their birth. The literature of Greece and Rome, their architecture, sculpture and painting, their political and legal institutions—these have never ceased to furnish the models and bases for European and, later, American societies, from the Renaissance to the present day.

Nevertheless—and here Jean Paul Barbier is right—it is true that for many civilizations, especially those without a written literature or whose language we are unable to decipher, their art is our only means of access. How fortunate we are to have it! And how fortunate is the reader who, in these lively and learned pages, will experience that imperishable initiation.

Jean-François Revel of the Académie Française

FOREWORD

Do you see it, humanity, that great caravan crossing the desert of the centuries? Along the way, one man finds a pebble and uses it to stun an iguana dozing in the sun. Another sees a parched prairie in flames and discovers the remains of an antelope exuding a heady new smell—the smell of cooked flesh! Thus comes mastery of fire. A third weaves together a few sprigs of wicker and makes a simple basket to hold wild fruit. The same person now seeks to keep their bowl from leaking and covers it with clay, leaving it beside the family fire. The wicker burns, leaving him with the first terracotta bowl.

The caravan and the walkers stand erect. God is closer now. They can hear him. He speaks, just like his creation. Ambition and its twin sister, avarice, make their entrance on the stage of the world.

The Neanderthals collected rare crystals and shells that our Cro-Magnon ancestors would make into ornaments or use to pay for a newly slaughtered bear. The economy lays down its laws, perhaps even earlier than we would imagine. Like us, these men respected the eternal rest of their kin, whom they laid piously in tombs.

Man without metal is the ingenuous and wily builder of this temple of ingenuity from which there radiate so many needs: elegance, harmony, efficiency, maneuverability. Any idea, any attempt to follow in the paths traced by our ancestors, any victory over the indolence that governs our instincts could be greeted in this Homeric manner: "Speak, Muse, of man with his thousand tricks, whose imagination pulls forward his underlying idleness!"

Terracotta figurine from the Danube. Vinca, Serbia, 4th millennium BC. H. 6". Musée Barbier-Mueller, Geneva, Switzerland.

At the same time, it was in a world of magic and religion that the creators of the great rock paintings gave birth to genuine works of art whose beauty it would be foolish to take as accidental. We might imagine that the very sensual integration of beauty into everyday life went hand in hand with other developments: that of language, no doubt, and the fruitful obsession that revolves around the questions "Who are we? Where do we come from? Where are we going?" The answer to which was a story: myth. Here, religion became poetry. We hobble around amidst dead cities, nameless bones, obsolete divinities, trying to find out if we, too, will one day be transformed into acceptable fossils.

Moving upstream through the millennia, we are guided by all those objects that answer our incorrigible penchant for Beauty. The concept that governed the raising of the megaliths at Stonehenge is no less complex or remarkable than the one we can observe in the Parthenon, in the bizarre "palace" constructed by the Facteur Cheval or the Eiffel Tower. All these examples attest the desire to create "something different" by referring to the attempts of known or guessed predecessors, the sole condition being that those attempts should have produced felicitous or recognizable results.

As Montaigne noted, we are always "interpreters of interpreters". No invention, however ingenious, was ever created outside a civilization. Walking on the Moon, we are acting out the dreams of Jules Verne and Cyrano de Bergerac, celebrating the genius of Galileo, Parmenides and Aristarchus. By shaping "idols" representing women with broad, fruitful hips, the Neolithic inhabitants of Anatolia and the Cyclades and those who dwelled along the Danube were rendering the image of a universal fertility goddess already portrayed in the Paleolithic period.

Even when looking at crafts rather than art, we can still be certain that man's concerns at the dawn of time went beyond merely sleeping, eating and surviving. We must be guided by these other concerns as we delve into past centuries. If the men of Lascaux had been interested solely in political maneuvers to ensure the election of their favorite

Stone figure
with broad hips.
Catal Huyuk,
Anatolia.
Neolithic period.
$2^{1/2}$ x $2^{5/16}$".
Musée Barbier-
Mueller, Geneva.

to the council of elders, then we would never have heard of them. Unless, like Genghis Khan or Adolf Hitler, they spill oceans of blood, no man or woman can hope to live on in the centuries beyond without creating a real monument, whether its name is Versailles, the Illiad, Hamlet or Petrushka. Octavio Paz put it all very simply: "Art survives the societies that create it. It is the visible part of that iceberg that is every lost civilization."

THE CHILDHOOD OF HUMANITY

According to current scientific knowledge, and assuming some dramatic discovery doesn't shift the focus towards an "Asian scenario," Africa is very much the cradle of humanity. Indeed, it would remain so even if we were to find that the common ancestor of apes and of hominids really was a creature from the Far East like the siamopithecus, which purportedly lived some 35 million years ago.

According to the prevailing theory, the Rift Valley, which cuts across East Africa from Egypt to Mozambique, and which is sometimes as much as nineteen miles wide, blocked out the western winds and engendered a dry area to the east. As a result, the hominoid apes split into two groups. The first tried to stay in the forests and settled to the west of the valley. These were the pre-gorillas. The second group split again into two sub-groups: the pre-chimpanzees and (our subject here) the pre-hominids. This hypothesis, generally known as the "East Side Story," is the work of the anthropologist Yves Coppens. However, it has long been disputed by other scientists because the only proof of the absence of hominid fossils to the west of the valley lies (or lay) in the fact that none had as yet been found!

In 1995, an *Australopithecus* mandible 3.5 million years old was discovered in Chad, and another, even more eloquent find followed. The researcher Michel Brunet immediately suggested that the East Side Story be abandoned, to which Coppens replied that Abel (the name given to the *Australopithecus* in Chad) was certainly more highly evolved than his contemporary Lucy, but that he was a

Entrance to the Arago cave near Tautavel, France. This was the habitat of our distant ancestor *Homo erectus*.

descendant of immigrants who came from the east, skirting the Rift to the south before moving back up into West Africa. And that is where things stand at the time of this writing. Doubtless, given the immensity of the lands to be explored, they will change radically in the future. But for the time being we must stick with what we know. The process began ten million years ago. Four million years later, the pre-chimpanzees and pre-hominids went their separate ways. We then lose trace of the latter for two million years until they reappear, four million years ago, in the form of the *Australopithecus gracilis*, the first biped (who has not heard of the famous and diminutive Lucy?), and the *Australopithecus anamensis*, who stands more surely on his or her two feet. In fact, there were several species of *Australopithecus* roaming East Africa. The one found recently in Chad was an *Anamensis*. But it would seem that all these existing types died out after the advent of a tough new cousin some 2.5 million years ago.

Some 5'7" tall (for males), this newcomer, *Australopithecus robustus*, certainly deserved his name. His thick skull had a bony crest and his powerful arms enabled him to climb trees with ease. *Robustus* enjoyed a long life—some 1.5 million years, compared with the few hundred thousand years (at best) of us Cro-Magnon types. He thus cohabited with the first man (*Homo habilis*, who appeared not much later) and even with *Homo erectus*.

"Clever" man and "Upright" man

It was *Homo habilis*, who appeared over 2 million years ago, who crossed the "cerebral Rubicon" which, in the light of his prowess, has been set at 36.6 cubic inches of encephalic matter. *Habilis* made simple stone tools which some have been tempted to attribute to *Homo robustus* because his fossilized bones have been found in the same strata. In fact, though, it would seem that the *Australopithecus* (apes turned bipedal) did no more than use stones, as do some great apes today.

South African biface made by a *Homo erectus* 800,000 years ago. 9 x 4$^{1/2}$". McGregor Museum, Kimberley.

Man was the only creature to "perfect" his tools and, above all, to reuse them. Memory makes us human.

Habilis had no bony ridge at the top of his skull. His arms were still powerful, but he was much smaller than *Robustus*. Both had short life spans. His larynx was certainly too high for a truly articulated language, but his brain was different: Broca's and Wernicke's areas (understanding and elaboration of language) are discernable in casts of the brain. This creature therefore communicated with his fellows, though he no doubt stopped short of electoral speeches. He very probably lost his hairy fleece when he quit the forests and his skin must have been very dark in order to bear the burning sun of his homeland. Likewise, his head must have been covered with hair to protect a brain that, in some specimens, was as big as 49 cubic inches. Omnivorous but not that strong, he made do with the

carcasses left by wild beasts: he was a scavenger, not a hunter. Nor was he much of an adventurer: remains of *Habilis* have never been found outside Africa. When, not long before *Robustus*, he died out some 1.5 million years ago, the last *Archanthropus* was already stalking the earth. This was *Homo erectus*, of whose remarkably vertical posture we are informed by Gallien, the author of an excellent synthesis of his colleagues' complex studies. *Homo erectus* emerged over 2 million years ago, still in East Africa. In his case we have an almost complete skeleton, found near Lake Turkana, Kenya, in 1985. It belonged to a 12 year-old boy who was (already) 5'3" tall and died some 1.5 million years ago. *Erectus* established camps, started out with a brain of nearly 61 cubic inches and, above all, had a larynx high enough to be able to use a fairly complex language. He thought and coordinated his actions and moved around hunting for game. Allowing that in a generation of 20 years (*Erectus* was not long-lived) he would have covered no more than 30 miles or so,
then he would have traveled 6,000 miles in 200 generations, i.e., in only 4,000 years. And if we slow him to half that pace, that would still leave us 3,726 miles in 8,000 years.

According to the journal *Science* (dated May 12, 2000), the first hominids to have peopled the European continent left traces in Dmanisi (Georgia) over 1.7 million years ago. Their features show that they emigrated from Africa fairly soon after their emergence there. They were still using Oldowan tools, which suggests that their migration was prompted by biological or ecological factors (a bigger brain and body requiring more protein-rich food). They then continued to move eastwards. This *Homo ergaster* is probably the ancestor of the first known Asian human beings whose traces date back to a period of between 1.8 and 1 million years ago (Lantian, China: 1.1 million years). The colonization of western Europe is a later phenomenon.

Remarkably, some 800,000 years ago, *Erectus* had attained the same degree of adaptation in every habitat. Moreover, this ancestor of

Preceding pages: Drawing of the evolution of bipeds. From left to right, in profile: Australopithecus, Homo habilis, Homo erectus, Homo neanderthalensis and Homo sapiens.

ours was about to domesticate fire. But then this will not be the last time that man, even in his most ancient forms, surprises us!

Over the next 700,000 years, his tools changed little. *Erectus* simply perfected the Oldowan "improved stones" used by *Habilis*. Then, seeking greater efficiency and aesthetic effect, he created, among other more sophisticated tools, perfectly symmetrical, almond-shaped stone bifaces. This quest for symmetry was exclusively human (see the illustration on p. 15). This production became known as "Acheulean," for the French site of Saint-Acheul, but it was widespread in Africa too.

It is estimated that, in this period, there were only a few hundred thousand pre-Anthropians living on the planet. Forming groups of about thirty individuals, they built huts out of branches

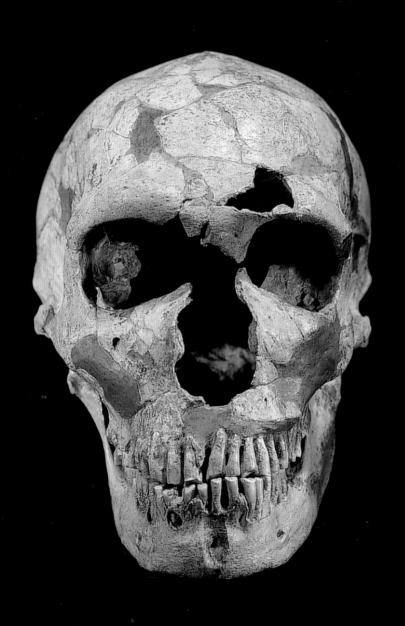

(the holes for their stakes have been found) under rocky shelters or in caves like the one at Tautavel, which has been made famous by the work of its discoverer, Henri de Lumley. After the Acheulean period came Levallois, which was remarkable for its finely worked flint tools.

Neanderthal Man: an *Erectus* who went wrong

From now on, *Erectus* evolved gradually towards *Homo sapiens*, or "Wise Man." In Europe, he gave rise to *Homo neandertalensis*, the famous Neanderthal Man or Neandertal, while in Asia and Africa other groups developed from *Erectus* that were fairly similar to the Neanderthals. These men spoke well, made fires, produced highly refined tools (still carved from stone) and manifested religious notions (they made tombs for their dead). But while they prefigure *Homo sapiens*, they are classified in a different category. In a word, this fine talking and pious *Erectus* had missed the evolutionary train: he is not one of the family. Besides, he was soon extinct.

Multicolored modern man

Having appeared (yet again!) in Africa, our true ancestors settled in Palestine some 80,000 years ago. There these proto-Cro-Magnon soon encountered the Neanderthals, who had fled the beginnings of the Würm glacial period in Europe. Traces of Neanderthal Man have been found all the way to the Caucuses. That was as far as they went.

Some 40,000 years ago, the Cro-Magnon, the true *Homo sapiens sapiens* (wise and clever man) reached Europe. There they found the Neanderthals, and it was thought that they eliminated them. It is more likely, however, that the Neanderthals were doomed to extinction because of their low population.

Still, one might imagine that there was interbreeding between the two species. Serious anthropologists have suggested that the beetle brow, sloping forehead and prognathous jaw of certain of our contemporaries (whatever their color) might

Preceding pages: Skulls of Neanderthal Man (left) and Cro-Magnon Man (right). Musée de l'Homme, Paris, France.

Opposite: The *Lespugue Venus* may be the world's oldest work of art (circa 25,000 BC). H. 5$^{5/16}$". Musée de l'Homme, Paris.

be a reminder of Neanderthal ancestors. The hypothesis is intriguing, if not "politically correct"!

Anyway, this is the point we have reached. On this planet there is now only one kind of human, and it is safer to take a transfusion from a Pygmy from the same blood group than from a neighbor who belongs to a different one. And while on the subject of Pygmies, some specialists hold that they were the first *Sapiens* in Africa. Whether whites from Europe, blacks from Africa or Australia, all these *Sapiens* shared the same passions. They painted fine images of animals and men on rocks. In Africa, the oldest images go back over 27,000 years. Cave paintings in Lascaux (France) and Altamira (Spain) are more recent, but Chauvet's cave has won the seniority trophy back for Europe. Although surely not for long.

Note that for the Americas, Australia and Africa, the age of rock art has been prolonged. Sometimes, the "Stone Age" continues into the present. But either way, African rock painting has given us some fine

Painting in the
Songo shelter
in Dogon country,
Mali, in 1999.
The rocks are
regularly repainted.

masterpieces: witness the big "Coldstream Stone" made by the San (Bushmen) and contemporaneous with the birth of Jesus Christ.

The men who painted on rocks also created sculptures as the focus for their religious belief or instruments of religious practice.

We have preserved "Paleolithic Venuses" from the Cro-Magnon era in stone, ivory and bone (see the photograph of the *Lespugue Venus*, p. 23), while all wooden Paleolithic objects have been lost.

Still, we know a lot more about the Neolithic period, which witnessed several of the civilizations presented in the following chapters.

Let us conclude this short survey with two remarks. Firstly, nowadays, the use of amulets conducive to the fertility of women and fields would prompt someone to write a big book on the subject.

As for the tradition of huge rock frescoes, it is perpetuated by certain "archaic" groups in Australia and Africa, such as the Dogon in Mali. But what this activity manifests is not some prehistoric hangover, but the spontaneous and unpredictable impulse to express the ineffable and the sacred in the most theatrical way possible.

THE ART OF THE CYCLADES

That ring of Greek islands, the Cyclades, enchants all those travelers who, like Ulysses, sail from creek to creek, from black sand to white beach, on the limpid waves of the Aegean Sea. The fortunate modern seafarer will be mindful that 5,000 years ago these same islands brought forth some remarkable marble sculptures that are close to the sensibility of our own modern art.

In around 4800 BC, small, crudely made idol figures began to appear in the Cyclades, usually shaped like a violin. This one, in marble, is nearly 2,000 years more recent and is the most perfect specimen from a small group to have survived the ravages of time. It was chosen for the poster advertising the only major exhibition devoted to Cycladic art, at the Badisches Landsmuseum in Karlsruhe, Germany, in 1976. It dates from circa 3000 BC, the earliest of the great epochs of Greek island art. H. 7¹/₈″. Musée Barbier-Mueller, Geneva. Acquired circa 1920. Formerly Jouvenel collection.

Towards 7000 BC, the shores of the Aegean were in the middle of the Neolithic period. The inhabitants of this part of the eastern Mediterranean lived by hunting and gathering wild berries and fruit. Man was about to become a farmer. Among his tools of hewn and smoothed stone we note blades of obsidian, a sharp-edged, glassy black volcanic rock that was still being used very recently by certain primitive peoples of the South Pacific. Surprisingly, though, recent research has shown that the obsidian found on continental Greece came from Melos, one of the Cycladic islands. Our hunters and gatherers therefore had boats capable of bold voyages across the sea. The interest of this discovery goes beyond archeology: it bears witness to the oldest known maritime activities, some 5,000 years before the invention of metalworking.

The dawn of Cycladic civilization

Coming forward 2,000 years, we find traces of human habitation in the area of Melos, on the islet of Saliagos, close by Antiparos. Traces of this "Saliagos culture" were found on Mykonos and Melos

as well. These fishing people also grew cereals and raised sheep and pigs, living in a way that is comparable to that of today's islanders. Makers of pottery, still without metal tools, these precursors used sand and pumice stones to polish marble and make containers and, already, small idols whose form is that of a simplified human figure rather like a violin. These represented women with broad hips, a symbol of fertility. Cycladic art was born!

The bright ring of Greek islands

Anyone who has sailed the Aegean in a small boat is sure to have wonderful memories. Like small, immaculately white cubes, constantly repainted houses huddle together on the sun-scorched hills strewn with sparse scrub. Everywhere sheer cliffs drop into the limpid water rippled by the "meltemi," the north wind. In Greek *kuklos* means "circle." It is in the words cycle and Cyclades—islands arranged in a circle. After the culture of Saliagos came that of Kephala, named for a necropolis on the island of Keos. Some thousand years more recent, it reveals that metalworking had begun to be known in around 3600 BC. No doubt this skill was imported from the continent, today's Greece, where beads of copper dating from the 5th millennium BC have been found in Macedonian graves. However, it was only in around 3200 BC that the inhabitants of the Cyclades distinguished themselves from their Greek and Turkish cousins. It was now that large quantities of vases, goblets and marble idols began to be produced. Thus, in a slow evolutionary process lasting over ten centuries, the objects that we admire today were created. Their function remains a mystery because we have no written documents from the period.

Following pages: The sun breaks through the sky over Naxos, lighting the bay at Grotta, seen from Aplomata, the richest necropolis for Early Cycladic II art.

From the Stone Age to the Bronze Age

At the end of the 4th millennium BC, which saw the appearance of the first violin-shaped idols cut from marble, their makers and users lived in modest villages. These initially consisted of wooden shacks, then of huts with walls of uncut stone and mortar. The partitions were thin, which implies that the roofs were light and thatched. The floor of these modest homes built at the same time as the pyramids of Egypt was of hard-packed earth, occasionally covered with slabs of stone.

A number of these marble figures were found in houses (were these studios turning out such objects, or was there a domestic idol cult?), but the sculptures held today by museums and fortunate private collectors all came from tombs. Cemeteries were located close to the villages, on the slope of the low hills. The tombs were vaults bounded by slabs (later, proper funerary chambers were dug into the rock). The oldest tombs are individual. Only after a few centuries did they become collective, when they were reused to bury the dead of the next generation.

Only rich tombs, housing the remains of a person of high rank, contained objects in marble (vases, bowls, statuettes and goblets). In one tomb, seven marble figurines were found; another (whose description goes back to the 19th century) yielded two statuettes of harp players accompanying two female "idols;" All these sculptures were found next to obsidian tools made in the Early Cycladic period. Then, in the first half of the 3rd millennium BC, bronze made its entrance and in the vaults were placed locally fashioned metal weapons and ornaments.

Although this period saw the islanders further develop the knowledge acquired by the navigators of the stone age, and although we have proof of trading links with continental Greece, Crete and the eastern Mediterranean, there seems to have been no attempt to find or import gold. Only one find has been recorded. All that has been discovered are a few small objects and ornaments in silver, as well as a few bowls made in the same metal, in tombs from the 3rd millennium BC.

Fishermen, farmers, wine-makers and, soon, possessors of the olive tree, which has been so intimately intertwined with the Hellenic

way of life in all ages, the only thing that distinguished the inhabitants of the Cyclades from their contemporaries in Western Europe or along the Danube was their massive output of these masterpieces, of these matchless plastic achievements that are the marble idols.

The idols of the Cyclades

It is a cliché to say that primitive peoples had no notion of art as art. And indeed, the religious or practical objects that they made were above all functional, and their beauty was inseparable from their effectiveness as objects.

However, we have no reason to believe that the inhabitants of the Cyclades at the end of the Neolithic period—no more, say, than the Papuans a hundred or more years ago—were indifferent to the formal perfection of the objects with which they furnished their world.

We had to wait until the 20th century to realize that "savage" ethnic cultures were worthy of comparison with the great civilizations.

Today, if we can admire a Cycladic violin-idol in the same way as a statue by 5th century BC Greek sculptor Praxiteles, that is because we have learned to see.

The variety of models of marble vases found in the Cyclades attests a constant concern to innovate and improve, to find satisfying plastic rhythms, to achieve an aesthetically pleasing equilibrium.

The question now is whether all this work was directed towards the creation of funerary objects, or whether these objects were for everyday use and then expected to accompany the deceased on his or her last journey.

Marble statuettes showing the evolution of these sculptures used mainly for funerary purposes throughout the 3d millennium (see table, p. 43). H. 10″ and 10¹ᐟ²″. Musée Barbier-Mueller, Geneva.

Everyday objects or funerary objects?

It is possible that during the first period (known as Early Cycladic I) statuettes would have been used for a domestic cult, albeit one about which we know nothing, while vases would have served as containers for ritual libations. Some of the latter, such as the globular vases with stems, had suspension lugs and may have served as oil lamps.

Many of the figures from this period bear marks of restoration (which are sometimes clearly visible), with holes through which a broken leg or head was tied back on. These repairs tend to indicate that the objects were much used but also precious enough to warrant fixing a limb that had snapped off in a domestic accident.

Of course, it could be argued that the sculptor, working with fragile material, had simply repaired an object he was making for the tomb of some distinguished figure. Only further archeological research can tell us whether these idols were objects of a domestic cult or were used in the shrines for which a certain amount of material evidence has now come to light. Such research would have provided useful information about their identity. As things stand, however, opinions diverge. Some consider the figures as effigies of divinities made to watch over the dead, others as new representations of a great goddess, the mother of all earthly fertility, whose cult emerged with the very buxom Aurignacian Venuses some 25,000 years earlier (see illustration p. 23). For others, finally, they are portraits of the deceased, substitutes for the body shucked off in death.

However, only 5% of the known figures are male. This very low proportion sits uncomfortably with the idea that effigies of male gods were placed in men's tombs and those of goddesses in women's. And it is equally at odds with the theory according to which these "idols" were portraits of the dead.

One things is just about certain: the production of figurines increased dramatically in the second period (known as Early Cycladic II), and this time the lack of repairs suggests that their function was indeed strictly funerary.

By now, the style of the statuettes is well defined. The only feature carved on the face is the nose. The arms are placed folded one above the other (and not crossing) under the chest, and the feet point outwards from the legs in a way that indicates they were not intended to stand, but rather to be laid horizontally in the burial vault.

The sculptors of this period were also ambitious: some of the marble

Statuette of a harpist. This is one of only half a dozen works showing the art of the Cycladic sculptures at its most sophisticated apogee. Badisches Landsmuseum, Karlsruhe.

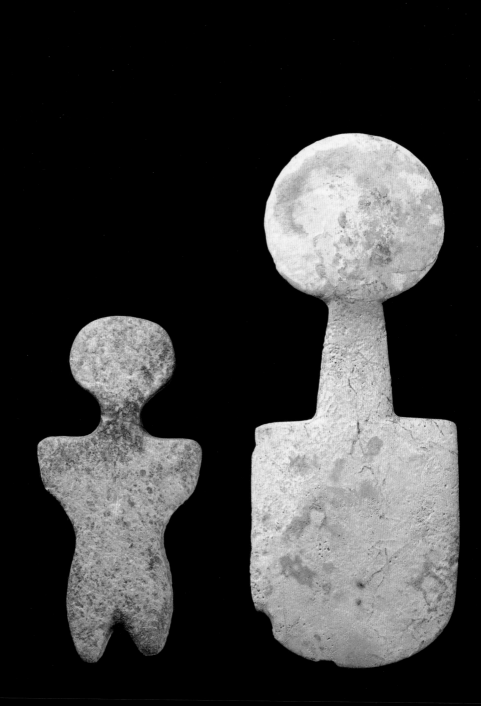

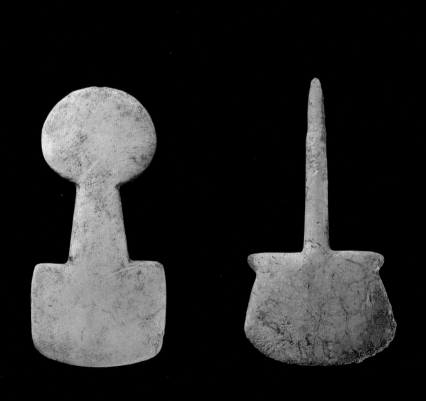

statues were so big that they had to broken so they could fit in
the tomb! The biggest known piece, at the National Archeological
Museum in Athens, is nearly five feet tall! One might assume that
if the sculptures were so big they were made for daily, religious use,
but unfortunately we have no evidence to support such an idea.
Over the last few decades there has been a growing interest in
Cycladic art and the sculptures and various objects found on the
islands, often by illicit excavators, have been listed and classified.
However, they remain shrouded in mystery. Displayed in their glass
cases, these idols with their unseeing faces can be admired all
the more freely because there are no academic arguments
to distract the beholder.

Preceding pages: Considerable quantities of "idols" of more recent origin
(2nd millennium BC) than the Cycladic "violin" sculptures have been found
on the coast of Asia Minor, and for quite a distance inland. The material (marble)
and function (funerary) are the same. These figurines found outside the
geographical perimeter of the Cyclades are distinguished by their rounded heads
or, if they have none, pointed necks. Terracotta pieces were also found.
H. (left to right): 5", 7$^{9/16}$", 4" and 4$^{1/4}$".
Musée Barbier-Mueller, Geneva.
Opposite: At Kolimbithres, near Plastiras, the sea and wind have combined
to produce surprising natural sculptures. Who knows, perhaps
these monuments stimulated the imagination of Cycladic sculptors and potters?

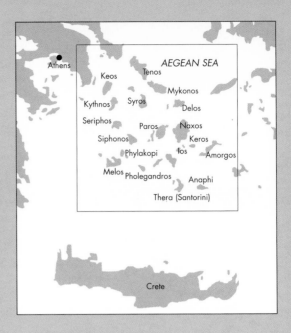

The Cyclades

Seafarers to metalworkers

"Early Bronze Age," the name sometimes applied to the first phase of Cycladic civilization, is deceptive. For while small quantities of metal were certainly used there to make ornaments and axes, the vast majority of tools and weapons were in stone. It is only in the tombs of the second, "Keros-Syros" phase, or Early Cycladic II, that we find large quantities of silver and bronze jewels, and that axes and daggers are increasingly replaced by swords. Whether for jewelry or cast and wrought metal objects, the forms and techniques were borrowed from Asia Minor and Crete rather than the Greek mainland. Axes were cast in open molds or in molds comprising two interlocking parts. The "lost wax" process was rarely used, even though it had been known in Crete since the beginning of the Bronze Age. So far, no farming tools have been discovered, but many weapons, tools and fishhooks have been found. We also know that the early inhabitants of the Cyclades cared about their looks as they left many toilet items, including tweezers.

Opposite: Table showing the chronology of the idols.

CYCLADES	END OF NEOLITHIC	ANATOLIA ASIA MINOR (TURKEY)

3200 BC

EARLY CYCLADIC I
ANCIENT BRONZE AGE I

2800 BC

EARLY CYCLADIC II
EARLY BRONZE AGE II

2400-2300 BC

EARLY CYCLADIC III
EARLY BRONZE AGE III

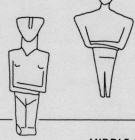

2200-2000 BC

MIDDLE CYCLADIC
MIDDLE BRONZE AGE

THE GREEK MIRACLE
from the origins to the Archaic period

We are all Greeks! The thought must have occurred to anyone who
has ever read or translated the writers of antiquity in high school.
And yet we cannot gauge the nature and importance of this heritage,
which lives on in the sculptures of a Maillol or in modern dramatic
reworkings of the Antigone myth by such as Anouilh, without taking
a closer look at the different Greek civilizations. Thus we will see
that the artists commissioned by Pericles in the 5th century BC
were steeped in a tradition in which the Hellenic element had
undergone numerous inflections due to the influences circulating
on Mediterranean trade routes.

King Minos was not Greek

Thanks to Herodotus, we all know about Crete and its Minoan
civilization, named for the legendary King Minos (though in fact the
name was more likely a generic title: Crete had its minos as Egypt had
its pharaoh).

For over a thousand years, superb palaces such as the one at Knossos
were filled with the treasures brought back by Cretan sailors from the
vassal lands of the Cyclades and continental Greece, or from Egypt
and other Mediterranean shores.

Circa 1750 BC, the
small kingdoms of
Crete were unified.
Their sovereign
reigned from
Knossos. Here, the
palace as restored
by archeologists.
Photo by
the author.

Among the Minoan ruins and tombs were found gold dishes, precious
objects in ivory and silver and delicate ceramics, along with mysterious
hieroglyphs. These riches were mentioned by Homer in *The Odyssey*:
"A land as fair as it is rich is the land of Crete, abundantly peopled,
with its ninety cities."

All this splendor and refinement seem synonymous with the glories of that Ancient Greece to which, ever since Roman times, we poor descendants of the Germanic, Alpine barbarians, or of Ligurian shepherds, have been in such admiring thrall.

And yet neither the Cyclades nor Minoan Crete were Greek. The civilizations that flourished there were built by men whose race and language we cannot name, but who were certainly no more Greek than their Sumerian, Babylonian or Egyptian contemporaries. It would seem that their language was not Indo-European and was closer to that of the Hittites in Turkey, who were beginning to establish themselves as a trading power in the first half of the second millennium BC—when the Minoan kingdom was at its glittering apogee.

The Achaeans: the "first Greeks"

The true ancestors of the Greeks came from the steppe of Southern Russia some time around the beginning of the second millennium. A few centuries later, they founded the famous cities of Mycenae, Tiryns and Pylos. Their civilization is known as the Mycenaean, after the first of these towns.

At first, these monarchic cities submitted to the authority of the powerful Minos in Crete. There must certainly have been trade between the mainland and the great island. But when a devastating earthquake destabilized Crete, did these newcomers, whom we name Achaeans, seize the opportunity to assert a new balance of power that was to their advantage? We know, in any case, that by some time around 1400 BC Crete was under Achaean domination.

This is the period of the tablets (commercial records or transactions) bearing inscriptions written in a new script known as "Linear B," of which large quantities were found both in Crete and in the sites of

Below: One of the gold funerary masks found by Schliemann in the royal tombs at Mycenae (c. 1500 BC). The German archeologist thought he had "looked upon the face of Agamemnon" but the person represented here lived several centuries before the Trojan War. National Archeological Museum, Athens, Greece.

Opposite page: This small bronze group (c. 750 BC) is considered the first purely Greek artistic masterpiece now known. The Metropolitan Museum of Art, New York, USA.

Mycenae and Pylos. We could easily have assumed that this script was used to convey messages in the Cretan language, had it not occurred to a young English architect, Michael Ventris, at the age of 22, that these inscriptions could be deciphered using the vocabulary of certain Greek dialects. In 1952, not long before his premature death, Ventris was able to prove the validity of his intuition. The syllabic signs on the Linear B tablets rendered an Indo-European language that was fairly close to Akkado-Cypriot. The Achaeans, those celebrated heroes of Homer's epics, were thus, historically, the first Greeks. Or at least, the first Greeks known to us today, since the other scripts found in Crete (hieroglyphs and Linear A) have yet to be deciphered.

The Dorian invasion

The Mycenaean civilization was less long-lived than the Minoan. A few hundred years after the conquest of Crete, at the beginning of the Iron Age, the Achaeans were harried by bands from Thessaly and Macedonia. In the history of Indo-European peoples, it is a notable fact

Below:
The Lion Gate is all that remains of the splendor of Mycenae.

Opposite page:
This tablet (with inscriptions in Linear B) is from the period when Crete was occupied by the Achaeans, who destroyed Minoan power. Deciphering has shown that it represents a Greek dialect. National Archeological Museum, Athens.

that destructive migratory movements often go from north to south, the Nazi campaign of 1939 being only the most recent *"Drang nach Süd"* ("Drive to the South")!

The newcomers were called the Dorians. They spoke a Greek idiom and justified their territorial claims by saying that they were the descendants of Heracles. According to these "Heraclid brothers," their ancestors had been driven out by the Achaeans, and it was now time for the latter to expiate their depredations.

Some of the Achaean towns were simply wiped off the map. Tiryns would never be inhabited again, and ancient historians imagined its walls to be the work of the

This bronze griffin protome with a bluish-green patina was cast using the lost wax process. It comes from the Peloponnese or Samos. 610-600 BC. 6⁵/₈". Musée Barbier-Mueller, Geneva.

Preceding pages: Thematically, this Archaic bronze sphinx is a Greek borrowing from the Near East, where such monsters were commonly represented. It may be from the Cyclades, the natural bridge between Asia and Greece. Late 6th century BC. 5¹/₂". Musée Barbier-Mueller, Geneva.

Cyclops. Meanwhile, other sites such as Athens gained a reputation as the refuge of the old traditions, bastions against the cultural dumbing-down brought on by the Dorians. Driven out by the invaders, the inhabitants of the Mycenaean cities head towards Attica and, across the Aegean, to Ionia on the coast of Asia Minor. A strong rivalry grew up between the Ionian and Dorian traditions, of which the disastrous war between Athens (considered to be Ionian) and Sparta (a bastion of the Dorian Peloponnese) was one manifestation.

The settlement by the Dorians was followed by "dark" centuries which are similar to our own Early Middle Ages. This period lasted roughly from the 12th to the 9th century BC. The Achaean traditions, with their Oriental and Cretan influences, were largely obliterated. This really was a "new beginning."

Gradually, innovations were made. The central area of the Mycenaean palaces was the *megaron*, a meeting area with an outlying courtyard and surrounded by other rooms. The Dorians used this space for religious purposes and, in what was either a deliberate or unconscious throwback to Minoan architecture, added a small portico with columns to this element when building their first temples. The stone sanctuaries built in the 6th century BC make this process of adaptation very clear, and it is still very manifest in the Athenian Treasury at Delphi, built in the early 5th century BC. In the sacred buildings of the Archaic period, wooden images (*xoana*) and bronze or terra cotta statuettes were dedicated to the cult of divinities that, in Mycenaean and Minoan art, had been symbolized by simple pillars or double axes, or perhaps animal attributes.

The great temples of the 6th and 5th centuries, which are still standing in Sicily, Paestum and on the acropolis in Athens, were all derived from the pre-Hellenic *megaron*. Its interior was divided up into several rooms while its front and back facades were adorned with columns and, in the so-called "peripteral" temples, as epitomized by the superb Parthenon (see photo p. 71), surrounded with columns.

Finally, the "proto-Geometric" pottery that began to develop in the 9th century BC was decorated with concentric circles until these gave way to Greek keys and meanders.

The Archaic period

Sculpture and bronze casting (of small pieces) did not emerge until the 8th century BC, which saw a real renaissance of the arts (sculpture, painting, literature). The "dark centuries" were over, even if there are certain parallels between Doric art and Hallstatt culture (the first Iron Age) in the Alps and Villanovan culture in northern Italy. A whole lexicon of figures with religious and magical connotations was deployed. This was essentially geometrical but also included sacred animals.

The Greek alphabet

The fragment reproduced here comes from the island of Thera (Santorini) and dates from the second half of the 7th century BC. It shows that little importance was attached to the direction (right to left or left to right) in which the inscription was read.

The list here features five names. The one at the top (REKSANOR) reads from right to left. This is confirmed if we look at the first, pennant-shaped character corresponding to the letter R. The same character reappears on the second line, except that the "pennant" is now pointing rightwards. This line therefore reads from left to right: ARKHAGETAS. The third name reads in the same direction: PROKLES. And so on.

The Phoenician alphabet, which comprises a mixture of 22 signs and sounds, must have been adapted by Greek traders who sailed to the coasts of today's Libya and Syria in around 770-750 BC. There was, for example, a Greek trading post at Al Mina.

The alphabet was used essentially for trade and politics and not for transcribing the literary works of the great Greek poets. It was not until the 6th century BC that the Athenian tyrant Pisistratus had the Homeric epics put into written form.

The ancient historians set the beginnings of Greek history in the year 776 BC, date of the first Olympiad. The centuries that followed, known as the Archaic period, were rich in events: monarchies were replaced by aristocratic governments or tyrants, use of an alphabet based on the Phoenician model became increasingly widespread (see preceding double page), maritime trade developed apace and, above all, colonies were established in Sicily and Italy, as well as in the western Mediterranean. Finally, we should remember that the 9th or 8th century BC witnessed one of the greatest geniuses of all time, Homer, who related the siege and destruction of Troy by the Achaean heroes, and that his verses were sung by generation after generation.

The visual arts in the Archaic period

As we have seen, early Archaic Greek art was very much the reflection of Iron Age Europe in general. It owed nothing to the brilliant achievements of the Mycenaeans, which it either excluded or forgot. The little bronze animals, particularly horses, of which large quantities were found at Olympia, the oldest dating back to the 8th century, are similar to pieces found in central Europe. Similarly, the fibulae consisting of a double spiral of thick bronze thread were common not only in Greece but also on the Danube and in northern Italy.

The 6th century BC saw a return of the Oriental influence that had been so widespread in the Bronze Age but forgotten since. This was due to close trading links with the Near East, either directly or via Cyprus, which had been settled by refugees from the Dorian invasion. There was a proliferation of fantastic animals such as griffins (see p. 52) and sphinxes (p. 50-51) which had been a part of Oriental mythology since the most remote past and had been depicted in Crete a thousand years earlier. While there was no large-scale statuary in the 8th century, its potters worked wonders. From the painted decoration on certain huge pieces of Dipylon pottery, whose geometrical style is named for a cemetery in Athens, we can gain an idea of the funerary ceremonies organized to establish the social standing of the deceased in the "world of the dead." By the end of the Archaic period these feasts had become so extravagant, and the sums spent on funerary goods so great, that the legislators of several towns decreed sumptuary laws limiting the number of pieces of fabric and pottery that could be put in tombs.

Large-scale marble statuary made its appearance in the first half of the 7th century BC, during a period of intensive trading relations with Egypt. This was also the time when the Egyptian pharaoh Psammetichus I (664-610 BC) recruited large numbers of Greek mercenaries. The famous *kouroi*, those early Greek statues of naked men, have the stiff realism of pharaonic representations, from which they have indeed taken a

The cemetery at Dipylon yielded a number of giant Geometric style ceramics like the one here (8th century BC). Staatliche Antikensammlungen und Glyptothek, Munich, Germany.

vestiges of Archaic temples show that these buildings already had colonnades, but in wood. It was during the 6th century BC that architects started to use durable, noble materials: calcareous tufa covered with stucco (the Temple of Concord at Agrigento, for example) or marble (the many temples built on the Acropolis in "the century of Pericles").

The first two big Ionic temples built in the 6th century BC would inspire countless others over the coming centuries. They were the Temple of Hera at Samos, built by Rhoikos and Theodoros in 570, and, at the same date, the first Temple of Artemis at Ephesus, which Theodoros built with the aid of his Cretan colleagues Chersiphron and Metagenes. These highly decorated Ionic sanctuaries stood in contrast to the severity of Doric constructions.

The Doric style developed in the Peloponnese, and may well have been an adaptation of the Mycenaean colonnade, which was itself influenced

by Crete. Towards the end of the 7th century BC, the columns were in wood with stone capitals. Within a few decades the golden rules for temple building had been laid down as embodied in the huge tufa and marble constructions still to be seen in southern Italy and Sicily. The fluted, cylindrical columns of the Doric order supported friezes in which triglyphs alternated with metopes, the square spaces between the triglyphs which were decorated with paintings terracotta panels or panels of carved stone. In contrast, the more slender Ionic columns ended in a capital with

two volutes and, rather than alternate metopes and triglyphs, the frieze above them was continuous.

As for the third order, the Corinthian, it is sometimes wrongly assumed to be a much later addition. While its capitals decorated with acanthus leaves may not date back to the Archaic period, as the Doric ones do, we nevertheless find a single Corinthian column placed in the middle of a wall facing the entrance of the Ionic temple built in around 420 BC by Ictinos, the famous architect of the Parthenon, at Bassai in the mountains of Arcadia. It is thought that the acanthus leaf decorative scheme, which can also be found on silver and gold objects, was invented by Callimachus, a renowned caster working in Athens towards the end of the 5th century BC.

number of features: a purely frontal perspective, arms held at the sides with clenched fists and one leg forward to suggest a movement that the rigidity of the work as a whole is unable to express.

Beyond the superficial Egyptian influences, though, these monumental statues were undeniably Greek, a continuation of the tradition manifest in the small, purely Dorian "geometric" sculptures. French art critic Elie Faure has written that "with the Dorian Apollo, Greece moves from primitive art to archaism in the strict sense [...] The Peloponnese becomes the great nursery of Archaic marble-workers. Sparta, citadel of the Dorian ideal, becomes the center of Greek thought, before Athens. But Hellenism will be unable to find nourishment there. Sparta is far from the routes of the Old World, imprisoned in a lonely valley [...] Whereas Athens is, on the contrary, at the center of the eastern Mediterranean and close to the sea. It is the meeting point of the positive, disciplined Dorian element and the Ionian element which, through the filter of the islands, brings the artistic spirit of Asia, made supple and subtle by the habit of trade, diplomacy and smuggling."

The role of the artist in Archaic Greece

This marble statue, bigger than life-size, is one of the oldest of its kind (580 BC). These youthful figures (*kouroi*) are nowadays recognized as portraits of heroes, since only gods and heroes could be depicted in images. We may note a certain Egyptian influence here in the position of the arms, the clenched fists and advanced leg, which mark a change to the old Doric traditions. The Metropolitan Museum of Art, New York.

Nowhere else did sculptors, potters and casters manifest such determination and pride in producing a personal body of work. Whether they were Maya or Assyrian, other ancient artists worked anonymously (like tribal artists), for the glory of their leaders or gods (even if we do know the names of a few Egyptian sculptors who, like the scribes, were public servants). Here, for the first time in history, the artist felt superior to his fellow men, while his work continued to express a mixture of religious feeling and magic. Potters and painters (and sometimes both) proudly put their names to fine ceramics representing the divinities and heroes sung by Homer. Euphronios, the greatest painter of terracotta vases in the late 6th century BC, enjoyed such prestige that his colleagues measured their prowess against his. Thus Euthymides (whose amphora is kept in Munich) boasted that he

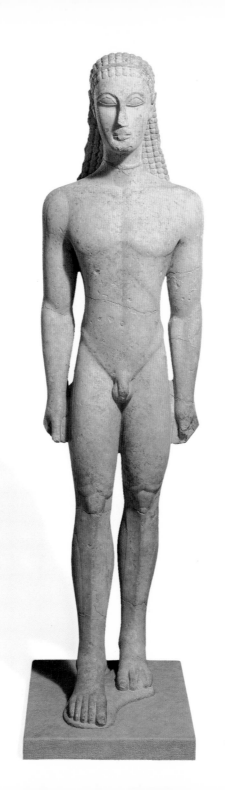

had made a piece "unlike anything Euphronios has ever done!"

The poets, we hardly need to recall, became immortals. A Terpander or a Hesiod were praised to the skies well before their verses were put in writing.

Architects, too, were well considered. Nobody remembers who designed the hanging gardens of Babylon, but the historians of antiquity knew very well that the great Temple of Hera on Samos was the work of Rhoikos and Theodoros. Here, admittedly, we have reached the last phase of the Archaic period: circa 570 BC. This was when the sculptor Achermos engraved his name in human memory by virtue of his outstanding talent.

The end of the Archaic period

The second half of the 6th century BC thus saw the Archaic period come to an end in an extraordinary burst of creativity. As well as small, vivid figurines (like the famous figurine of a man reclining at a feast, or Banqueter, now at the British Museum in London: see p. 64-65), mirror handles, toilet articles and metal vases, including some huge pieces with separately cast and riveted decorations and handles (this was the technique used for the superb krater found at Vix, in a Celtic tomb: see opposite page), the bronzeworkers now also made monumental statues, the oldest of which is a life-size bronze kouros dating from circa 530 BC and found in Piraeus in 1959. The period when the "tyrant" Pisistratus held power in Athens (560-527 BC) was a happy and fertile one indeed, and seems to point the way to the "century of Pericles." The date 530 BC is also given as the—naturally, somewhat approximate—point at which the "red-figure" vase-painting technique was invented and replaced the "black-figure" style that had been favored since the 7th century BC. Both types have left us many masterpieces. The painter Kleitias was the author of the François Vase (circa 570 BC)

Below:
The Orientalizing style of Corinthian pottery (early 6th century BC) was soon replaced by black-figure vases of Attica. H. 4$^{1/4}$"; D. 5$^{1/2}$". Musée Barbier-Mueller, Geneva.

Opposite page:
This huge bronze krater, which was no doubt cast in several parts in Magna Grecia (southern Italy), was found under a funeral mound in Vix, Burgundy, where it was placed in a chariot in the tomb of a Celt princess. H. 5'3". Late 6th century BC. Musée de Châtillon-sur-Seine, France.

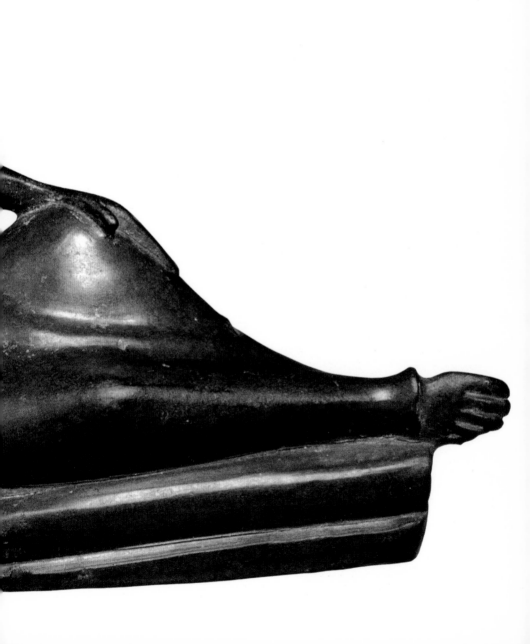

decorated with narrative scenes describing the adventures of mythological heroes. Such themes gradually replaced the animal friezes painted in Corinth under Oriental influence, making Athens the "capital" of black-figure vases and bowl making. After Kleitias, Ergotinos and Lydos, the "Painter of Amasis," came the great Exekias, who produced pottery for the table alive with characters from Homeric epics and full of an elegance and realism that was utterly new.

We are only twenty years from the construction of the Temple of Zeus at Olympia, which marked the transition from Archaism to the Severe Style that was the forerunner of the Classical Style. And we are only fifty years from the construction of the Parthenon, whose sculptures had all the freedom and movement sketched out by the artists of the late Archaic style, such as Onesimos, the Berlin Painter or the Brygos Painter.

Preceding pages:
The famous bronze of a reclining banqueter. Circa 530 BC. British Museum, London, Great Britain.

It was now, at the beginning of the 5th century BC, that the Greek world came very close to disappearing in the horror of the Persian invasion and all-out war. Miraculously, though, it survived, and from the ruins there arose a Classical Style that was the worthy heir of the traditions described here, and whose brilliance, boldness and freedom never cease to dazzle.

Opposite:
Up until circa 530 BC, the ground remained a natural ocher color and the characters were painted in black, with white and red highlights. As can be seen from Exekias' famous vase at the British Museum, London, the folds in the clothes were incised.
Above:
After 530 BC, the ground was usually painted in black, leaving the figures in red.
This allowed for a more delicate rendering of the details. This vase by the Brygos Painter from around 490 BC prefigures the art of the Classical period. Musée du Louvre, Paris.

Greek coins

Herodotus, that inexhaustible fount of information whose exactitude has been confirmed on countless occasions by modern archeology, states that the Lydians (the inhabitants of Asia Minor, governed by King Croesus, who has famous for his wealth), were the first to mint gold and silver coins. So far, there has been nothing to contradict this assertion.

It would indeed seem that in the 7th century, they began to mint coins in the coastal area of today's Turkey, where "Barbarians" such as the Lydians rubbed shoulders with Greeks from the cities of Ionia.

Before the invention of coinage, goods were paid for with ingots of metal.

The oldest known coins are in electrum (an alloy of gold and silver). The minting of pure silver coins began in around 550 BC, followed by pure gold.

From this period we have the oldest coins struck on the continent—or rather, on a small trading island near Athens: Aegina.

The second half of the 6th century BC saw workshops spring up all over continental Greece: having its mint was a way for a city to assert its independence (opposite, Athena, goddess of Athens).

Above: In about 550 BC the Greeks began minting coins in silver then in pure gold. The coin shown here comes from the small island of Aegina. Cabinet des Médailles, Bibliothèque Nationale de France, Paris.
Below: Coin bearing the effigy of Athena. The obverse shows an owl. Circa 450 (?). D. 1". Musée Barbier-Mueller, Geneva.

GREECE
from Pericles to Alexander

By the time the Persians set out to subdue the Greeks, the latter had raised their civilization to new heights of refinement. They had built magnificent stone temples as far afield as their colonies in Sicily and southern Italy, and their artists had produced life-sized statues in bronze and marble. Now, following their victory over their oriental enemy, the Greeks overcame the last limits placed on them by their tribal past. In only a few decades, Phidias, Aeschylus, Sophocles and Herodotus had laid the foundations of modern Western culture.

At the beginning of the 5th century BC, the great Persian empire founded in 559 BC by Cyrus the Great was still governed by the Achaemenid dynasty. Cyrus' dramatic rise, described in chapter 11, brought the whole of the Near East, including today's Turkey and Egypt, under the control of the "king of kings." However, the Greek cities on the Ionian coast continued to resist and appealed to their racial and cultural brothers on the Greek mainland for help. But only Athens, which was Ionian at heart, sent forces to these cousins over the sea. Other cities remained neutral, still others declared their sympathy for the Persians, with whom they were engaged in busy and fruitful trade.

The Persian Wars

When the Greeks stepped up their support to the Ionian cities, the then Persian emperor Darius issued an ultimatum to those who defied him. Now the immense Persian army rumbled into motion. The islands of the Aegean—the Sporades and then the Cyclades—were conquered.

The Acropolis, Athens.

Next they landed in the bay at Marathon. Athens appealed for aid to the Spartans, who were unable to send reinforcements in time. However, the inhabitants of Plataea, in Boeotia, came to support the Athenian army whose commander, the cunning tactician Miltiades, now pretended to weaken his center. The Persians charged into this false breach and were trapped. The slaughter among the attackers was atrocious. The Greeks lost only 92 men.

This was in 490 BC. The victory at Marathon looked resounding indeed, for Darius withdrew to Asia Minor. In reality, he was planning revenge. And he had the resources he needed.

What happened next is well known: the Spartan sacrifice at Thermopylae, the capture and sack of Athens and, finally, the Greek naval victory at Salamis where the Persian fleet was destroyed. Its date, 480, is arbitrarily taken to mark the end of the first Archaic period. Xerxes, who had taken over the command from his father Darius, fled, leaving his treasure in the hands of the victors. One might have expected the Hellenic cities to take advantage of these circumstances to unite and form a powerful new nation. But no, these temporary allies were more concerned to preserve their selfish independence. This was stronger than their ethnic bonds, stronger than the religion whose divinities they all shared, as they did the holy places and the pilgrimages to Delphi, Olympia and other sites. There games and festivals were held in honor of Zeus. It was said that they were founded by Heracles, and the date of their "restoration," 776 BC, was to the Greek world what the year of Christ's birth would be to the Christian: the end and the beginning.

In reality, the autonomy of the city and island-states was merely a fiction. Alliances turned into leagues despotically dominated by the most prestigious and powerful of the member cities.

The 5th century BC, which could easily have seen the birth of a brilliant Hellenic confederation, closed with a clash between two great leagues led, respectively, by the intellectual and democratic Athens (where the Ionian element had introduced a certain Eastern refinement)

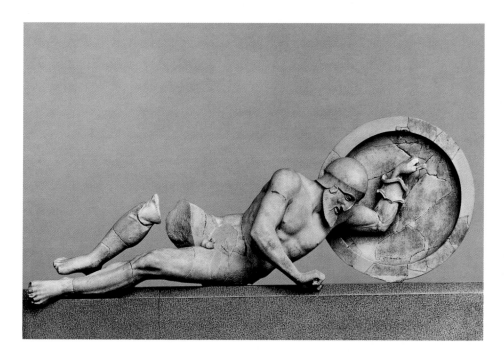

This Dying Warrior comes from one of the pediments of the temple of Aphaia at Aegina. Circa 490 BC. Staatliche Antikensammlungen und Glyptothek, Munich.

and the frugal, militaristic and oligarchic Sparta, heir to the pure Dorian tradition.

Towards classicism

This turn of the 5th century BC which saw the Persian kings' dreams of conquest end in failure, also saw Greece poised to become the cradle of Western humanism. The Greek warriors, those successors to the heroes of Homer, were also fascinated by the adventures of the mind. Aeschylus, the father of tragedy, had fought valiantly at Marathon and Salamis. According to tradition, he introduced the second actor (the first being Thespis) and was the first to use scenic effects and costumes and to combine spoken text with music. Reducing the importance of the chorus, he put the emphasis on individual characters (his *Prometheus Bound* is an illustrious example of this) facing their destiny and epitomizing the uniquely human combination of fragility and strength in the face of cruel fate. Just as, in the tragedies of Aeschylus, the individual overcame the trials of life at the price of extreme physical

73

suffering, or by renouncing his very physical existence, so, under the fingers of the sculptor, the faces and bodies in marble escaped the limitations of Archaic frontality.

Contemporaneous with the first plays of the great tragic poet, the bearded warrior from a pediment on the Temple of Aphaia at Aegina (c. 490 BC) is an excellent example of the artist's sense of wonder at the living strength expressed by his chisel. The soldier's body, whose modeling points to classicism, is miles away from the old conventions, even if his face is inexpressive with its copy of a copy of a smile and its empty eyes. What is remarkable and moving about this monumental work is the surprising realism with which it shows the limp, strengthless hand on the shield, thus suggesting that final moment of agony when the spirit is about to leave the flesh, that fatal moment when the marvelous machine of muscles and reflexes will be reduced to an inert mass of flesh. This moment is summed in that one single detail, expressing the eternal renunciation of the mortal's ambitions (which are in this case warrior-like).

Sculptural representations of the human form now began to echo this profound awareness of individual responsibility in a community that, unlike tribal societies, no longer believed in the flawless homogeneity of the edifice formed by religion, politics and obligations. When man starts thinking, he starts wanting gods that think. Mythology had reached the end of the long evolution that transformed it from divine law to a poetic lesson which, however much it was respected, no longer obliged each member of society to rehearse its tenets through ritual. The same freedom could be felt in sacred images. They acquired movement. First, bodies balancing on a single leg, with the other one bent, the foot no longer placed flat as in Archaic statues. Soon, the whole body would seem to sway, the sculpture creating a sense of both restrained *élan* and movement in space.

These stone figures were set within the limits of a human being making measured gestures. At the same time, the exquisite delicacy of some of

Archaic style sculpture from the Acropolis. It was discarded when Pericles began the construction of the Parthenon. Circa 500 BC. Acropolis Museum, Athens.

These *metopes* are from Selinunte in Sicily. The one on the left, from a 6th-century BC temple, is in the Archaic style; the one on the right is in the Severe style, dating from the early 5th century BC.

these sculptures and their refinement prove that Athens was influenced by Ionia and by the Cycladic artists working in the Ionian style.

The Severe style

It is true of course that men were also shown in action, and women dancing, during the Archaic period. But everything about such representations suggests that they are based on conventions that sculptors reworked ad infinitum. The flat ground offered no illusion of depth (see top left). All that had changed by the early 5th century BC (see top right). Soon, the trend was towards vivid, realistic works free of artifice and conceived as an organic whole. These were the sculptures of the Severe style, which we can see emerging in the dying warrior from the temple at Aegina and which reached its apogee with the famous

Charioteer at Delphi. This style, which developed during the decades leading up to the Classical style, as immortalized by the sculptors of the Parthenon (after 447 BC), is often overlooked in popular books on the subject. However, connoisseurs are well aware of its importance. It has given us some of the masterpieces of Western art. It is a great pity that there is no space here to show the Charioteer in full, or the *metopes* of the Temple of Zeus at Olympia (circa 470-456 BC), which was the first building to be erected after the victory over the Persians.

The Athenian age of enlightenment

With the Persians gone, the victors were left licking their wounds. Athens lay in ruins. The temple dedicated to the city's tutelary goddess had been devastated (the marvelous sculpture shown here as an

Sculpture in the 5th century BC

It is a mistake to think that the frontality and rigorous symmetry of Archaic statues ruled out any representation of movement. The *metopes* of 6th-century temples show figures in the throes of action, although their poses are conventional and lifeless. The *metope* from a temple at Selinunte in Sicily shown on page 76, depicting the slaying of the Gorgon, is contemporary with the bronze banqueter on pages 64-65, and yet the latter is so much more alive and less stereotyped. In fact, this man reclining at a feast prefigures the revolution that took place at the beginning of the 5th century and was illustrated by the sculptures on the pediment of the temple at Aegina. As we have noted elsewhere, the will to idealize man was evident at the end of the Archaic period in the dreaming face of the young woman sculpted circa 500 BC (p. 74) whose full eyes contrast with the empty sockets of the dying warrior, made only a decade earlier (circa 490 BC), at the time when the Persian armies were repelled for good and when the Severe style was born. The progress this style made in the decade or two that followed can be seen from the finesse of the features on the Charioteer from Delphi.

The Greek Classical canon was established by Phidias and, soon afterwards, Polykleitos, in the middle of the 5th century. In addition to features such as *draperie mouillée* (the garment clinging to the body as if wet), one of the most remarkable inventions of Classicism was the technique of representing the body with its weight shifted onto one leg, instead of having it rest equally on the two feet as it did before. This displacement of the center of gravity, with one "supporting" and one "free" leg, implied consequent adjustments of the hips and shoulders.

The procedure was amplified in the century that followed with the introduction of artificial rests (tree trunks, rocks), allowing an even more marked shifting of the center of gravity, as can be seen in Praxiteles' famous sculpture, Hermes Holding the Infant Dionysos (see p. 82-83).

The famous Charioteer from Delphi in the Severe style. Detail. Circa 480 BC. Archeological Museum, Delphi, Greece.

example of Archaic art was knocked down by the invaders). Everything had to be rebuilt. The credit for employing the greatest artists of the age in this task must go to Pericles, who begin to edge out his rivals in 460 BC so that by 444 BC he alone was in charge of public affairs. It seems very clear that all the sculptors from the regions under Athenian domination were brought in under the direction of Phidias to sculpt the *metopes* and friezes of the Parthenon.

For this city razed by the Persians to become a great maritime power with a virtual monopoly on trade with the Near East, and to do so in a matter of decades, must have taken a prodigious effort. The most remarkable thing, though, is that, in its dogged effort to assert its hegemony over the Delian League, Athens should have accompanied its political undertakings with a real cult of the arts. This phenomenon is almost unique in the history of humankind.

Need we recall that at the same time as Pericles was commissioning the architect Ictinus and the bronze maker Phidias to build and decorate the Parthenon, crowds were gathering round to hear the stories of the historian Herodotus, that ancestor of all reporters who was paid handsomely in order to induce him to settle in Attica?

And that young and old alike were captivated by the tragedies of Euripides and Sophocles, then at the zenith of a glory that will attach to their names forever?

It is interesting to note that from 444 BC to his death in 429 BC, the only official post held by Pericles was that of *strategos* (general). For there were several such strategoi, and this military function did not bring with it the kind of power wielded by Pericles by virtue of his natural authority, during the decades when he made Athens the capital of a genuine empire, a prosperous sea power and a spiritual beacon of the Mediterranean world.

This empire was founded on the league formed by some 150 cities spread around the Aegean Sea. At the first meeting of the member cities in Delos in 477 BC, there was no mention of forming a confederation to oppose Sparta which, up to now and however

The Parthenon friezes represent the quintessence of the early Classical style. The team of gifted sculptors no doubt produced the marble bas-reliefs using the clay models made by the bronze sculptor Phidias (circa 440 AD). A number of these artists came from islands allied with Athens. Acropolis Museum, Athens.

disturbing its own militaristic tendencies, had been Athens' ally against the Persians.

From the Athenian historian Thucydides we learnt that the Delian League was formed to collect a contribution paid by all the Greek allies in order to avenge the destruction wrought by the Persians. The treasure thus acquired was kept in Delos. Its main use was to fund work on boats in order to strengthen the power of the Greek navy. Under the command of the Athenian Cimon, the allies thus liberated numerous Greek cities that had remained under Persian power. Cimon, it so happened, was a well-known friend of the Spartans. It was after his exile in 461 that a fratricidal enmity grew up between the Peloponnese,

Sculpture in the 4th century BC

In 2,000 years from now, if asked who dominated 20th-century Western art, no doubt we would name Picasso. Just as surely, the most famous sculptor of the 4th century BC was Praxiteles (known as "the Younger" to distinguish him from his grandfather, a rival of Phidias). Unlike Phidias and Polykleitos, Praxiteles was not a maker of bronzes. Instead, his intimate knowledge of marble enabled him to play with the laws of balance and gravity, as can be seen in his Hermes Holding the Infant Dionysos, in which the slender, slightly effeminate body of Hermes leans naturally on a tree trunk hidden by a draped coat. This trunk is a vital support because the group's center of gravity is to one side of Hermes' legs.

Below:
The Apoxyomenos by Lysippus (Roman copy). Vatican Museum, Rome, Italy.

Praxiteles was the first sculptor to dare show female divinities unclothed. Pliny tells us that Knidians came to Athens to buy an effigy of the goddess Aphrodite. Its nudity at first caused a scandal but then became a source of profit as people flocked to Knidos to behold the beautiful nude goddess by Praxiteles.

Praxiteles' contemporary Scopas became famous for the qualities of movement in his battle and hunting scenes. Here the serenity of Classical faces is clouded by the pathos and tragedy of human destiny. Gods and heroes alike are shown suffering.

The last great sculptor of the 4th century BC was Lysippus, a maker of bronzes whom Alexander chose as his official portraitist. He is said to have produced over 5,000 works, none of which has survived. The Apoxyomenos is a Roman copy of one of them.

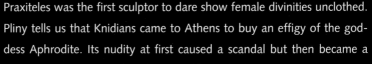

Right:
Statue by Praxiteles showing Hermes Holding the Infant Dionysos. Archeological Museum, Olympia, Greece.

dominated by Sparta, and the Delian League, led by Athens.

In 454 BC, Athens seized on some dubious pretext to have the allies' treasure transferred within its city walls. The fund served to finance the construction of the monuments with which Pericles wished to embellish the city. Soon, thanks to his wise governance, Athens would be overflowing with riches. The olive groves destroyed by the Persians were replanted. Above all, almost limitless resources flowed from the newly discovered silver mines at Laurium. Meanwhile, agriculture and apiculture developed apace and were soon substantial exporters.

No sooner had he established and consolidated his power than Pericles made plans to rebuild the temples, the monuments destroyed during the war. A new Parthenon (temple of Athena Parthenos) would rise up on the site of the old, whose damaged statues were—much to the delight of later archeologists (this was where the charming marble statue of a young girl shown on p. 74 was found)—piled up in the hardfill.

The architects mandated to design this major work were Ictinus and Callicrates. They chose the Doric order, and decided to use the local Pentelic marble.

The Parthenon is not the biggest temple in the Greek world, but it is certainly the most perfect. Its dimensions are the result of precise mathematical calculations based on the "golden mean." In order to conceive decoration worthy of the project, Pericles appointed Phidias, who must be seen as the true master builder of the sanctuary on which construction began in 447 BC.

In fact, Phidias was a bronze caster. It is likely that he first made models for the sculptures on the pediments and *metopes* and that these works, which were so new in their inspiration, were executed by stone carvers, many of them from the Cyclades.

Preceding pages:
The caryatids on
the Erechtheum,
the most refined of
the temples built
on the Athenian
Acropolis.

Inside the temple was placed a giant statue in chryselephantine, i.e., gold and ivory, 49 feet high, of the patroness of the Athenians, made this time by Phidias. However, the Athena commission saw him fall from grace when he was accused of having embezzled some of the precious metal to be used for the sculpture. The reality was that he had traveled to Olympia to make another chryselephantine statue representing Zeus. Some moving relics were recently discovered on the site of his Olympian workshop: blocks serving to shape hammered gold leaf and, above all, a modest terracotta drinking cup bearing the inscription: "I belong to Phidias."

Now a majestic entrance, the Propylaea, was built on the Acropolis, the fortified rock where generations of Athenians came to implore the protection of the gods and take refuge in times of danger.

Soon, there were other temples surrounding the Parthenon. Among them, the temple of "Athena the Victorious" (Athena Nike), in the Ionian style, built in the time of Pericles, and the famous Erechtheum, also in the Ionic style, built not long after the death of the great strategos, whose caryatids (statues that serve as columns) around the building's southern porch are perhaps the most admired and frequently photographed monument in the world (see preceding pages).

Through to the present today, these constructions have embodied the strength and grace of classical art, whose influence has been felt through the centuries, surviving the invasions of savage barbarians on whom it imposed respect (through the channel of a Roman Empire besotted with Hellenism) to revive 2,000 years later in Renaissance Italy.

After Pericles

Athens' wealth and the authority it wielded over a league comprising some 200 towns made others jealous. In 461, war broke out with Sparta.

In 449 BC, Pericles had "long walls" built, linking the city to its port, Piraeus. Construction of the Parthenon was well under way. But, one by one, the allies left the Delian League, complaining of high taxes and knowing full well that their contributions were being converted into marble columns and statues to decorate the Athenian temples.

In 435 BC, a prohibition was placed on members of the Peloponnesian

League forbidding them to trade with any port or counter of the Athenian Confederation. This created a situation so tense that the outcome, in 431 BC, was merciless war. Setting aside a short truce in 421-420 BC, the conflict lasted more than 25 years. While Athens held sway on the sea, it was threatened on land because of the Spartans' numerous alliances, notably with Thebes.

Skirmishes were followed by massive destruction, terrestrial expeditions by maritime raids, with one side attacking and then the other. In 429 BC, Pericles died in the plague that decimated the population of Athens. In 416 BC, Alcibiades persuaded his Athenian compatriots to mount an expedition against Syracuse in Italy. Sent into exile after accusations of debauchery and profanation of sacred statues, this disloyal subject now went to Sparta and convinced the enemies of his homeland to send

Below:
Coin showing Alexander the Great as a semi-divinity. Musée Barbier-Mueller, Geneva.

Opposite:
Head of goddess, known as the Laborde Head. Classical style sculpture, circa 420 BC. Musée du Louvre, Paris.

their own troops to Sicily. The Athenian general and historian, Thucydides, who left us a detailed account of the Peloponnesian War, has related the sorry fate of the Athenian soldiers routed outside Syracuse in 413 BC. The lack of mercenaries meant that it was no longer possible to defend the silver mines at Laurium, Attica's only remaining resource as its olive groves had been destroyed yet again. The last hope was the once powerful fleet. But no, in 405 BC, it succumbed to a surprise attack and was destroyed by Sparta and her allies while lying at anchor at Aegospotami. A prolonged siege followed and, in 404, Athens surrendered. Spartan hegemony lasted about a quarter of a century. Then, in 378 BC, Athens formed an alliance with Thebes, a rising power, forming a new league against the Peloponnese. An elite troupe of Theban soldiers, who practiced homosexuality as a military discipline, mounted an offensive under the orders of a chief named Epaminondas. This remarkable general was so sure of his power that in 371 BC, when Athens and Sparta signed a peace treaty, Thebes refused to adhere. The city inspired such fear in its former allies that, in the end,

Pliny the Roman on Praxiteles

"This artist was not just a maker of bronzes: he was also a sculptor of marble and in his works in this medium, he not only surpassed his rivals; he surpassed himself. [...]

Imitations of his manner can be seen in ceramics in Athens: but, above all in, let us say, the Venus of Praxiteles or, rather, the Venus of the whole world; for is there any country from which men did not set sail for Knidos to admire this Venus? The artist sculpted two of them and put them up for sale together. The people of Kos chose the clothed one, even though they could have had the other one for the same price. No connoisseurs in this art, they imagined that the one they saw was severe and modest in comparison to the other. But the Venus neglected by the people of Kos was not neglected by those of Knidos, who bought it. [...]

This Knidian Venus is of greatly superior value to the other. This was understood by King Nicomedes who set his mind on buying this master-piece from the Knidians, offering to pay their national debt, which was immense. The Knidians preferred to endure the worst rather than agree to such a treaty, and they were not mistaken for the fame of their town is entirely due to this one work by Praxiteles, placed in a temple that is simple circular colonnade. Without walls, open on all sides, it reveals the effigy of the goddess at whatever angle one looks from, and this magic of art passes for a supernatural wonder, as if Venus herself were about to produce this illusion. [...]

But the true wonder is that from whatever side one looks at it, this statue is a true masterpiece, admirable in every way."

Roman copy of The Aphrodite of Praxiteles
The original dated from around 340 BC. Vatican Museum, Rome.

the Athenians allied with Sparta (369 BC). But Theban power barely outlived Epaminondas, who died in 365 BC. Weakened and exhausted, the Greek cities were incapable of resisting the initiatives of Philip, king of Macedon, the unifier of Greece and father of Alexander the Great.

From Classical to Hellenistic art

The 5th century saw the first treatises on art. In his Canon, Polykleitos described the significance of the rules he had discovered by observing matter. His concern to codify his research explains the fact that he is credited with discovering the impression of movement produced by showing the body shifting its weight on to one leg and leaving the other one "free." This artist in the Classical tradition was some fifteen years younger than Phidias. The latter was an acknowledged master of the period associated with the Severe style, from whose limitations he freed himself with the authority we have seen. As W.H. Schuchhardt has written: "The two artists shine like a double constellation, over the period when Greek genius was at its greatest. Phidias, forerunner of the Attic spirit in all its power and magnificence; Polykleitos of Argos, representing Doric art with its clarity and logic, its rigid structure and its refined sense of aesthetic laws."

This cult of the individual—a lucid vision of the progress from birth to death based on the cosmic order, founded as it is on immutable cycles (the daily resurrection and death of the day)—was also a cult of liberty. For artists, man's freedom excused and justified every invention or perversion. Thus the sculptor Lysippus and the painter Apelles, both protégés of Alexander the Great, were able to give free rein to their creative genius. It may have worn a religious disguise (thus Alexander was represented with the features of Zeus), but profane art—art as art—had well and truly arrived. And with it appeared a new race of individuals. These were collectors, men with a special quality or gift: the ability to see.

This ivory type limestone statuette from the Greco-Roman period embodies all the qualities and excesses of Hellenistic art with its draperie mouillée, deeply folded garment and pronounced movement of the hips. The treatment is highly precious. H. 8". Musée Barbier-Mueller, Geneva.

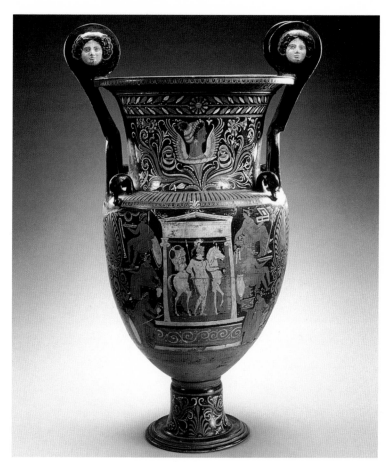

In Italy, at around the time of Alexander's death, Greek painters were decorating huge vases (this one is more than 40″ high) with teeming patterns and figures showing an absolute *horror vacui*. The exaggerations of the Hellenistic period began to appear in 330-320 BC. H. 4′1″. Musée Barbier-Mueller, Geneva.

The 4th century BC saw sculpture move towards a mannerism that tended to exaggerate the inventions of Classicism, and which eventually led to Roman art. The painted decorations on vases now became increasingly complex, with teeming masses of characters illustrating mythological scenes at the same time as the period's *horror vacui* (abhorrence of the void).

In architecture, the construction of temples slowed down whereas increasing numbers of public buildings and theaters were erected. However, this general principle should not make us overlook the fact that both the temple of Artemis at Ephesus and the tomb of King Mausol at Halicarnassus, two of the seven wonders of the ancient

world, date from the middle of the 4th century BC—or, in other words, from the late Classical period (which, by convention, is taken to end with the death of Alexander the Great in 323 BC).

The expansion of Hellenism

The great dream of empire, an empire that was certainly heterogeneous and retained its local cultural identities within a binding framework of Greekness, was only partially achieved, and Alexander's successors, the generals who shared his kingdom, proved incapable of preserving its political unity.

Their rivalries and constant internecine wars made any deep-reaching Hellenization of the Near East and beyond impossible.

The sovereigns of the only durable post-Alexandrian dynasty, that of the Ptolemies in Egypt, soon became "pharaohized" and, far from imposing Greek religion and mores, adopted the religion and customs of their subjects.

Only Pergamum under the Attalid kings played a leading role in the Hellenistic world. There philosophers, historians and poets vied with the sculptors who perpetuated the ideas of Scopas and Lysippus, while inflecting them with the heightened expressionism, mannerism and taste for excess that are typical of Hellenistic art and are exemplified by the famous tanagras in cast terracotta, the languid bronze effigies of goddesses at Alexandria and the figures in the friezes at Pergamum.

In 133 BC, Pergamum was absorbed into the Roman sphere of power. Pliny tells us that during the Romans' conquest of Greece, King Attalus, who at the time was their ally, was ready to spend vast sums to acquire the Greek artistic masterpieces (sculptures and paintings) auctioned off by the victors in order to finance their campaign. However, the Romans too had a passion for beauty and Attalus' plans were thwarted.

Statue of King Mausol from the famous Mausoleum built a few years before the campaigns of Alexander. British Museum, London.

Hellenistic art enjoyed tremendous freedom and artists were able to explore every register, style and theme as they sought to express their gifts. Some sculptors returned to an Archaic style, others sagely measured themselves against Classical sculptors. This was the case with

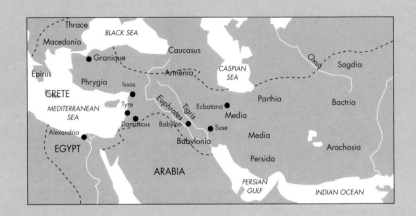

Alexander the Great: the philosopher and the conqueror

Few destinies are as extraordinary as that of the young son of King Philip of Macedon, whom the Athenians dismissed as a semi-barbarian, or at least who, while he boasted of belonging to the Greek cultural sphere, reigned over a motley band of coarse tribes.

Philip conquered the neighboring countries one by one: Epirus, Thrace and Thessaly. This powerful kingdom enabled him to impose his will on Thebes and Athens, winning acceptance as the new chief of a confederation founded in 337 BC that would once again go to war with the Persians. But Philip died the following year. His great design was carried out by his son, Alexander.

Born in 356 BC, Alexander was a brilliantly gifted child. And his father had the good fortune to be able to choose as his tutor one of the finest minds of the day: the philosopher Aristotle.

From 342 to 335 BC, Aristotle gave Alexander the wisdom of his encyclopedic teaching (the Greek philosopher's interests ran from poetics to zoology, from physics to politics). When the young king set off to conquer Asia, Aristotle returned to Athens, where he founded a school in the Lyceum garden (whose name has become synonymous with senior schools in many Latin languages). His treatises were translated into Arabic and Latin, becoming the great scientific and intellectual references throughout the Mediterranean world through to the Middle Ages. As for Aristotle himself, he fell into disgrace after Alexander's death in 323 BC and was exiled for "collaboration with the Macedonian power." He retired to Chalcis, where he died in 322 BC, accused of impiety just as Sophocles had been 70 years earlier.

Alexander's great adventure profoundly changed the cultural configuration of the Near East. Its effects were felt as far as Afghanistan and India, with the development of Greco-Buddhist art.

Alexander's heirs were his generals, all of them Greek. They dismantled his great empire in order to create their own kingdoms, founding dynasties which not only failed to support one another but actually tore each other apart and exhausted themselves in internecine wars. As for the Greek spirit, however, it proved indestructible.

the famous Venus of Milo which, like the works of the great
5th-century BC sculptors, is made to be seen frontally. Others took
on descriptive themes, adopting a verist style exemplified by the
extraordinary "drunken old woman" mentioned by Pliny (see p. 101)
and of which, alas, only Roman copies remain (the best one being in
Munich).

As regards architecture, the preeminence of the Ionian cities led to the
generalized use of the Ionic order, to the detriment of the Doric. It was,
however the Corinthian order that developed most spectacularly.
Appreciated for its richness, it was adopted by the Romans, who used it
through to the Late Empire.

The imperial era and the Greek heritage

It is difficult to put a date on the end of the Hellenistic period.
The date 31 BC (when Octavian/Augustus triumphed over
his rival Antony at Actium) is generally taken as the beginning
of the Roman imperial period. Fascinated by Greek civilization,
Augustus' successors and their close circles ensured the survival
of what barbarians would surely have destroyed.

Thus the Greek heritage was passed on to us in its totality,
without betrayals or distortions, by a deeply admiring
and respectful Roman world.

This is why we should refrain from criticizing the flatness of
Roman copies of Greek sculptural masterpieces, for they
constitute the encyclopedia from which we draw most of
our knowledge. Still, it is true that Rome failed to
penetrate the secret of Classical sculpture's intimate
sensuality. They were too much taken with the excesses
of Hellenistic art, an art whose grandeur we can
nevertheless value if we look beyond its exaggerations
and see that it speaks to us of a past where
everything was order, intelligence and sensibility.

The "Drunken Old Woman" is mentioned in Pliny.
Today we have only Roman copies of the 2nd-century BC original.
Staatliche Antikensammlungen und Glyptothek, Munich.

The Greek world

The Olympic Games were a pan-Hellenic festival; in other words, they brought together participants from throughout the Greek world. The superb bronze statue known as the Charioteer at Delphi (the head of which is shown on p. 79) was part of a life-size monumental group which also represented the horse and chariot of the race winner. It was dedicated to Zeus in around 470 BC by Polyzalos, the tyrant of the town of Gela in Sicily. The colonization of Magna Grecia (southern Italy) began in the 8th century BC. Founded in 689 BC, Gela had become so powerful that it was able to create its own colony further west along the southern coast of the island, at Agrigento, whose ruins can still be seen outside the modern town.

The Greeks of Asia, including the Phocaeans, were the most active in the colonization of the Mediterranean rim. They established Alalia in Corsica, using it as a springboard to found Elea, south of Naples, which became famous for its school of Eleatic philosophers, and Marseille (Massalia), which still likes to call itself "the Phocaean" city. In 474 BC, Hiero, the king of Syracuse, inflicted a crushing naval defeat on the Etruscans. In 413 BC, an Athenian expedition to Syracuse (a Corinthian colony allied to Sparta) was massacred, dealing a fatal blow to the city's power. A few years later, the Syracusans defeated the Carthaginians, thus strengthening their grip on the western part of Sicily.

The sculptors, ceramists and gold and metal workers of Magna Grecia had a profound influence on Etruscan civilization and, subsequently, on Rome.

The Peloponnesian War viewed by Thucydides

After the victory of the Persians (480 BC), the alliance between Athens and Sparta lasted for a few decades but then degenerated into hostility and, soon, outright war. The whole of the second half of the 5th century BC was punctuated by fighting and truces between Athenians and Spartans.

The history of his war between Peloponnesians and Athenians was related by an Athenian contemporary, Thucydides. Following the war from its out-

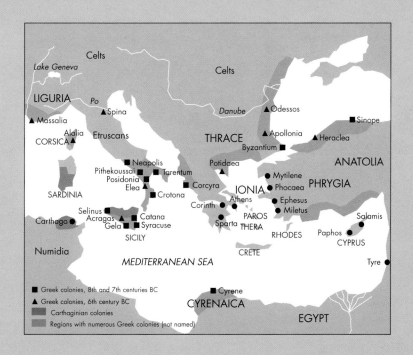

set, he observed these two states at the height of their power fighting on land and sea, with each side drawing in allies from all around the Greek world. Those cities that had yet to take sides stood poised to do so.

Although himself an Athenian general, Thucydides was remarkably objective. He wrote: "Hostilities between the Athenians and the Peloponnesians began after the breach of a thirty-year peace treaty. Concerning the motives for this breach, I have begun by presenting the grievances of the two adversaries and their disputes, so that it was not a mystery why a war on this scale broke out among the Greeks. But the truest cause (and also the one that was most seldom put forward) lies, in my opinion, in Athenian expansion, which aroused the fears of the Lacedaemonians (Spartans) and thus forced them to fight."

IN ITALY BEFORE THE ROMANS
The Etruscans

During the first Iron Age, in the first millennium BC, Italy was an ethnic mosaic. Soon, it would experience Greek hegemony. While many of its the tribes spoke Indo-European languages (including the Latins, the Sabines and the Venetes), the Etruscans, exceptionally, did not: indeed, their tongue is still not understood.

From prehistory to history

The prehistory of Italy has been much studied and yet it continues to present a nagging mystery that scholars have tried in vain to elucidate: the origin of the Etruscans. The key question concerns the intrusion of an Oriental-style funerary art in the "Villanovan" tombs of today's Tuscany, combined with local production which, under Greek influence, moved towards Etruscan art, along with the first inscriptions in circa 650 BC of an incomprehensible language: Etruscan.

Italy in around 500 BC

The situation in the Italian peninsular in around 500 BC is relatively easy to understand. The young Roman republic was fenced in by the confederation of the twelve Etruscan cities to the north, by the Greek colonies to the south and, wherever there were no Greeks or Etruscans, by Sabines and Samnites, whose wars with the Romans spread over several centuries. These tribes all practiced the *ver sacrum*—in other words, the mobilization of their youths in the spring in order to conquer new territories.

They were loath to accept Roman dominance and often allied

Tumulus built over one of the underground tombs at Cerveteri. 7th century BC. Photo by the author.

themselves with the Etruscans in order to combat the expansionist Republic.

Curiously enough, the rich Greek cities of southern Sicily were less alert to the danger. It is true that when that handful of Latin villages joined forces to constitute the city of seven hills that would one day hold sway over the Mediterranean world, they were already very well organized. In 734 BC, Syracuse was founded by the Corinthians. In 706 BC, Sparta founded Tarentum. And it was not until 506 BC that Rome drove out the last of its three Etruscan kings, to whom it in fact owed the cult that it would now devote to the Hellenic gods of Olympus who, thanks to Etruria, had all been Italianized.

From Villanovan art to Etruscan art

The techniques that were developed during this first millennium, with the introduction of metalworking, were not specific to the region bounded by the Po, the Arno and the Mediterranean. They could also be found in the Alps and the plains of the Danube. The art of making religious and funerary recipients in riveted sheet bronze was no doubt imported from the Orient: cauldrons and vases of this kind have been found in Iran and Urartu (Turkish Armenia). The art of lost wax bronze casting was practiced throughout Italy, across the Alps and in Greece. Helmets and urns were typically Villanovan—a term taken from a site

near Bologna, in northern Italy, which seems to have developed later than the Tuscan south, which is where the great towns of Caere (Cerveteri), Vulci, and Tarquinia grew up on the site of Villanovan villages.

Burial chambers from the early 7th century BC onwards (such as the famous Regolini-Galassi tomb at Cerveteri) have been found to contain a mixture of Villanovan-style objects and objects imported from Asia Minor or copied from Iranian, Cypriot or Phoenician prototypes. The first Etruscan inscriptions date from this "Orientalizing" period. The Etruscans (who gradually forgot their Villanovan heritage) would soon discover Corinthian ceramics and reproduce the lost wax casts of post-Geometric Greece. Greek merchants were active in Etruria from 700 BC, and Greek inscriptions have been found at Tarquinia. Etruscan cities adopted a geometrical, square plan and grew rapidly under the reign of their princes (the kings or priest-kings known as Lucumoni).

Founded (according to legend) by a Greek, the Tarquinius dynasty began its rule over the city of Rome in 616. Further south, Etruscan domination stretched as far as Campania, where they founded Capua.

To the north, they colonized the plain of the River Po and advanced as far as the Adriatic (Ravenna is an Etruscan name). In circa 540 BC, chamber tombs decorated with paintings were built at Tarquinia.

Beginning in around 575 BC, the Archaic period followed the Orientalizing epoch.

Etruria enjoyed a long period of prosperity thanks to its maritime activity. The Greek influence, which was marked by imports of large numbers of objects of every kind (most of the figurative Greek vases in our museums were found in Italy), swept away for good the archaism inherited from the Villanovan period.

The result, at the end of 6th century BC, can be seen in the superb terracotta sarcophagi showing a deceased man

A Villanovan biconical vase made by hammering and riveting together sheets of bronze. This funerary vase is identical to certain vases found in the Hallstatt culture, north of the Alps, from 750-700 BC. H. 16¼". Musée Barbier-Mueller, Geneva.

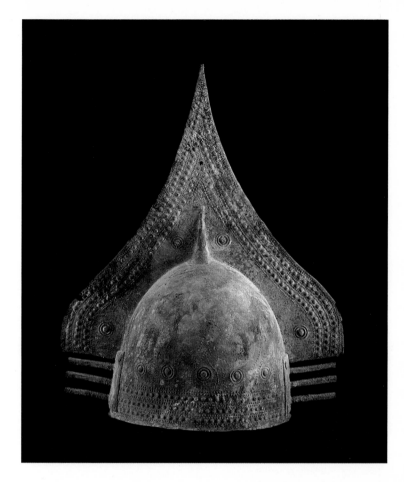

and woman, one of which can be seen at the Villa Giulia in Rome.

The decline of the Etruscans

In 474 BC, the Etruscans were defeated at sea by Hieron, the tyrant of Syracuse, who marked the event by having an inscription written on a helmet captured from the Etruscans and subsequently placed in a Greek sanctuary (and, luckily for us, found by archeologists). Now the Etruscan Confederation was no longer the maritime power that had conquered Corsica from the Phoenicians. Its cities fell one by one. The Romans took Veies in 396 BC and, in spite of the Gaulish invasion and the capture of Rome by the Barbarians in 390 BC, it was followed by his much-debated question also interested the ancient historians. In the 5th century BC Herodotus stated that the Etruscans had migrated to Italy from Lydia in Asia Minor. He was seconded by Pliny the Elder, whereas Denis of Halicarnassus, writing in the century of Augustus, argued that they autochthonous. But what answer do archeological excavations offer? Before the Iron Age, which began in around 1000 BC, the coast north of Rome seems to have been only sparsely populated. The people who settled there were known elsewhere in Europe for having propagated an "urn burial" culture (i.e., they incinerated their dead).

These strangers are known as "Villanovans", after a site near Bologna. They built villages of huts which are sometimes represented on their terracotta and bronze urns. On the site of these villages there developed the Etruscan villages. This was the time when huge tombs were dug into the tufa—genuine "underground residences" where the deceased were buried with all the goods they had enjoyed during their lifetime. Typically Villanovan artifacts continue to be found in these tombs where urns containing ashes stand side by side with the remains of bodies that were not cremated.

The first Etruscan inscriptions date from around 650 BC. They are legible because they are written in an alphabet based on Greek, but incomprehensible since, unlike Latin, Umbrian, Samnite, etc., Etruscan does not belong to the Indo-European family of languages.

Also at this time, Villanovan artifacts begin to disappear and give way to a more Orientalizing style.

Should we therefore conclude that the Villanovans were themselves Etruscans? That they were (from the linguistic viewpoint) Indo-Europeans who, at some uncertain moment, were infiltrated by immigrant (Etruscans?) from the East? No one knows, but the discovery of inscriptions in a language similar to Etruscan on the Greek island of Lemnos, which is located on the route from Asia Minor to Italy, has certainly sparked fresh

We need to imagine the Italy of the last few centuries before the birth of Christ as an ethnic mosaic. Italic tribes who came from the Danube region during the second millennium BC occupied the entire peninsula. In the far south, and in Sicily, Greek colonies had been in existence since the 7th century BC. One of them, Syracuse, inflicted a crushing defeat on the Etruscan fleet in 474 BC, thus putting an end to their commercially profitable domination of the sea.

In 90 BC, a league of Italic peoples tried to put an end to Roman imperialism. The result was the so-called "Social War", which ended with the victory of Rome in 88 BC.

This was when all the inhabitants of today's Italy became Roman citizens, including the Etruscans, whose aristocratic and wealthy families settled in Rome. Latin being the official language, Etruscan, Umbrian and Samnite all fell into disuse and died out.

This phenomenon can be compared with what happened in France when Breton or Gascon nobles came to live in Paris while their authority in the regions was replaced by magistrates and state appointees mandated by the central power.

Caere (Cerveteri) in 351 BC. In 308 BC, proud Tarquinia was subjugated, and Vulci became Roman in 273 BC. The destruction of Volsinii in 265 BC marked the end of the last major Etruscan stronghold. At the end of the 3rd century, one last tomb was dug in the necropolis at Tarquinia, that of the daughter of a magistrate, whose funerary objects prove that the Etruscans had adopted Roman mores.

The Classical period and decadence

The Classical period began in around 470 BC, not long after the Etruscan defeat at Cumae. Greek art remained an influence, but the gracious drapery and supple forms of Greece in the age of Pericles were a long way from the realities of Etruria. Unlike Greek temples in the same period, religious edifices here still used perishable materials with wooden columns and beams and brick walls. As for private houses, they were a long way from the luxury of Roman homes. Still, their furniture was no doubt very rich. A number of vaults have been found to consist

Etruscan rites

Prosperity in the afterlife

Setting aside the extraordinary life-size group sculptures in terracotta that adorned the temples and a few monumental bronze sculptures, Etruscan art is best known for its funerary goods.

During the Villanovan period, urns containing ashes were placed in a stone-lined trench or buried in a rough-hewn stone container known as a *ziro*.

Burial chambers began to be used in the 7th century BC (see photograph opposite). Initially covered with false vaults, they were soon completely dug out of the rock. Some of them, as at Cerveteri, were surrounded with a wall of dressed stone and covered by a tumulus (see p. 105).

In these multiple-chambered tombs, which reflect the new mode of burial, bones of historically known Etruscans have been found. Later, the importance accorded to the afterlife led to increasingly lavish decoration, as can be seen from the painted tombs at Tarquinia.

The Etruscans laid out their tombs like real apartments dug into the tufa. The dead were represented reclining and feasting. This recreation of a late tomb at Volterra full of sarcophagi is at the Museo Archeologico in Florence, Italy.

of a succession of small rooms reproducing the houses of the same period, and containing the same objects. At Cerveteri, for example, a famous underground tomb dug into the tufa has walls decorated with stucco models of the various tools and instruments that no doubt once hung on the walls of the rooms of those buried there.

As during the Archaic period, the bronze figurines are votive and represent worshippers of a divinity. The major works known to us from this period include the almost human-size figure of the god Mars found at Todi (Umbria), which carries an inscription in Umbrian (its closeness to Latin will be quite apparent here): *Ahal Trutiotis dunum dede* ("Trutius Ahala donated this"). It embodies a new realism which was one of the sources of Roman portraiture. Finally, this evocation of the Classical period would not be complete without a mention of the many engraved bronze mirrors found in numerous museums, and of the unique and extraordinarily "realistic" *Wounded Chimera* from the mid-4th century, which Benvenuto Cellini repaired after its discovery in 1553 (see p. 124-125).

It may seem surprising that so few of these pieces should have come down to us when we have conserved so many marble Roman goddesses. One things is clear: alongside the major workshops turning out pieces for priests, kings, the nobility and rich merchants (an inscription on the right side of the *Chimera* proves its votive function) there was a multitude of more or less talented craftsmen turning out figurines, paddles, stamps, sieves, mirrors, fibulae and all kinds of vases and beauty instruments and accessories. Some of these objects are very refined, but if we consider the huge quantity of small human statuettes excavated by all the intensive digs since the 18th century (when Etruscology spread like a new and rabid virus!), we cannot but admit that most of them are rather crudely fashioned and at the same time lack the rustic charm of small Sardinian or Iberian bronzes. However, these last two sets of artifacts can be seen as the "cousins" of the Etruscan and Umbrian ex-votos, for they too are the result of the Archaic Greek influence on the old Ligurian stock, as it changed in

This large Etruscan terracotta vase, dating from around 600 AD, was one of a series. Its decoration was stamped on, and features an animal frieze inspired by Greek Archaic art. H. 32¹ᐟ⁴". Musée Barbier-Mueller, Geneva.

accordance with the various fashions brought in by immigrants since the Bronze Age. Thus, while popular art forms coexisted with those urban studios that were steeped in respect for Greek models, we must hasten to add that this phenomenon is neither a sign of archaism, nor a sign of degeneracy. The phenomenon can be explained by the simple fact that, in an excessively stratified society such as this one, ordinary people had no contact with the upper classes. In the tombs of the latter, however, and right through to the 2nd century BC, we find works of art of a quality and originality such that the Romans, those fanatical imitators of Hellenic models, could achieve only in their civil portraits, and never in their sacred art.

As an example of Etruscan taste, we might mention the bronze group representing a dead, naked young man being carried by a man and a woman, whom it would be tempting to think of as his parents (were it not for the fact that we know the object to be the handle of a cist, i.e., a cylindrical bronze chest for domestic use, and that the scene represented need not necessarily refer to mourning, and may allude to a mythological event), or the Head of a Bearded Man Called *"Brutus,"* which is the fount of all Roman portraiture (p. 122).

The production of such pieces was the last activity to die out. With it dies the Etruscan tradition. After all, do we not have one of these cists, an intact piece discovered in old Praeneste (today's Palestrina), which is signed by its maker and, what's more, indicates the town where he worked: Rome!

Given that Palestrina is located south of the Italian capital, we can see that—even after the foundation of the Republic, when the Latins shook off the domination of their prestigious neighbors throughout the Latium region and even beyond, within a wide circle whose center was Rome—the cultural, if not political domination of the Etruscans continued to make itself felt through the creation of models for temples or the production of artworks (such as the cists) that were particular to their culture.

Etruscan painted tomb at Tarquinia. Circa 550 BC.

The two figures adorning the terracotta lid of this sarcophagus are life-size. Tradition records the existence of big terracotta statues made under the kings of Rome and representing Zeus (Jupiter) and other gods imported from Greece by the Etruscans who were the contemporaries of this work. The influence of Greek Archaic art is very marked, with the almond-shaped eyes and smiling mouths. This is one of the greatest masterpieces of Etruscan art. 6th century BC. Museo Nazionale di Villa Giulia, Rome.

This moving work of art, known since the 19th century as the "Warneck bronze", is from the end of the Classical period (3rd century BC). It represents a man and woman carrying the corpse of a young man. It was the handle on the lid of a large cylindrical bronze cist and may represent a mythological scene. W. 5¹/²". Musée Barbier-Mueller, Geneva.

Opposite: Head of a Bearded Man Called "Brutus." Etruscan bronze. 3rd century BC. H. 27". Palazzo dei Conservatori, Rome.

Following pages: The strikingly "naturalistic" *Wounded Chimera.* The sculptor and caster have surpassed themselves in their detailed rendering of this lion-like monster. Mid-4th century BC. The tail was restored by Benvenuto Cellini. W. 4'. Museo Archeologico, Florence.

The end of the Etruscans

In around 330 BC, Hellenism spread all around the Mediterranean after the conquests of Alexander, thus putting an end to the Classical period. Soon there began the first of three Punic Wars, which ended with the destruction of Carthage in 146 BC. Rome extended its power throughout an Italian peninsular impoverished by war. Still, 2nd-century Etruria was still a rich land with its great estates worked by slaves. A contemporary author notes that then the Etruscans "had moved away from the valor they had prized in the old days." They continued to engrave mirrors and cists (albeit with less vigor), and to decorate with paintings their last tombs, in accordance with their traditions. Ever since the last great revolt that united the Etruscans, the Samnites, the Sabines and the Umbrians in 298 BC, and ever since their coalition had been crushed by a Roman Republic also engaged with the Gauls and soon to be confronted with the Greek invader Pyrrhus, the truncated confederation lived in the shadow of its great neighbor. Its art and tongue disappeared at the turn of the 1st millennium AD. The Etruscans were now wholly Latinized.

THE IBERIANS

The Iberians were contemporaries of the Etruscans and just as mysterious, even if they have not aroused such passionate debate. Their first appearance in historical records is around 600 BC (compared to 650 BC for the Etruscans). No doubt we will long remain uncertain as to whether they came from the Tartessian culture that preceded them or whether they were immigrants from North Africa who took over this hospitable land and transformed it to their benefit.

In Spain, as in Italy, we find marked traces of Near Eastern influence in 7th- and 6th-century BC culture. It was the same sources that gave Greece griffin's heads and sphinxes with curved wings, as well as lions with highly graphic modeling of the muscles. But does the contribution of eastern Mediterranean traders suffice to explain the blossoming of Iberian art and civilization? It is not at all certain.

Tartessos, a mythical kingdom

The Bronze Age in Spain lasted into the 7th century BC. It was followed by a first Iron Age, when the metal was rare, but with marked Orientalizing influences as mentioned above. In 550 BC, the Iberians make their appearance in Andalusia and in the southwest as far north as Tarragona. To the north of the peninsula, the Celts were about to make their entrance, bringing with them the so-called "Hallstatt" culture of the first central European Iron Age.

There is nothing to indicate that the Tartessian culture which preceded the Iberian one in the Guadalquivir basin had began to develop organized

The famous stone bust known as the *Dama de Elche* shows signs of Phoenician and Greek influences. The heavy jewelry worn by this princess or goddess was certainly not just dreamed up by the artist. Prado, Madrid, Spain.

forms before the Phoenicians from Tyre founded the future Cadiz in around 1100 BC.

The decision by these keen-witted Levantines to set up a trading post at such a great distance from their base was certainly a well-considered one: the region was rich in gold, silver and copper (the still operational mines of the aptly named Rio Tinto, or "Red River"), while the precious tin that enabled them to make bronze came overland from the north in large quantities.

What was the reality of this Andalusian kingdom whose riches so excited the imagination of ancient writers like Herodotus, who was writing less than a hundred years after the ruin of Tartessos? Some claim that this was the Atlantis described by Plato, and generations of archeologists have dreamed of exhuming the lost capital of the Tartessians. Perhaps it never existed.

Perhaps the sovereign of one of the richest of the small towns in the region was referred to by foreign traders as "the king of Tartessos," rather like Argantonios, whom Herodotus refers to, and who is thought to have reigned in around 600 BC and protected the Phocaean sailors, who were the rivals of the Carthaginians. Note, incidentally, that his name is Celtic and not Iberian: *argantos* means silver in Celt, and Argantonios "king of silver."

To sum up, what we can say with most confidence is that Tartessos was either a state or a confederation of towns which, during the early centuries of the first millennium BC, established themselves and grew rich as the suppliers of the Phoenician traders. In the 7th century BC, when the Phoenician towns crumbled under the assaults of Assyria (and their role was taken up by Carthage, a former Phoenician colony), there was a string of Phoenician encounters on the coast where we now know Malaga, Almeria and Alicante. Inland, the odd and, alas, very rare monument recalls the grandeur of Tartessos and reminds us how strong the Oriental influence was on the predecessors of the Iberians: witness the stone funerary tower (*pillar-stela*) found at Pozo Moro, the base of which is decorated with four lions in the purest neo-Hittite style.

Iberian stone
doorway at
Tarragona, Spain.
Photo by the
author.

Tartessos and the rivalry between Greeks, Etruscans and Carthaginians

Driven out of Asia Minor by the Persians, the Phocaeans, a Greek people,
began to ply the western Mediterranean where the Carthaginians had
taken over and reinvigorated the old Phoenician colonies. Phocaean
competition also angered the Etruscans, who were themselves an
important trading people. They consequently formed an alliance with the
Carthaginians and, with their navy of 120 warships, inflicted considerable
damage on the Phocaean fleet in the strait of Sardinia. Although the
victory was by no means conclusive, the Phocaeans abandoned Corsica
and their decline also weakened the kingdom of Tartessos, which
disappeared at the end of the 6th century BC, no doubt as a result of

Iberian inscriptions

The writing system used by the Iberians, which was subsequently adopted by the Celtiberians, comprises 28 signs, of which twelve are alphabetical and the other sixteen correspond to syllables: ba, be, bi, bo, bu, etc. At first glance there is an obvious affinity with the Phoenician alphabet, from which the Greek and Etruscan systems were derived. But Tartessian (Hispanic I) and Iberian (Hispanic II) also include borrowings from the Aegean systems, which converge on Cypro-Minoan. We can see here a Celtiberian silver coin bearing the name of the town Arecorta, near present-day Guadalajara.

This inscription should be transcribed as follows: ꟼⱉ ᴌⵝ♢ꟼⵝ

Below is a simple table showing the meaning of each character and the corresponding character in Tartessian and Phoenician.

1 = English transcription

2 = inscription on coin

3 = Iberian variants

4 = Tartessian

5 = Phoenician

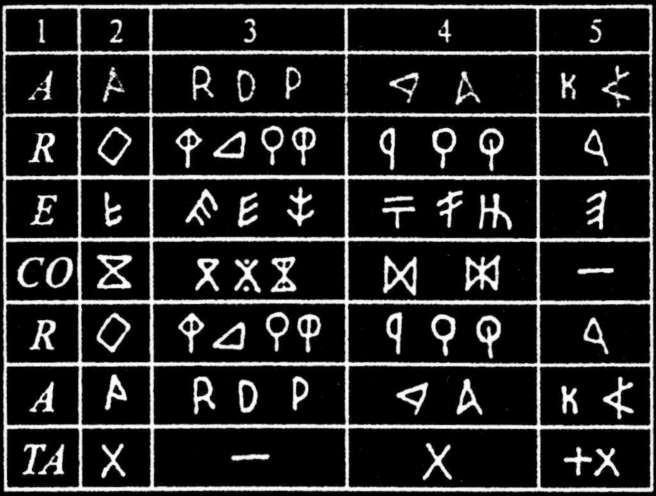

1	2	3	4	5
A	ꟼ	R Ɗ P	◁ Λ	Ƙ ⳤ
R	◇	Ⴔ◿ ΨΨ	۹ Ϙ Ϙ	◁
E	Ᏸ	⋏ Ɛ ⳩	⊤ ꓒ Ⱨ	ꓱ
CO	ⵝ	ⵝ ⵝ ⵝ	Ꙏ Ꙏ	—
R	◇	Ⴔ◿ ΨΨ	۹ Ϙ Ϙ	◁
A	ꟼ	R Ɗ P	◁ Λ	Ƙ ⳤ
TA	X	—	X	+X

Iberian coin.
Musée Barbier-Mueller, Geneva.

The Mediterranean: a little history

In the 13th century BC, the eastern Mediterranean world was shaken by an event of great consequence: Nordic invaders, probably of Indo-European origin, spread through Asia Minor, where they laid the foundations of a Hittite empire. They ravaged Syria and pushed on to the Nile delta. There Ramesses III, the Egyptian ruler, crushed those whom his victory monument refers to as "the Sea Peoples."

This was the period when metallurgy spread through the Near East. And what of western Europe? It was in the middle of the Bronze Age. Farming communities lived in villages of primitive huts, as in France and Italy. In Spain we find signs of a certain Mycenaean influence from Greece in the construction of funerary chambers with stone vaults covered by great tumuli.

This was the period when the Phoenician cities dotted along the coast of today's Lebanon, who had escaped the invasion of the Sea Peoples, took control of maritime trade and set up their trading posts (the first being Cadiz, in circa 1100 BC) wherever there were natural resources to be exported, and especially metallic minerals. It was not for another 300 years that competitors to the Phoenicians emerged in the form of the Greeks, who had adopted the Phoenician alphabet.

The Phoenicians kept western Sicily and the Greeks took the eastern part. The Phoenicians also settled in Sardinia, leaving Corsica to the Phocaeans. All traded busily with the peninsula.

As a result of these relations, the predecessors of the Iberians (who appear only in around 550 BC) created a civilization in Andalusia whose wealth impressed the ancient world. This was the (lost) kingdom of Tartessos.

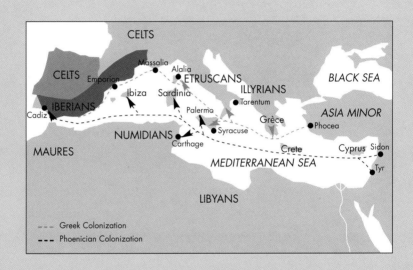

The Iberians had dealings with the Phoenicians and the Greeks along the coast. Colonies (often competing ones) were founded by both continental Greeks and Asian Greeks (Phocaeans). The Phoenician trading posts (Cadiz was founded in circa 1100 BC), which were older than the Greek ones, were taken over by Carthage. The Iberians mixed with Celtic immigrants, becoming the people known as Celtiberians.

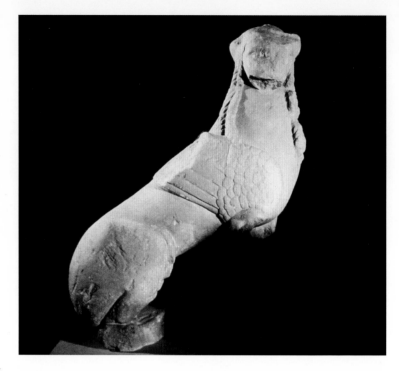

The *Argost Sphinx*, found in the province of Alicante (above) is an Iberian work in which Greek influences remain manifest in spite of the ravages of time (its curved wings have been broken off). This can be seen from comparison with a sculpture found and now kept at Delphi (opposite page), the inscription on which indicates that it was an offering from the inhabitants of Naxos. The geographical position of this island explains its Oriental stylistic influences: sphinxes, griffins and lions were of Asian origin. Archeological Museum, Delphi.

Carthaginian dominance along the Spanish coast all the way to Gibraltar. The Roman writer Pausanius gives us reason to believe in the cultural independence of the Tartessians. He informs us that at Olympia there was a treasure of bronze objects weighing, all in all, some thirteen tons, and wonders if it was made uniquely by the craftsmen of Tartessos: in other words, the fact that he merely expresses a doubt indicates that in antiquity the Tartessians were considered capable of the kind of prowess that is evidenced by the treasure of El Carambolo (see p. 138), which was without a doubt locally made.

Who were the Iberians?

The precious tale of a 6th-century BC Phocaean navigator, as preserved by the late Roman historian Avienus (4th century AD) establishes the Iberians as quite distinct from the Tartessians. And yet the writing used by the Iberians, which we know from various inscriptions but are unable to decipher for lack of knowledge of their language, is derived from the

half-alphabetical and half-syllabic signs used by the Tartessians.
One thing is certain: the Iberians, and the Tartessians before them, did not speak an Indo-European language. In this regard they are close neither to the Phoenicians, who were Semites, nor to the Greeks or Celts, who were Indo- Europeans. Research into the possible links between Iberian and Basque, another non-Indo-European language, has so far proved inconclusive.

With the disappearance of Tartessos in the 5th century BC, Iberian settlements appear to proliferate. A number of Iberian towns and villages have been found in easily defendable positions on hilltops or cliffs. They were covered by solid ramparts with towers and, sometimes, as at Tarragona, positively Cyclopean gateways. A number of these towns, such as Osuna, form the kernel of modern developments.

Iberian houses were built to a rectangular plan. The walls were originally drystone or cob the drafting of large stones (as in the wall at Tarragona) dates from shortly before the Roman conquest and not, as used to

be thought, from the beginnings of Iberian civilization. The Iberians practiced cremation and so their tombs offer no clues as to their racial type. The dead were buried in specific cemeteries corresponding to their social class. The rich or members of aristocratic families had vaults with several compartments or chambers, redolent of Etruscan tombs, where their urns were arrayed in lines on benches. As was the case during the transition from the Villanovan to the Etruscan Archaic period, Andalusian burial vaults sometimes contain evidence of both the cremation and the burial of bodies, as practiced by the Phoenicians. In conclusion, then, there is no evidence to prove that the Iberians were not the descendants of Bronze Age Spaniards, but nor can we rule out intermixing with the proto-Berbers of North Africa.

Iberian art

There is an abundance of stone lions and bulls from Cordoba to Alicante. These elegant yet rustic creatures show thoroughly local traditions becoming freighted with Oriental and Greek echoes. This is borne out by comparing the Greco-Iberian sphinx of Argost (Alicante) and the sphinx donated by the people of Naxos to the temple at Delphi (see p. 134-135). Naxos, an island open to ideas from Asia, was no less "Oriental" than Cyprus, that essential staging post for Phoenician traders on their way to Spain. There is not enough space here to show how styles and major mythological themes were passed on and transformed, but the similarities in terms of choice of animal linked to religious beliefs, such as the sphinx, lion or bull, and in the way they were represented, are enough to establish certain correspondences which owe nothing to the imagination.

The anthropomorphic representations draw on a much wider range. There are the stone heads of the Cerro de Los Santos, and there is the *Dama de Baza* ("Lady of Baza") or the famous *Dama de Elche*. Let us consider

Golden ornament belonging to a treasure of more than twenty pieces found at El Carambolo near Seville, and which was possibly part of a heavy necklace. It attests the virtuosity of Tartessian art. Museo Arqueológica, Sevilla, Spain.

the latter for a moment (see p. 127). This universal masterpiece representing a priestess (or, as is now thought, a goddess) was discovered quite by chance in 1897. Laden with precisely rendered jewelry, its face has a serenity that seems thoroughly indebted to Greek art, while the overall effect recalls the splendor of the Orient.

This enigmatic bust was at first given a very remote date (6th century BC) and subsequently brought forward to the 3rd century BC. Current moderation argues that it should be attributed to an intermediary period: perhaps the late 5th century BC. In those days Greek art had still to produce any busts, and yet, notwithstanding various hypotheses on the subject, the *Dama de Elche* never had a body. The handsome face with its slightly lowered eyelids is from the hands of an artist who was familiar with Greek art but the jewelry with which she is laden is too similar to that of figures found throughout the Tartessian area for us to entertain the thought of Phoenician (Carthaginian) inspiration. The goddess is without a doubt Iberian, as is the sphinx of Argost. Never mind the cultural mixes that shaped it.

In conclusion, a quick overview. Let us remember that the decoration of Iberian ceramics, although highly individual, is infused with the kind of Orientalism we find in other Mediterranean cultures. Here we will limit ourselves to a single example.

The bronze ex-votos

Large numbers of these were found in sanctuaries dedicated to unknown gods (some of them, no doubt, had merged with Phoenician or Punic divinities, such as Baal-Melqart, or Oriental ones such as Ishtar-Astarte. The common people made pilgrimages to their shrines and, once there, would buy bronze figurines representing the donor in a position of prayer or adoration, arms folded or hands outstretched, palms open wide. Usually the work was crude and simple, but on occasions the modeler-cum-caster rose to the level of his Etruscan or Sardinian contemporaries, and produced a charming, delicate figure—in other words, a work of art. The work on the very unusual figures representing riders is especially

Following pages:
Left:
Ex-voto: bearer of offerings influenced by the Greek korai and Phoenician Astarte. H. 3".
Right:
Small bronze horseman, ex-voto offered by an aristocrat. H. 2³/⁴".
Both: Musée Barbier-Mueller, Geneva.

139

meticulous. It on doubt reflects the need to do full justice to the donor, since ownership and use of a horse denoted a higher social status than that of a simple pedestrian.

In spite of the apparent implications of the above lines, the Phoenician-Carthaginian influence was less important than contact with the Greek world and the development of an Iberian style, or styles (with the exception of gold and silver work).

Spain and the Celts

The first Celts probably arrived in the region of the Pyrenees in around 550 BC. They had already settled throughout Western Europe, notably in England, as well as in France, where they were known as Gauls. Since the Iberians occupied a part of Catalonia, alongside the Ligurians, the first inhabitants of the Mediterranean coast from there to Genoa, the newcomers had to fit in behind them and head for Galicia. Within a few decades, they had reached today's Portugal, as well as the western half of Spain. Writing in around 450 BC, Herodotus signals the presence of the Celts in Spain. And, at the end of the 4th century BC, Aristotle designated the mountain region of Iberia as "Celtic." These pastoral and warrior-like Celts were soon trading with their industrious neighbors, as can be seen from the Greek and Phoenician objects found in their cemeteries, and the fact that they adopted a number of Iberian tools and arms, including the round shield.

Iberian expansion, the Celtiberians

While the Celts settled to the west of the Iberians, the Iberians themselves pushed northwards, crossing the Pyrenees at the beginning of the 5th century, driving out the Ligurians from the sea shore of today's Languedoc, a region in Southern France. They captured and razed the town of Bezera (Béziers) and pushed on to the banks of the Oranus River (the Hérault). They also headed inland and founded towns which bear witness to this Iberian past: Elibere (Auch), Tolosa (Toulouse) and Carcaso (Carcassonne). This Iberian drive northwards deprived the Spanish Celts

Sombrero de copa-shaped vase from La Guardia, Alcorisa (Teruel). 150-125 BC. H. 15¹ᐟ⁴″. Museo Arqueológica, Teruel, Spain.

of their main lines of contact to their fellow Celts in Gaul. Having arrived bearing the traditions of the first Iron Age (the Hallstatt culture), they were now cut off from the developments following on from the appearance of the La Tène culture, also known as the Late Iron Age, which developed in the second half of the first millennium BC. The gold torques (rigid necklaces) and fibulae particular to the La Tène Celts were rare in Spain. Nor have we found evidence of the iron broadsword, only small swords locally forged on the pattern of the antenna-hilted dagger. It was only at the end of the 4th century BC, no doubt, and after the Iberians had withdrawn to Catalonia (it is thought that they were driven out of the Languedoc by a Ligurians counteroffensive), that new bands of Celts appeared, bringing with them the materials for the second La Tène period: fibulae, swords, shields. Contemporary Mediterranean peoples soon started speaking of the "Celitiberians" (Timaeus was the first Greek historian to mention the name, in 260 BC). As of the 4th century, the

143

Iberian culture that had developed in the southern and eastern parts of the peninsula reached Castille, which was dominated by the Celts, after which this new Celtiberian culture advance northward.

Whatever their age, the famous "bulls of Guisando," together with other animal sculptures found near Avila, evince the continuation of a Greco-Iberian sculptural tradition that emerged in Betica. We may also note that the Lusitanians of present-day Portugal put up stiffer resistance to the Iberian culture: the tombs there contain few elements that are not Celtic. After Hannibal's reconquest of Spain in 221 BC, the Celtiberians served as mercenaries in the Carthaginian army, fighting against the Roman conquest and responding to the military repression exerted around Europe against the Celtic peoples who had taken up the Punic cause.

The Roman conquest of Numantia was preceded by eight centuries punctuated by skirmishes, pitched battles and all-out war, prompting the frequent observation that the Iberian Celts proved a much tougher enemy than those of Gaul. However, this kind of comparison fails to take account of the circumstances of the respective conflicts: nevertheless, the Iberian element proved a unifying factor for the Celts in the peninsula, one which the Gauls lacked. The latter were consequently quick to take up opportunistic alliances and little inclined to pay heed to the reasoned, nationalist arguments of Vercingetorix.

Excavations have brought to light hundreds of bronze figurines like the ones shown here. H. from $2^{3/4}$ to 6". Musée Barbier-Mueller, Geneva

Inquisitive travelers to the town of Avila will note the imposing stone animals, which are either bulls or boars, a number of which are exhibited in the cloister of the cathedral or in noble houses. In all, 123 of these strange sculptures have been found in this region of western Spain and in Portugal along the Douro—in other words, within a diameter of about 60 miles around Salamanca, halfway between Avila and the Portuguese border. The biggest concentration of these monuments would seem to be in the area around Avila and in the province of which it is the administrative capital: no less than 65 animals are kept here, most of them highly eroded. The best known are the four "bulls of Guisando" which stand alone in the middle of a field 30 miles south of Avila. On the back of one of these granite sculptures is an inscription, which has been half worn away, which a number of archeologists have used to justify the attribution of a "recent" date to all the animals in the same style. In fact, these are more likely to be vestiges attesting the Iberian element in Celtiberian culture. There is an obvious kinship with the zoomorphic sculptures to be found around Andalusia, especially between Cordoba and Jaén, but which are also found on the eastern coast, towards Alicante, and whose pure Iberian origins are undisputed.

The bulls of Guisando, El Tiemblo. Celtiberian Art.

THE ART OF THE CELTS

Celtic art was highly original and—wherever it was not crushed by Roman domination (for example, in Ireland)—long-lived. It makes its appearance rather suddenly in southern Germany and Bohemia in around 450 BC. It is characterized by a pronounced taste for curvilinear decoration built from repeated, linked and interlaced motifs such as spirals. Hence its name, the "Continuous Vegetal Style." The major exhibition in Venice in 1991 and its catalogue managed to put the spotlight on the aesthetic values and creative talent of this people who are often confused with the Germans, and whose cultural heritage is something modern Europeans have every reason to be proud of.

It is 387 BC. Republican Rome is already a power to be reckoned with. It is busy undermining the strength of the Etruscan confederation that witnessed its birth. The Romans have just won a major military victory and have captured the rich Etruscan city of Veii. Suddenly, like a violent hurricane, an army of 30,000 Gauls comes out of nowhere and ravages everything in its way, going on to seize the future capital of Christianity. The Romans never forgot this nightmare. And never again, even in the direst situations, would one of their enemies, a Hannibal or a Pyrrhus, manage to get near to the city. Can it be said that the Celts made contact with Italy at the beginning of the 4th century BC?

In fact, recent research has shown that the Celts settled south of the Alps at the end of the Bronze Age. Thus the so-called "Golasecca culture" has been recognized as Celtic.

It was the Celts of Como and Sesto Calende who, acting as intermediaries

Mound with biface stela at Tübingen-Kilchberg (Baden-Württemberg, Germany), rebuilt as it would have been in the 6th century BC. In original location.

148

between the Etruscans and the Celts north of the Alps, made these towns rich.

We should hasten to add that these peaceful traders had nothing in common with tribes such as the Insubres (the founders of Milan), the Cenomani, the Boians and the Senones, the very bellicose peoples who later settled in northern Italy, known at the time as Cisalpine Gaul.

Who were the Celts?

At the beginning of his famous *Commentaries*, Caesar wrote that "We call them Gauls, they call themselves Celts." However, in the same sentence he also distinguishes the Gauls from the Belgae, who were in fact another branch of the Celt nation.

The oldest historical references to this mysterious people date back to 500 BC and the writings of Hecatea of Miletus (of which we possess only fragments) and, somewhat later, Herodotus. The latter offers some precise information: the Danube has its source in the land of the Celts, which stretches westward to the Atlantic Ocean. That is all the Greek historian has to say about these remote foreigners. It was not until the Italian campaign that Celtic pugnacity was acknowledged, so much so indeed that, after the sack of Rome, the Carthaginians and Etruscans, as well as the king of Syracuse (who followed their lead) hastened to recruit these fine soldiers as mercenaries.

There were many different tribes, and these groups would often split up so as to engage in different enterprises. Thus while the Boils (who gave their name to Bohemia) were involved in the sack of Rome, another group of Celts were busy settling in the Bordeaux area.

The Celts had no system of writing and only adopted the Latin, Etruscan or Greek alphabets fairly late in the day, leaving us few inscriptions. No doubt the Celts' original homeland was between the upper Rhine and Bohemia. Further north were the Germans (who also spoke an Indo-European language), with whom the historians of the ancient world often confused them.

When, in the 2nd century BC, the Cimmerians mounted a raid on Italy

This magnificent and original bronze wine flagon was made in 400-350 BC by the Celtic bronzeworkers of southern Germany. H. 18". Museum für Kunst und Kulturgeschichte, Salzburg, Germany.

there was talk of further Celtic depredations, when in fact these invaders were 100% Germanic. Linguistically, in fact, the Celts were closer to the Italic tribes than to the Germans. This confusion only came to an end with the conquest of Gaul by Caesar in the 1st century BC.

One thing is certain: the Celts were Europeans of ancient extraction. But were they the descendants and successors of their predecessors during the Neolithic period (3rd millennium BC) and the Bronze Age (2nd millennium BC), when they began to build mounds over noble tombs? The basic principle is this: although these Bronze Age or Hallstatt peoples may have been proto-Celts, the Celtic lands only become visible as such in around 450 BC, and stretch from central France to Bohemia.

This is the "La Tène" culture, named after a site on Lake Neuchâtel in Switzerland, which corresponds to the second phase of the Iron Age and (by pure convention) is said to end with the conquest of Gaul and the accession of Augustus (who, after his victory at Actium in 31 BC, became the first Roman Emperor).

Mounds and chariots

The building of burial mounds was a habit that may have been borrowed from the occupants of the steppe along the Don and Ural rivers, where such mounds had been built since the Bronze Age. During the First Iron Age, or Hallstatt period, this trend took on astonishing proportions, whereas cremation became increasingly rare (until then, nobles had been buried and commoners were burned). From now on, bodies were buried with varying amounts of funerary gifts, and in anything from modest tombs to underground chambers, depending on their rank.

During this period the Celts occupied an area extending from Champagne in France in the west to present-day Hungary and Slovenia in the east, and from the mountains of central Germany (above which lived the Germans) in the north to the valleys of Lombardy in Italy in the south. No less than 6,700 burial mounds have been listed in Württemberg alone. At the end of the Hallstatt era, the grave goods that Celtic princes and princesses took with them into the afterlife show that great material wealth had been amassed. The masters of the fortified settlements near the main communication routes (those that were used to transport tin from the British Isles to Italy, or silk from the eastern steppe, traces of which have been found in a Hallstatt tomb) levied a tax on the traders' caravans. They also commissioned these merchants to bring back bronze flagons or containers that had been made fashionable by Greek coppersmiths and were produced in the Greek workshops in Italy or by the Etruscans, the heirs to the Villanovan tradition. The incredible discoveries made at Vix in Burgundy and at Hochdorf in the Neckar Valley illustrate the splendor of the Celtic princes just before the emergence of Celtic art as such—before the La Tène period. The two tombs in question are more or less contemporaneous. The one at Vix housed the remains of a young woman while its neighbor

Left: Dagger from Hochdorf illustrating the Celtic geometric style. La Tène period. Württembergisches Landesmuseum, Stuttgart, Germany.

Right: One of the figures supporting the Hochdorf couch (following pages). The anthropomorphic legs of this seat reflect a tradition close to the "geometric" art of Greece and Italy. Württembergisches Landesmuseum, Stuttgart.

at Baden-Württemberg held those of an unusually tall man. Both had been carried to their final resting place in a four-wheeled wagon which was then taken apart and put in the tomb. The two tombs also contained large bronze vases in the Archaic Greek style (6th century). The man in the Hochdorf tomb rested on a remarkable bronze couch, which is perhaps the most important archeological vestige from the 1st millennium found in Central Europe.

The art of the Celts

"Classic" Celtic art is highly decorative, favoring plant motifs, or motifs "redolent of plants," into which it fits human faces and bodies of fantastic animals metamorphosed into tendrils that are knotted and unkotted, at first symmetrically, and then asymmetrically. When we refer to the

Large bronze
seat from the
Hochdorf tumulus
(circa 520 BC).
Württembergisches
Landesmuseum,
Stuttgart.

"Oriental influence" thought to have inspired the development of the
"continuous" curvilinear Celtic style in around 450 BC, we are of course
referring to the same Orientalism that infuses Etruscan art from the end
of the 6th century, with the appearance of griffins, sphinxes, animals and
animal tamers and palmettes (symbolizing the Tree of Life) and other
motifs that came over the seas from the Near East. These transfers can be
explained by the trading relations established during the Bronze Age
between the countries north of the Alps and the Italian peninsula (along
with Greece). However, they do not take into account the contact
between the inhabitants of the Danubian regions and the inhabitants of
the plains of today's Russia. The Thracians and Scythians lived alongside
and traded with the Hallstatt period Celts, while at the same time the

Scythians organized raids as far as Assyria and Iran. It is hardly surprising, therefore, that the Scythian manner of breaking up animals' bodies, and the half-human and half-animal Celtic creatures with their clearly defined articulations and muscles, should recall both the strange wild animals made by the bronzeworkers of Siberia and the cast iron pieces of Luristan made by Indo-European nomads who settled in the mountainous regions of western Persia during Iron Age I. There is therefore no need to assume the existence of migratory movements like those we know of from historical times in order to explain the transplantation of certain ways of doings things, and certain graphic and plastic vocabularies whose presence is unlikely to have been due to spontaneous reinvention (always a possibility when only simple motifs such as spirals, crosses or key patterns are involved).

Above:
Head of a man
from the "Dejbjerg
wagon."
Nationalmuseum,
Copenhagen,
Denmark.
Right:
A famous stone
head found in
Bohemia. These
two sculptures are
several centuries
later than the
Hochdorf couch.

Early and classic Celtic art

The great bronze seat on which rested the Celtic prince in the recently excavated Hochdorf mound gives no signs of what we might call "classic Celtic art." Hochdorf is a tomb from the end of the First Iron Age (not long before 500 BC) and the decoration of the objects is exclusively geometric and angular, as can be seen from the golden sandals and dagger. The legs of the couch are anthropomorphic, in keeping with a tradition that we can link to the Geometric art of Greece and Italy.

This tradition, which is a long way from the Continuous Vegetal Style developed by the Celts who left those human faces with eyebrows ending in spirals, can also be observed in Italy, during the First Iron Age, in the decoration of Villanovan bronze containers and ceramics.

From European angular geometrism to the Celtic curvilinear style

To simplify, we can sum up the emergence of a unified "Classic" Celtic art over the vast territory concerned by saying that in around 450 BC, with the Second Iron Age (La Tène), the angular geometrism of the Bronze Age and First Iron Age (Hallstatt), gave way to a pronounced taste for curving motifs which are typical of what is described as the Continuous Vegetal Style because of the constant presence of intertwining spirals and volutes forming a compact pattern on the surface of the objects. Above, from left to right: an early Bronze Age vase, a vase from the First Iron Age and a vase from the Second Iron Age (La Tène culture). The differences pretty much speak for themselves. The continuing geometrical decoration on the first two vases contrasts sharply with the lyricism of the broad spirals painted on the third.

It is interesting to recall that while 2nd-century Europe was luxuriating in squares, lozenges and saw-tooth patterns, there were civilizations at the eastern end of the Mediterranean that had developed a passion for "conti-

nuous curvilinear" decoration. The stone containers of the Cycladic period (circa 2500 BC) have adjoining spirals, a motif that also features abundantly in Mycenaean Crete, whose contacts with western Europe in the middle of the 2nd century BC have been conclusively substantiated.

Similarly, a "geometrical" style has been observed in Greece in the first half of the 1st millennium BC (at the time, therefore, of the Hallstatt civilization north of the Alps). This is superbly attested by the large funerary vases found in Attica. And yet, at the same time, large vestimentary fibulae in the form of double inverted spirals have been found in both Geometric Greece and Villanovan Italy.

No one knows why the Celts were the only culture to draw eyebrows and moustaches as spirals, in the process creating such a powerfully original style of art that one soon forgets its borrowings from Etruria and Scythia as one admires its exuberant mixture of interlacings and leaf-like forms which bring to mind the (re-)inventions of a Guimard or a Gaudi only a century ago.

Celtic religion

To what extent do such works reflect religious concerns? Are they not, rather, talismans whose function was to ward off the mysterious and ill-defined forces threatening an individual or community? Like the Scythians, of whom Herodotus gave a precise description, Celtic tribal societies must have been very similar to the "non-literary" societies of Africa and the Pacific that we have had occasion to study through to the present day. They have their gods and revere them, but there are no temples, no clergymen.

Perhaps we have been deceived by the very precise observations recorded by Julius Caesar, who presents the Celtic pantheon through a loosely applied Roman lens, writing that the god the Gauls worshipped most devoutly was Mercury, along with Apollo, Mars, Jupiter and Minerva. Less an ethnologist than a strategist, the famous general forgets to give us the corresponding Celtic names. We might assume that he chose those divinities whose functions or attributes seemed closes to those of Mercury, Apollo and Mars.

Historians have been studying this question since the 19th century, but so far their only conclusion is that the Celts had a number of gods of varying importance. This impression is no doubt heightened by the fact that two different tribes could easily worship the same divinity, but under two different names. All this ties in with Caesar's remark: "Natio est omnis Gallorum admodum dedita religionibus" ("the people of the Gauls is excessively inclined to religion"), which could well apply to people who were busy with all kinds of magico-religious practices without however being devoted to specific cults in the Roman manner. From inscriptions we can be sure of the names of a number of gods such as Epona,

Below:
Large silver phalera (boss) found at Manerbio sul Mella (Brescia). First half of 1st century BC. Museo Civico Romano, Brescia, Italy.

Opposite:
Spirals and triskeles are common motifs in Celtic art. Detail of a bronze bracelet. Museo Civico Romano, Brescia.

the "equine goddess" (possibly an avatar of the Oriental "mistress of animals"), Sucellus, the "god of the hammer," Cernunnos, the "wearer of deer's antlers" and Taranis (whose name was bestowed on a now-demolished Parisian alleyway, the rue Taranne, opposite the well-known Café de Flore in the Latin Quarter). For a number of these gods worship involved human sacrifices. Other gods from the Celtic world, such as Lug (who gave his name to many a town, and notably Lugdunum-Lyon), continued their career in the British Isles and Ireland, whose myths, as transcribed in the early Middle Ages, are a source of information as precious as they are dangerous: for how can we be sure that nothing has been lost, nothing transformed, fused or altered, between Prague and Dublin, and in the ten centuries during which the Celtic contemporaries of Pericles grew into the subjects of the Irish kings?

The end of the Celts

While Celtic religion, customs and art were able to survive in the regions that remained outside the *Pax Romana*, such as Ireland and Scotland, Celtic civilization began to undergo profound changes in the 1st century BC as a result of the Roman victories in Gaul and the pressure exerted by the Germans. By the end of the La Tène period, the Celtic territories had changed considerably. Real *oppida*, or fortified towns, had grown up along the major trade routes. The temples housed statues of gods while thick ramparts protected the houses of the rich. The different craftsmen—blacksmiths, ceramists, jewelers, etc.—were grouped together in specific districts. This unity began to disintegrate with Caesar's conquest of Gaul. The Continuous Vegetal Style mentioned above would disappear from the continent, surviving only in the British Isles.

For a full idea of this European past, we would need to be able to bring back the buildings, painted hangings and wooden statues that have been lost to time. The extraordinary beech-wood woman's bust found at Chamalières in France gives us some idea of what

Preceding pages: Silver plaque from a large cauldron comprising several panels with different decorative schemes. It was found in Denmark, which was German territory, and was no doubt imported from the Celts. Its origin has been much debated, although it seems likely that the man with the deer's antlers is the Celtic god Cernunnos. Danish Nationalmuseum, Copenhagen.

we have lost. But let us not lament: ignorance is the nursemaid of imagination, and enough has been preserved to nourish our dreams.

This bronze figure found at Bouray appears to be a Celtic god. For all its realism, due no doubt to Roman influence, it remains very much a Gaulish sculpture. Musée de Saint-German-en-Laye, France.

REPUBLICAN AND IMPERIAL ROME

Never a true democracy, and always fascinated by dictators, the proud Republic was always likely to fall into the hands of an adventurer, especially when, like Julius Caesar, he was a direct descendant of the goddess Venus. Only a thousand years separate the first, legendary Romulus, the founder of the city, from Romulus Augustulus, the last emperor who was toppled by a barbarian. But in the course of those ten centuries the Roman adventure changed the course of human history for ever.

It is quite possible that the traditional date, 753 BC, is in fact pretty close to the time when a few Latin shepherds settled on the Palatine Hill. Did their leader go by the name of Romulus? That seems unlikely. Livy claims that Romulus marked out the limits of a city with a furrow, and then appointed a hundred senators, but 8th-century BC houses were no more than round or oval huts built on clay foundations: nothing to warrant the name of city.

The centuries of legend

The Via Appia (Appian Way) was named after Appius Claudius, a censor of the Republic who also built this gateway, which is one of the few pre-imperial monuments in Rome. Photo by the author.

It was only after 600 BC that a larger town grew up. Not in the hills, but at their foot, where the Forum now stands. There they built the Temple of Vesta, whose form for many years evoked the modest huts of the early days. The Sabines, who were culturally and linguistically close to the Latins, no doubt lived nearby, if not in one of the villages that have recently been rediscovered. Tradition states that the successor of Romulus, Numa Pompilius, was a Sabine. Was he the son of one of

the Sabines abducted by his predecessor? Or the avenger of his people, who vanquished the Latins of the future Eternal City?

One thing is certain: we can start speaking of a city with the advent of the three Etruscan sovereigns, who were the last in the list of the seven legendary kings. It cannot have been very difficult for a neighboring Etruscan prince to conquer these seven, strategically advantageous hills once he had set his heart on them. The tiny Latin tribe was not strong enough to repel this people whose trading ships sailed all around the Mediterranean.

Frescoes in the most famous Etruscan tombs at Vulci relate how the brothers Vibennae set out to free their ally Macstarna, who was held prisoner by Cneve Tarchu Rumach—i.e., Cnaeus Tarquinius of Rome. A chronicle of the imperial epoch tells us that Macstarna was the Etruscan name of Servius Tullius, the second Etruscan king of Rome, who came between the two Tarquins. Roman historians, who were not familiar with the tomb at Vulci and its inscriptions, say that Servius Tullius was deposed by the last Tarquin, Tarquinius Superbus. In other words, the great Etruscan nobles fought one another for control of Rome. The Republic was very probably founded in the first half of the 5th century BC.

Wars of survival, wars of conquest

When the Republic was founded, Rome was little more than a few villages surrounded by a wall. The Latins (for Rome was not the biggest of their cities) was one small tribe among other fairly primitive Italic groups, wedged in between the confederation of Etruscan cities and the Greek colonies of southern Italy.

At first, then, the Romans had no plans to conquer Italy, let alone the known world—notwithstanding what historians of the imperial period say or imply. No, their priority was survival and the first step was to establish their hegemony over the other Latin cities. After that they had to keep the Sabellian people at bay (this is the blanket term for the Indo-European tribes of central Italy, the Samnites, Oscans, Volscians,

The Via Appia. Photo by the author.

Eques and others) and to loosen the Etruscan stranglehold, for their former masters were only a few miles further north. In 396 BC, the indifference of its Etruscan neighbors left the Romans free to take Veii. A few years later, however, they were thrown back by the Celtic invasion as Gauls swept down south of the Po, ravaging Tuscany and seizing Rome. This terrible memory left an indelible scar and, from now on to the end of the Empire and the barbarian invasions, Rome would always be carefully guarded.

Volsinii, the last independent Etruscan city, fell in 265 BC. Now it was time to look south. Seeing the threat, the rich Greek city of Tarentum called on the king of Epirus, Pyrrhus, for help. This self-proclaimed defender of Hellenism duly landed with his well-trained army and his elephants and defeated the Romans twice, in 280 BC and in 279 BC. But these "Pyrrhic victories" were to cost the Greek king dear. When he sailed homeward in 275 BC,

Tarentum was taken. Now the entire peninsula was Roman.

Rome's only remaining rival was Carthage, a Punic (i.e., Phoenician) colony in present-day Tunisia. The two cities had already drawn up several treaties defining their respective spheres of influence. Sicily was in the Carthaginian sphere, except that the city of Messina was now occupied by mercenaries from central Italy who had become independent of their Greek masters and were threatened by Carthaginian forces. By accepting their pledge of allegiance, Rome was breaking its treaty with Carthage. The first Punic War broke out in 264 BC. Rome made alliances with Syracuse and then Marseille, posing as the champion of Hellenism when it had only just liquidated the Greek colonies in Italy and defeated their champion, Pyrrhus! It was a curious turnabout, but by no means an illogical one. Amidst all those village-like, tribal societies, was not Rome like a great beacon that had just been lit?

The Romans hastened to build a fleet so as to meet on equal terms an enemy that was greatly experienced in naval strategy and well armed to

boot. After various ups and downs, Rome emerged victorious. In 241 BC, Carthage yielded Sicily and paid a tribute. Both towns were in dire financial straits. Carthage even had to suppress a revolt by its unpaid mercenaries. To do this it had to seek assistance from its former enemy, ceding it Sardinia in exchange. The events of the Second Punic War (218-201 BC) are well known. Setting out from Spain, whose Mediterranean coast had been colonized by the Carthaginians, Hannibal, son of the famous Hamilcar Barca, crossed the Pyrenees and then the Alps. Having started out with 80,000 mercenaries, he reached Italy with

only 26,000 men and yet, while greatly outnumbered, still managed to inflict two defeats on his Roman enemy. In 217 BC came the disaster of Lake Trasimene, when 15,000 Romans were killed. In 216 BC, Hannibal inflicted the worst defeat in all Roman history: out of 80,000 soldiers, 25,000 were killed, 20,000 were taken prisoner, along with one of the two consuls, and only 15,000 were able to make it back to the city.

In this dire predicament, Rome's alliances proved brittle. A number of Italic cities as well as Syracuse and Tarentum now changed sides while, in Macedon, Hannibal managed to obtain the help of King Philip V. Never was Roman tenacity so sternly tested and proven as in the years that followed. Town by town, region by region, it forged new alliances, won back territories. Soon, it was laying siege to and—eventually—capturing Syracuse (one victim of the battle being a certain Archimedes).

Hannibal's luck, too, was bound to change. In 202 BC, he was defeated by Scipio Africanus at Zama. It was left to Scipio the Younger, known as Scipio Africanus Minor, to deal the fatal blow to Carthage. Although this long conflict had brought considerable economic problems, Rome did not rest on its laurels. First of all, it set about conquering Cisalpine Gaul, founding Bologna in 189 BC; then it subdued the Ligurians, a non-Indo-European people living on the Mediterranean coast around Genoa and as far as the Languedoc. The Roman provincia would one day become Provence.

At the same time Rome, the most powerful city in the western Mediterranean world, also began to look east. Its first victim was Philip V of Macedon. Having defeated him, the Romans declared the Greeks free of the Macedonian domination that they had experienced ever since the days of Alexander the Great's father.

The process of methodical empire-building had begun. The map in this chapter (p. 187) graphically illustrates

Bust of Scipio Africanus. Museo Archeologico Nazionale, Naples, Italy.

the success of this undertaking that was pursued obsessively from one generation to the next.

The time of rebellions

The troubles that broke out in the second half of the 2nd century BC prefigure many a popular revolt in modern times. The wealthy *optimates'* monopoly on the land stirred such discontent among the *populares* that it was impossible to repress. This group found a spokesman and champion in the person of young man of high birth: Tiberius Gracchus. Although of plebeian origin, his father had held important positions and had risen into the nobility.

Elected tribune of the plebeians, Gracchus sought to pass a law limiting the size of arable holdings allotted to individuals. The land that would have thus been regained was to be distributed to poorer citizens.

The Senate reacted violently and the troublemaker was executed.

But Tiberius had a brother who was ten years his junior, Gaius Gracchus, who now took up the project. However, he was no more successful

and lost his head in the attempt. The Gracchi, as they are called, had failed. Nevertheless, the seeds of resentment had been sown in fertile soil. The rebellion in North Africa, backed by the Numidian king Jugurtha, was to reveal another of these popular heroes. The second in command in Africa, Gaius Marius, was a man of modest origins and little learning, but a fine soldier and leader, and too powerful for Jugurtha. In between battles, he managed to discredit his superior and have himself made a consul. Once in Rome, he spoke out freely about the Jugurtha's bribes to various magistrates and senators. Taking advantage of his consular power and popular support, Gaius set about a complete overhauling the army's recruitment system. Initially, no one foresaw the tremendous consequences of enrolling the poorest citizens to serve the flag, when hitherto they had always been barred from doing so. Before 107 BC, the year of Marius' reforms, the army had been constituted by five classes of men, divided up according to their personal wealth, for soldiers were expected to provide their own equipment and the more modest citizens were not obliged to do military service. From now on, thanks to Marius' reforms, the army would include poor wage-earning soldiers who, while they had no estate or property to defend, would exploit the circumstances of war to climb the social ladder. Moreover, when they were demobilized these soldiers were awarded a plot of land, a free recompense for which their general stood as guarantor. Now we can understand why the troops were so devoted to Marius, Pompey or Caesar: no old-style army could ever have been prevailed upon to cross the Rubicon!

Below:
As victor over the Gauls, Gaius Julius Caesar had coins minted with his name on. D. 1/4". Musée Barbier-Mueller, Geneva.

The Republic confiscated

Nothing could be further from the truth than the idea that Caesar and his heir Octavian (the future Augustus) acted like upstart tyrants, transforming an old democracy into a monarchy. In the first place, the Roman Republic was no democracy: the success of the plebeians in gradually wresting power from the patricians had not changed

the oligarchic nature of the government. While Rome certainly offered opportunities to rise above one's station as a reward for great deeds, once you became a general, consul or senator, your heirs would automatically belong to the happy few. These are very much the workings of an oligarchy.

By seizing power and having his consulate established as a lifelong office, Octavian was not flouting republican principles. For centuries it had been the practice to elect dictators in periods of danger and to vest in them the most exorbitant powers, including the power to decide whether their fellow citizens should live or die. Octavian followed Caesar in becoming a permanent dictator. Imperator, the title bestowed on him by the Senate, had already been taken by many a victorious general. The word does not mean the same as our "emperor."

We come closer to it with the other title that was thrust on Caesar's great-nephew: Augustus.

Julius Caesar

The pithy, colorful portraits penned by Lucien Jerphagnon and Pierre Grimal show us the superior intellectual qualities of the man who, in a single year (45 BC) both reorganized the administration of the provinces and allied or subject cities and weakened the power of the Roman nobility and senators (by raising their number to 900 and promoting even sub-officers to their ranks).

That same year, Caesar also reformed the calendar, setting the year at 365.25 days (thus giving us our modern calendar, which was only very slightly modified by Pope Gregory XIII in 1582). He founded Seville in Spain and Bizerte in Africa and granted Roman citizenship to the inhabitants of Cisalpine Gaul (northern Italy centering on the River Po). However, the tasks of checking corruption and administering what was now an empire led him to reduce the privileges of the elite—the Senate and the nobles, who represented less than 1% of the citizens. Caesar's severity made many discontents.

Consul, dictator, pontiff and augur, Caesar was also on several occasions proclaimed *imperator*, a title bestowed on victorious leaders.

Debate continues as to whether Caesar's goal was to arrogate all power and, after four proud centuries of republicanism, to restore the monarchy for his own personal advantage. Certainly, he did not disdain the white-braided crown of the eastern kings when, much to the disapproval of the crowd, it was placed on his head by Mark Antony on February 15, 44 AD. Indeed, he even had this contested crown placed on his statue in the Capitol.

This moment was perhaps a test, for the dictator was no man for idle games. That, certainly, is how his adversaries understood things: a month later, on March 14, 44, Caesar was stabbed 23 times. And, while Antony organized a magnificent funeral, the weakened but relieved nobles jeered, as did Cicero.

Bust of Caesar. Green basalt. Mid-1st century BC. H. 16⁵/₁₆″. Staatliche Museen, Berlin.

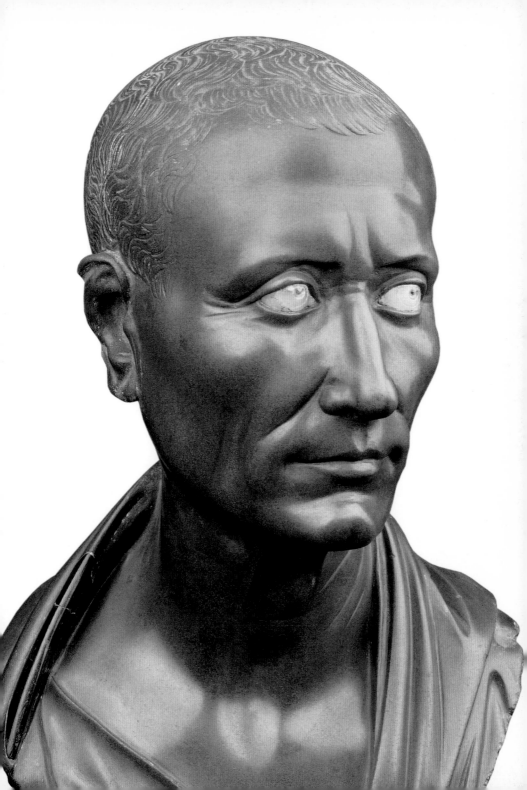

The grandeur of this title was unprecedented, unsurpassable ("Romulus" was one alternative that had been considered). And yet the Senate continued to function, and the various magistratures and institutions of the Republic were either maintained or gradually reinstated—all the consuls, quaestors, praetors, tribunes and censors. No matter that most of their functions were now attributed to Augustus. They had been to Caesar, too. And so, after eliminating his rival Antony, who was driven to commit suicide along with his mistress Cleopatra, Octavian Augustus took in hand the destiny of the *res publica*. This was a very different proposition from our modern "republic." Although the words translate as the "affairs of all men," the *res publica* was nonetheless managed by a small group of men who owed their power to noble birth and also, but almost never exclusively, to the talents with which nature had endowed them. Since Caesar, the *res publica* had been the business of one man only. And since that man was authoritarian and omnipotent, he tended to treat each individual either in accordance with that person's merit, or simply as the fancy took him. Dictatorship would weaken the power of the great families and make the humble less humble. Of this we have firm proof in the *Res Gestae*, written by Augustus at the end of his life. There we read: "During my sixth consulship, having put an end to the civil war using the absolute powers entrusted to me with the consent of all, I conveyed the Republic from within my own power to that of the Senate and the Roman people."

The emperor modestly adds that in reward for his meritorious act, "I was named Augustus."

The Late Empire and the fall of Rome

The Late Empire is generally said to begin with the death of Commodus in 192 AD. Before the accession of Diocletian in 284, numerous crises shook the huge and disparate ensemble whose structure had been built by Augustus. For some fifty years now, the pressure from the barbarians on the Danube frontier had

Below: This bust of a Roman officer wearing a baldric and a paluda mentum shows the influence of imperial statuary in the period of Trajan. It dates from around 100 AD. H. 18½". Musée Barbier-Mueller, Geneva.

Opposite: Though conquered by Caesar, Gaul was not perfectly pacified and Augustus found it necessary to take military action. This trophy at La Turbie was built to commemorate his victories there, six years after the birth of Jesus Christ.

To begin with, each citizen belonged to a small family nucleus. These nuclei were joined to form an extended family, or clan. This was the gens whose name was taken by each member (gentilice).

The gentes (plural of gens) united to form curae, and ten curae in turn formed a tribe. At the beginning of the monarchy, that is to say, in the 5th century BC, there were three tribes. It has been supposed that they may have represented the three ethnic groups present in the town: Etruscans, Latins and Sabines. Servius Tullius, an Etruscan and the penultimate king of Rome, is credited with replacing the three original tribes with four new tribes, organizing gentes in accordance with their place of dwelling. The word "tribe" thus became almost a synonym for ward or parish, and the number of gentes grew constantly. There were, however, limits. Alongside the citizens (necessarily members of a gens) was the crowd of outsiders, the traders or craftsmen who formed the Pleb, and who constituted their own groups. In addition to the Curiate Assembly (comprising three tribes, and thirty curae), he created five classes on the basis of wealth and set up an assembly for the entire population, the Comitia Centuriata.

The classes included varying numbers of centuries. In the first there were 80 centuries, who provided the army with its cavalry (on top of which there were 18 centuries of horsemen, not included in the class) and were the richest citizens. Since there were 193 centuries in all, and as votes were attributed by century and not per capita, the middle classes and the poor (excluded from the army) were automatically in a minority. Moreover, this system reduced the power of the older families in favor of the new rich. Clearly, the number of tribes had increased in keeping with the extension of the Republic's territories. In the third century there were 35 tribes, four urban ones and 31 rural ones. Freemen and new citizens were registered in the plebeian urban tribes. To join the patrician class one had to be adopted

Etymologically, the patricians were the descendants of the patres, that is to say, members of the Senate during the monarchy (by around 200 AD it was considered that the original patrician families had ceased to exist). By the beginning of the 4th century BC, the plebeians, who were in open conflict with the patricians, had gained the right to become consul or censor. Former magistrates automatically became members of the Senate.

This was how the nobilitas (nobility) was formed, from the important patrician and plebeian families. For even if a plebeian family had included several consuls, that was not enough to make it patrician.

The equestrian class is a social category that illustrates the complexity of this hierarchy. Its members included cavalrymen whose nobility entitled them to a "public horse," which they were to look after and ride during military campaigns, but also those whose wealth had given them access to this status, but who were required to pay for their own steed (equo privato). In 225 there were twelve thousand cavalrymen, of whom only 800 were entitled to a "public horse."

The workings of this system show the importance of the censors. Appointed for a five-year term, the role of these magistrates was to assess the standing of each citizen and to place them in one of the above-mentioned classes. The censors kept the register, or "album" of the Senate, whose 300-odd members they either confirmed or designated. Their extensive powers ran to excluding or transferring individuals from their tribe because of their behavior. They also approved adoptions, which were the only means of access to the patrician class (we know that, in his testament, Caesar adopted Octavian, the future Augustus, into his family, the Julia, which claimed descent from the goddess Venus).

Every five years, then, the censor "filtered" or "purified" the entire Roman citizenry. This process was known as the *lustrum*.

been growing irresistible. Breaches had been made and the Goths had begun moving southwards through the gaps in the Roman defensive system.

In 193 AD, a general of North African origin was proclaimed emperor. Septimus Severus achieved many worthwhile things but had the weakness to marry an eastern princess who was constantly bringing to Rome new, exotic gods and cults from her home country. One of his descendants took the name of a Syrian god whom he venerated (Heliogabalus) and indulged in the excesses of a cult involving extremely perverse relations between priestesses and believers. But the reign of the last Severiuses also saw the spread of the teachings of one Chrestos, or Christus, who had been crucified in Palestine two centuries earlier. In 235 AD, Alexander Severius was assassinated. Chaos reigned. Diocletian (284-305 AD), the persecutor of Christians, was the first to attempt to redress the situation. A second, more marked revival occurred under Constantine the Great, who granted the disciples of Jesus the right to practice their religion freely in his Edict of Milan

(313 AD). This princeps founded Constantinople on the site of ancient Byzantium. Another important date is 394 AD, when Theodosius closed the pagan temples: the persecutors of yore were now themselves the persecuted.

The empire, though, was on its knees. German barbarians were settling throughout and Rome struggled to keep face by issuing imperial authorizations for these migrations that had already occurred.

In 402 AD, Ravenna was made capital of the Western Kingdom.

In 451 AD, the Huns were held back only with the help of the Goths. The guards watching over the emperor were themselves barbarians and one day, one of them, Odoacer, decided to put an end to the charade that was the Italian imperial power. In 476, he deposed the last emperor and sent his crown and scepter in a parcel to the eastern emperor, Zeno, at Constantinople (was this an act of flattery or mockery?).

The eastern emperor did his utmost to reconquer the peninsula, but Byzantium was too far away and the emperors were now Illyrians, Greeks fascinated by the splendor of the Orient. They imitated the king of Persia and imported Chinese silk to make rich, heavy brocades that the rough-hewn heroes of the Republican epoch would have mocked.

How far the Empire had fallen! In the west, Gothic tribes were fighting over the rich cities left by Rome. In the east, potentates now spoke Greek instead of Latin and were perfectly indifferent to Italy and Gaul. Indeed, they had new enemies to worry about: the Bulgars, Slavs and Turks (Mongols from furthest Siberia, distant relations of the Huns). Ancient Rome was no more.

Covering as it did the whole Mediterranean, Roman imperial power soon acquired a rather incongruous hodgepodge of symbols. Here the lion's head emblematic of power is endowed with the horns of the Egyptian god Amon. Musée Barbier-Mueller, Geneva.

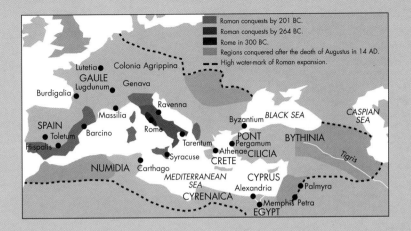

The Romans and religion

As citizens of a Republic where you were either a soldier or a nobody, the Romans had little time or inclination for mysticism and had ceased to worship the gods of their remote Indo-European ancestors. Under Etruscan domination, they adopted the triad of gods that their neighbors had themselves taken from the Greeks: Jupiter (Zeus), his wife Juno (Hera) and Minerva (Athena). Under the Republic, the Romans showed little concern for metaphysical problems: their nationalism was practical and realist, and they filled their pantheon with whichever gods they thought would help them control the supernatural forces threatening individuals or the nation. Sometimes, before laying siege to a city, the Romans would pay homage to its protective god or goddess. The system was, as we know, highly effective! In the same way, magical practices were adopted whenever they seemed effective. Everyday life in Rome was cluttered with rites that owed nothing to religion and everything to superstition. While there were priests responsible for certain cults, the clergy was not an organized body. Purifying rituals were organized to avoid contamination (*piaculum*) and to prevent the sacred (*sacrum*) from interfering with everyday life (*profanum*). Thus the Roman contemporaries of the Greek philosophers behaved pretty much as the Papuans always used to in recent centuries. If Stoicism appealed to them, it was because it posited the principle that the divine order imposed on mankind was irrefutable.

Chronological outline

Beginning of 1st millennium BC – The Italian peninsula is inhabited by various Indo-European tribes. To the north of the future Rome, Villanovan culture carries the seeds of the Etruscan Confederation whose brilliant civilization influenced—and was ultimately destroyed by—Rome. To the south, Greek colonists begin to found cities. The first, in 775, is thought to be Ischia.

753 BC – According to legend, Romulus traces the furrow on Monte Palatino that would mark the boundaries of the future city called Rome. It is said that after him came three Latin or Sabine kings. In fact, all that existed were a few villages of huts, the remains of which have been excavated and dated.

616 BC – Accession of the first of Rome's three Etruscan kings.

509 BC – Tarquinius Superbus, the last king, is sent back to his native Etruria. Birth of the Republic. Soon, executive power is wielded by two Roman consuls occupying yearly terms.

474 BC – Syracuse defeats the Etruscans, speeding the decline of their economic and political power.

450 BC – After the conflict between patricians and plebeians, the "Law of the Twelve Tables" establishes relative equality between Roman citizens. However, the prohibition on intermarriage between patricians and plebeians remains.

396 BC – Veii is the first city of the Etruscan Confederation to be taken by the Republic.

390 BC – A lightning invasion by the Gauls culminates in the capture of Rome.

367 BC – From now on, one of the two consuls can be a plebeian.

326 BC – Beginning of the Samnite Wars.

312 BC – The censor Appian Claudius orders construction of the Via Appia.

280 BC – Designs on the Greek town of Tarentum, which is defended by Pyrrhus, king of Epirus. The whole of southern Italy falls to Rome.

265 BC – Fall of the last Etruscan city.

260 BC – Beginning of the Punic Wars. Carthage is destroyed in 146. Spain becomes Roman.

148 BC – Conquest of Macedon.

146 BC – Conquest of Greece.

107 BC – Marius reforms the army. The general becomes a kind of god for the soldiery.

105 BC – Numidian War. Defeat of their king, Jugurtha.

91 BC – The Social War. The Italian tribes make their last attempt to save their independence.

90 BC – Roman citizenship granted to all inhabitants of the peninsula. Ethnic and cultural particularities are at an end (disappearance, for example, of Etruscan civilization, script and language).

60 BC – Formation of the first triumvirate: Pompey, Crassus and Caesar.

59 BC – Caesar becomes chief consul. War on Gauls.

52 BC – Pompey proclaims himself sole consul. Caesar marches on Rome and crosses the Rubicon. He defeats Pompey at Pharsalus in Greece.

44 BC – Dictator since 47, Caesar is murdered by conspirators.

31 BC – Caesar's great nephew and adoptive son, Octavian, breaks with his former ally, the consul Mark Antony, and crushes his fleet at Actium. Cleopatra, Antony's mistress, kills herself.

27 BC – Octavian is given the name Augustus by the Senate. The Republic is confiscated and Augustus becomes *princeps* (or "first citizen," a more appropriate term than emperor).

68 AD – Death of Nero, great grandson of Augustus and last of the Julio-Claudian *princeps*. The struggle for power between the generals Galba, Otho, Vitellius and Vespasian ends in the triumph of Vespasian. The first emperor not to emerge from the old aristocracy, this capable general founds the Flavian dynasty.

96 AD – Death of Domitian. The Flavians are replaced by the Antonines. Their reign is marked by the conquests of Titus and Hadrian.

192 AD– Death of Commodus, son of Marcus Aurelius. End of the Antonines and the Early Empire. The Late Empire is marked by the threat from the Germans on the borders.

212 AD – Caracalla grants Roman citizenship to all freemen of the empire.

260 AD – The Romans are defeated by the Persian king Shapur.

284 AD – Accession of Diocletian. He chooses to rule with a second Augustus, Maximian, and then adds two junior emperors, the Caesars, to form the Tetrarchy.

305 AD – Diocletian voluntarily abdicates. The Tetrachy ends in quarreling between the different Caesars and Augustuses.

312 AD – Constantine triumphs over the Tetrarchs. He grants the Christians freedom of worship and founds Constantinople on the site of the ancient Byzantium (today's Istanbul).

394 AD – The emperor Theodosius closes the pagan temples.

395 AD – Death of Theodosius. His sons Arcadius and Honorius reign, respectively, in Rome and Constantinople. There is now a Western and an Eastern Empire, each with its own capital: Rome and Constantinople.

402 AD – The Western capital is transferred to Ravenna. Everywhere, the barbarians are flooding over the borders. Visigoths, Ostrogoths, Burgundians, Franks and Lombards make a mockery of an enfeebled empire as they carve out their own kingdoms. Rome itself is no more than the seat of the pope.

476 – Romulus Augustulus, the last Western emperor, is deposed by the Barbarian who commands his guard. The emperor in Constantinople will remain, in name at least, the sole successor of Augustus until the fall of the Eastern Empire in 1453.

Rome and the arts

As Horace observed, Roman sculpture and painting were both daughters of Greece. However, the finest Roman art, the portraits whose truthfulness and realism are unmatched by those of any Greek artists, came from Etruria. We know that Tarquinius Priscus, the first Tuscan king of Rome, had a full-scale terracotta statue of Jupiter raised on the Capitol square. We are familiar with such works from those that were found at Veii and are kept at the Villa Giulia. It seems highly likely that this magnificent vision of the "king of the gods" (imported from Greece via Etruria) made a profound impression on the subconscious of the new nation. The Romans never denied their debt to the Etruscans. Indeed, what is no doubt the oldest work of art made in the city (by one Novos Plautios in circa 320 BC) is a large box whose cylindrical form and decoration are typically Etruscan.

"Conquered Greece conquered its fierce victor
and brought the arts to rustic Latium." Horace

The two sculptures shown here both date from the beginning of the Empire, i.e.,
the first centuries BC and AD. The one on the left (50 BC-50 AD, H. 6$^{1/2}$") typifies
the Hellenistic influence on Roman religious art. In contrast, the kind of ancestor images
exemplified by this matron on the right (110-120 AD, H. 6"), which only nobles
and not plebeians were allowed to own, were made with a vigor and lack of prettification
which indicate a very different tradition. This goes back to the Etrusco-Italiot portraits
of which the most famous example is the bronze "Head of Brutus" (see p. 123) in
the Vatican Museum, Rome. Here the Greek influence is combined with a distinctly
Italic coarseness. Both works here: Musée Barbier-Mueller, Geneva.

OUR ANCESTORS THE BARBARIANS

Two years before the celebrations marking the bicentenary of the fall of the Bastille, 1987 witnessed rather more modest festivities recalling the coronation of Hugh Capet exactly 1,000 years earlier.

Admittedly, unlike 1789, that distant regal event is shrouded in the mists of a past where only historians can find their way. And if we try to forget the bloodshed and failures of the Revolution and think only of the equality and freedom acquired when the *sans-culottes* became members of the bourgeoisie, then memories of Capet's accession boil down to the image of a dynasty that became identified with French history: its Germanic roots are quite simply forgotten. For French memories are more enthusiastic and more faithful when it comes to their "ancestors the Gauls" than when considering the people who gave the country its name: the Franks.

These two wooden statues, discovered in a marsh in northern Germany, represent the gods of the Braak and date from the 5th century. The faces bring to light a little-known aspect of this tribal civilization. Indeed, would we not spontaneously tend to associate them with the rituals of some contemporary "primitives"? Archäologisches Landesmuseum, Schleswig, Germany.

In order to understand what forged the character of western Europe, readers unfamiliar with the Early Middle Ages would need to go back to the end of the Western Roman Empire. In 395 AD, the vast realm conquered by Augustus and his successors was officially divided into two halves: an Eastern Empire, with its capital at Constantinople, and a Western Empire centering on Rome. For two centuries now, the legions posted on the Germanic borders had been keeping an anxious eye on the considerable migratory movements going on around them. In the middle of the 3rd century AD, the Franks settled on the banks of the Rhine. In 276 AD, 70 towns in Roman Gaul were wiped out by a great surge of those to whom the Romans applied the blanket name

From tribal art to Christian art

The historian Tacitus confirms that the religion of the Germans did not require them to make images. If we considered only the readiness with which the Franks or the Lombards proceeded to adopt architectural and artistic traditions from the Greco-Roman world, it would indeed be tempting to believe him. But we also possess sculptures that give the lie to Tacitus' assertion. Modern archeologists thought that these "idols" (two of which are shown on the previous page) represent gods identified in the writings of ancient historians: Thor, Nerthus, Wotan or Freya. But are they not, rather, "fetishes," guardians that served to ward off malevolent spirits? It would not be surprising to find magical—as opposed to religious—objects amongst tribes for whom the evidence of human sacrificial prac-

tices goes back to earliest antiquity.

A form of "primitivism" remains in evidence in certain funerary or religious monuments found in Germany and dating from a period, the 7th century AD, when the Franks had already been converted to Christianity. One would not imagine the stela shown on the right to be contemporaneous with, or even later than, the small ivory plaque on the left. Both works are Frankish, but the second is from a region influenced by Gallo-Roman traditions. Here is clear evidence of the passion with which these hardy northerners took to the sensuality of the Mediterranean world and to the glorious Hellenistic heritage, all of which explains the ease with which they embraced Christianity.

Left: Plaque representing Saint Peter or one of the Evangelists. Ivory. 6th century. H. 9¹ᐟ⁴″.
The Metropolitan Museum of Art, New York.
Right: Frankish stela. Rheinisches Landesmuseum, Bonn, Germany.

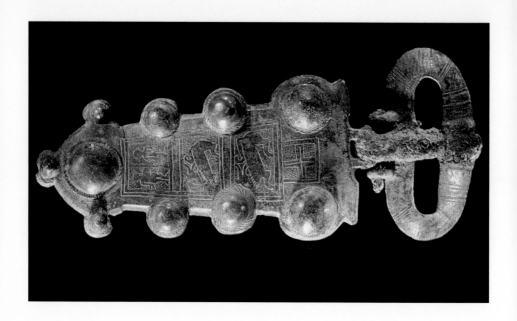

These two bronze buckles, one Merovingian (above, south of the Loire, 7th-8th century. W. 7"), the other Burgundian (Burgundian kingdom, 5th-6th century, W. 4¹ᐟ²") show the influence of the Scytho-Siberian steppes on barbarian body ornaments. However, the winged figure surrounded by lions on the Burgundian buckle is the Old Testament prophet Habakkuk. Both: Musée Barbier-Mueller, Geneva.

"barbarians." This term designated genuine Germanic peoples such as the Franks, Goths and Alemanni, but also groups from the steppes of central Europe or Russia such as the Sarmatians and the Alans as well as Turko-Mongols like the Huns and Hunnigars.

At the turn of the 5th century Alaric, king of the Visigoths, invaded Italy and the Emperor of the West was unable to resist. The capital was transferred from Rome to Milan and then established at Ravenna.

In 451 AD, the threat of the Hun hordes led by Attila prompted a new alliance between Romans and Visigoths, which managed to beat the invading forces at the Catalaunian Plains (near present-day Châlons-sur-Marne, in eastern France). But that was not the end of it. The Franks and Burgundians, too, were attracted to the mild climate of Gaul.

As for the Western Emperors, they tried to fight barbarians with barbarians. Indeed, the imperial guard was itself composed of the strongest barbarians and it was indeed their chief, the Herulean Odoacer, who eventually deposed the last successor of Augustus, Romulus Augustulus, in 476 AD, and sent his insignia to the emperor of the East.

That date, 476 AD, is generally accepted as marking the end of antiquity and the beginning of the Middle Ages. The new medieval age lasted until 1453 and the collapse of the Eastern Roman Empire, marked by the Turkish capture of Constantinople, which now became the capital of the Islamic world.

It is important to note that this barbarian Europe was Christian, even if some of these ferocious warriors, such as the Visigoths, upheld the Arian heresy. Clovis, the famous king of the Franks, was converted in 596 AD and, when the Carolingians followed on from the Merovingians, the only remaining pagans were the wild Saxons (whom Charlemagne baptized by force in 785 AD). We may remember that in 380 AD a decree by Theodosius made Christianity the Roman state religion and prohibited worship of the old Greco-Roman gods.

In this mix of peoples, this seedbed from which the future European nations would grow (Visigoth Spain, Frankish Germany, the Lombards in northern Italy, etc.), the illiterate masses were under the intellectual domination of monks and bishops. The barbarians, who were cattle-raising people from the north, never had any real architecture and

Following pages:
The baptistery of Saint Jean at Poitiers (7th century) shows how the Franks, who had no architectural tradition of their own, based their buildings on Roman models.

adopted that of the Late Roman Empire. If we compare the last monument of antiquity (the mausoleum of the empress Galla Placidia in Ravenna, built in around 450 AD) and the brick churches built in the same town under Ostrogoth domination, we get a good idea of the Germans' capacity for assimilation. In fact, it may well be that the only building from this period to break away from the Roman tradition is the tomb of Theodoric, an imposing rotunda perhaps designed to imitate the mounds of stone and earth once laboriously assembled to seal the tombs of nobles and chiefs in central Europe or in the Russian or Siberian steppe.

Merovingians, Carolingians and Robertians

It was Clovis and his four sons, the descendants of Meroveus, who were the first to create a kingdom that, from a geographical point of view, pretty closely resembled today's France, albeit with the addition of the Franks across the Rhine. However, divisions among Clovis' descendants led to endemic warfare, enabling "mayors of the palace" such as Charles Martel to become veritable heads of state. It was Martel, in fact, who founded the Carolingian dynasty, which was followed by the Capetians.

Hugh Capet

When Hugh the Abbot (or Hugh the Great, grandson of Robert le Fort, count of Paris and Blois) died in 956, his responsibilities were taken up by his son Hugh. He was nicknamed "Capet" because of all the lay abbot's capes inherited from his father. The latter was a man who had never pressed claims to his father's royal crown (Robert, son of Robert Le Fort), resting content with the title "Duke of the Franks." Capet himself was not much pushier. His beginnings were modest, and over the decades that followed his succession, his power indubitably declined. His suzerainty over Aquitaine, for example, was a mirage, for his liege man there, Duke William "the Tow-Headed," refused to acknowledge him. As one historian has tellingly noted, "It was the very

Built in 450—two centuries before the baptistery of Saint Jean at Poitiers—the tomb of the empress Galla Placidia at Ravenna is no doubt the last building of antiquity. Photo by the author.

Early medieval architecture

After the fall of the Western Roman Empire in 476, architecture regressed in all the lands held by the barbarians: having no traditions of their own, they merely copied existing Roman constructions. Since the barbarians were also Christians, their first buildings were churches (with the exception, that is, of Theodoric's mausoleum). During the Carolingian period, the Visigoths of Asturia built a strange royal residence, the palace of Naranço, the facade of which has a series of raised semicircular arches in the Romano-Byzantine style (circa 840).

The traditional forms of the basilica and rotunda had already been used for the rotunda church (or "mausoleum") of Santa Costanza in Rome, which dates from the imperial period (340-355). This domed building is surrounded by an ambulatory with external porticoes. Such porticoes were to constitute one of the key characteristics of early medieval religious buildings, becoming standard annexes of the basic church structure. Built by a Roman architect shortly after Theodoric's rise to power, the church of San Vitale at Ravenna (between 530 and 546) is based on an octagonal plan which would later be used for the Palatine chapel at Aachen (Aix-la-Chapelle). It is to be noted that the central octagon has a hexadecagonal precinct. This chapel built for Charlemagne by Eudes of Metz illustrates the growing complexity of religious architecture.

Religious buildings gradually moved away from the classic style inherited from Rome and towards a much more complex form that would blossom into the glory of the Romanesque period.

Opposite: Photograph of the palace at Naranço in northern Spain.
The facade is of Romano-Byzantine inspiration (circa 840).
Above: Plan and section of the church of Santa Costanza in Rome.
Side, from top to bottom: Photo, plan and section
of the church of San Vitale at Ravenna. Plan of the chapel at Aachen.

decline of Robertian power that determined the election of Hugh Capet," since this reassured the great feudal lords. In fact, there was another factor in Capet's favor. Asserting his Carolingian legitimacy, Capet's king, Lothair, the son of Louis d'Outremer, had the reckless idea of making war on Otto II while laying claim to Lorraine (the first in many a Frankish dispute over this region). Capet, though, stood by his rash lord who, against all expectations, made it all the way to the imperial capital, Aix-la-Chapelle (Aachen), which he duly pillaged before turning back without pressing his advantage any further.

Otto was furious and summoned all the lords of Germany. In 978 he unleashed his troops on France, devastating the north and sacking the royal palace at Compiègne. Seeing them poised to take Paris, Lothair fled. In his place, Hugh Capet organized the defenses whilst awaiting the reinforcements he had requested from his brother, the Duke of Burgundy. But Otto sensed that his luck had changed and turned back. Capet's troops had the satisfaction of pursuing and massacring his

rearguard. Thus Lothair's failure was followed by Otto's. As was often the practice in those days, Lothair decided to share the royal function with his son. The latter thus became Louis V at his coronation in Compiègne in 979. Lothair's decision was partly motivated by the desire to protect his heirs against the claims of his brother Charles, Duke of Lorraine.

For all his devotion, Hugh Capet now began to show his claws. Abused by a monarch for whom he had done so much, he sought a rapprochement with Otto. And Otto was only too glad to oblige.

At this juncture, Lothair died of appendicitis, leaving his throne to the 19 year-old Louis V. The sobriquet later attached to him, "the Do-Nothing," was in fact deeply unjust. Louis had little time to prove himself as his reign lasted only a year, but his decisions were sound. Aware of Hugh Capet's barely concealed sympathy for the German Emperor, Louis decided to neutralize him rather than look to him for support. Unfortunately, Louis' political acumen was accompanied by a great passion for hunting. The young king died from the wounds incurred when pursuing game.

It so happened that the synod of French bishops was meeting at the time to judge the behavior of the archbishop of Reims, a powerful figure devoted to the cause of Otto. The prelate grasped this opportunity to kill two birds with one stone and managed to have himself acquitted by arranging the election of Hugh Capet to the throne.

Eliminating the first Carolingian pretenders

Charles of Lorraine, an authentic descendant of Charlemagne, and uncle of the deceased young king, argued his own legitimacy in vain: Hugh was acclaimed king at Senlis in 987. However, as long as his crown was disputed by Charles the Carolingian, there were always important nobles ready to hesitate between the legitimate heir to the throne and the "duke of the Franks," even if the astute archbishop had managed to demonstrate that among the Franks royalty was not hereditary.

Opposite:
Gold ewer crafted by Carolingian goldsmiths and decorated with enamel. According to local tradition, it was donated to the monastery of Agaune by Charlemagne. Abbey of Saint-Maurice.

Following pages:
Paten (Late Empire) made with serpentine (1st century BC or AD) (serpentine) and (paten). From the court of Charles the Bald (second half of 9th century: mount). Serpentine inlaid with gold, precious stones, pearls, stained glass, filigree, garnets and copper. D. 6³/₄". Musée du Louvre, Paris.

It was, then, only in 991, once Charles had been eliminated for good, that King Hugh could begin thinking of consolidating his power and ensuring that it was preserved for his descendants. In the year after his own investiture, he singled out his son Robert II, a practice that would continue until the older child's claim on the throne was taken as automatic.

As a key figure in French history, a skilled politician and dogged defender of his possessions and privileges, Hugh Capet's renown is well deserved. However, it also tends to overshadow his forebears, the Dukes of Neustria, who had been gradually shoring up their position in France over the last four generations, thus laying the foundations for Capet's success. After all, was Hugh not the grandson and great nephew of two French kings?

His great masterstroke, immediately after his election, was to claim God as his sole master and, more audaciously, his sole "elector." Apparently, the Eternal was not too displeased, since Hugh' son, Robert, reportedly had the power to cure scrofula.

We might ask ourselves if the Almighty plays by the rules of democracy and gives his blessing to the presidents of the Republic, the latest successors of the Merovingians. But then did anyone ever see Messrs. Auriol or Mitterrand curing scrofula sufferers on the day of their investiture? In contrast, the most maladroit of the Capetians performed miracle upon miracle. To which you may reply (and you would be right) that kings and presidents have always had a remarkable talent for amnestying dishonest ministers or promoting obscure servants, which only goes to show that they are indeed equal before God!

Detail of a miniature by Jean Fouquet, showing Hugh Capet, who was crowned at Senlis in 987, thus founding the third dynasty of French kings. The portrait, needless to say, is imaginary. Bibliothèque Nationale de France, Paris.

THE DISMEMBERING OF THE ROMAN EMPIRE *MEDITERRANEAN SEA*

The Barbarians and the beginning of the Middle Ages

When the barbarian general Odoacer deposed the last Roman emperor of the West in 476 AD, no one in Italy considered this a turning point. It is simply that historians now agree to take it as marking the end of antiquity and the beginning of the Middle Ages. At the time, for inhabitants of the peninsula the word "barbarian" was synonymous with "soldier" because the army was made up of a great mixture of the peoples nominally under Roman rule. Stilicho, the general who put up such stiff resistance to the Visigoths (although he was unable to prevent them from taking Rome in 410) was himself a barbarian. Similarly, it would seem that Odoacer acted as he did only in order to ensure that his men received the land that was their due and whose

attribution was being called into question. One thing is certain: he unambiguously claimed to be exercising power in the name of the Emperor of Constantinople, who bestowed on him the title of patrice. Italy did not suddenly become more barbarian after 476.

When Odoacer became too ambitious, Zeno, the eastern emperor, decided to rein him in by sending a young Ostrogoth prince of illustrious line, Theodoric, who had been raised at the court of Constantinople as a hostage. The young chief's irresistible campaign at the head of his people ended up with him conquering not only Italy but a part of Provence, central Switzerland and a considerable chunk of present-day Austria and (former) Yugoslavia (see map above). But although he was proclaimed king by his fellow countrymen after capturing Odoacer (493),

Theodoric was not the sovereign of the Romans of Italy. His coins were stamped with his monogram but minted in the name of the emperor. The main problem affecting the peninsula was due to the fact that the Ostrogoths had adopted the Arian heresy, and were thus opposed by the clergy. As the only Roman Catholic sovereign in the barbarian world, Theodoric's contemporary Clovis had no such problems and consequently enjoyed full submission from his Gallo-Roman subjects.

Merovingian France

Fifty years after the fall of the Western Roman Empire (476), the chief of the Franks, whose triumphant advance from Germany had taken them as far as the Somme River, was Clodion. We are not quite sure of the nature of his relationship to Meroveus, who gave his name to the dynasty under which France became a melting pot of the Celtic (Gaulish), Roman and Germanic traditions which, with the conversion of Clovis, were soon to be bound together by Christianity. In any case, in 481 Clovis, who was Meroveus' grandson or nephew, inherited a kingdom that stretched from Catalonia to Belgium.

At his death in 511, his kingdom extended all the way to the Pyrenees. Only Burgundy had been spared (in fact, he had married a Burgundian princess). Power was divided up between his four sons in the traditional Frankish manner. Consequently, there were soon four Frankish kingdoms: Neustria in the northwest (Salian Franks), Austrasia in the northeast (Ripuarian Franks), Burgundy in the southeast and Aquitaine in the southwest, which was contested by the Visigoths.

The Merovingian monarchs were consequently weakened by constant warring and power was increasingly in the hands of their ministers, known as "mayors of the palace." Finally, in 751, Pepin the Short, the son of one such mayor, Charles Martel, deposed Childeric III and became king of the Franks.

Francia occidentalis. Kingdom of Charles the Bold
Francia media (Lotharingia). Kingdom of Lothaire
Francia orientalis. Kingdom of Louis the German

Carolingian France

Pepin the Short pursued an interventionist policy in Italy, where he was the sole support of the popes against the constant threat of the Lombards, the Germanic barbarians who had settled in the Po valley after 568. By now the emperors of Byzantium were Roman only in name, being either Greeks or Armenians, and were incapable of defending the papacy. In 800 Pope Leo III unexpectedly placed the imperial crown on the head of Pepin's son, Charlemagne, then visiting Rome. Thanks to the pope, the king of the Franks thus became the heir of the Caesars. Henceforth, the masters of the Holy Roman Empire would, after the election and coronation in Aachen, come down to Rome to be consecrated. The reign of Charlemagne's son, Louis the Pious, saw a real cultural renaissance. However, divided up as it was into over 200 pagi (districts), the empire was poorly administered. The counts wanted independence and their titles to be hereditary. Louis' three sons eventually divided up their kingdom, in accordance with ancient barbarian custom. The result was three more homogenous kingdoms: "eastern France" (Germany), ruled by Louis the German, "western France " (former Gaul) ruled by Charles the Bald, and Lotharingia (i.e., Provence, Burgundy and Italy) by Lothair, the nominal emperor.

Capetian France

The ancestor of the Capetians was Robert "the Strong," a valorous warrior who had been invested with several important counties by Charles the Bald in 857. No doubt the son of an important noble family in the Rhineland, he married a princess of Carolingian blood and distinguished himself by repelling the Normans.

In 888 the Franks decided that the grandson of Charles the Bald, Charles the Simple, was not up to the job and elected Eudes, the son of Robert, to replace the Carolingian. The move was approved by the emperor, Arnulf. However, on his deathbed Eudes requested that the crown be returned to Charles the Simple. Back on the throne, Charles covered Eudes' brother Robert with honors, but this did not save him from being dispossessed of his throne once again, this time in favor of Robert, who was elected king in 922. When Robert died, his son Hugh the Great, or "the Abbot," approved the accession of Charles the Simple's son, Louis d'Outremer, who reciprocated by making Hugh Duke of the Franks. When, at the same time, the German Carolingian line died out the imperial title went to Otto I of the House of Saxony. Hugh the Great never sought to take power and his son Hugh Capet himself bided his time. His moment finally came when Louis V, grandson of Louis d'Outremer, died in a hunting accident.

IMMORTAL EGYPT

Everything about the history of Egypt, that fertile corridor traced by the Nile in the middle of the desert, seems miraculous. Barely emerging from prehistory, its sovereigns could call on the most gifted sculptors, the most daring architects and the most skilled goldsmiths. When western Europeans were living in modest lakeside villages, three Egyptian kings, whose names every schoolchild knows, built those incredible, indestructible monuments that are the pyramids.

Is it in the slightest bit surprising that, ever since antiquity, travelers should have been overwhelmed by such wonders? The decision to include the word "immortal" in this chapter's title was a considered one. But the Egyptians did more than leave the ineradicable proofs of the exceptional gifts showered on them by nature; they also managed to sustain their traditions for 3,000 years. These are what underlie the remarkably homogenous yet never monotonous monuments and works of art so many of which can still be admired on the sites where they were conceived, built and sculpted. And we can venture that these marvels, which dazzled the travelers of ancient times, will forever continue to convey their message of faith in the success of all the undertakings dreamed up by humanity, however ambitious, transcending the vicissitudes and incidents that are no doubt needed to stimulate our will to survive and progress.

Opposite:
The pyramids of
Mycerinus and
Chephren at Giza.

The dawn of civilization

The Predynastic era, which ended some time around 3200 BC,

was marked by the coming together of the different clans, each of which had its own emblem (falcon, ibis, etc.). Some of these emblems were also taken as the physical manifestation or symbol of the guardian divinity of the clan capital or its symbolic object. The clans were at the origin of a certain number of the 42 nomes, or provinces, of Pharaonic Egypt, for some of these provinces were the result of regroupments or creations decided by the Pharaonic administration over the centuries. By the end of the Predynastic period, certain chiefdoms had already risen to a dominant position. The kings of Upper Egypt were distinguished by a long, white crown, while those of the Nile delta wore a low, red crown. The Scorpion King, identified by his mass of weapons with decoration featuring the falcon god bringing the obeisance of the inhabitants of the Delta, wears only the crown of the South. On a ritual makeup paddle that belonged to his successor, Narmer (often identified as the legendary Menes known to the Greeks, the founder of the first dynasty) we can see hieroglyphs indicating his name but also showing him wearing the bulb-shaped crown on one side and, on the other, the low crown, thus indicating that he was the king of the Two Egypts.

This was the "Thinite" period, named after Thinis, near Abydos, the capital of the first two dynasties. This period saw the beginnings of metalworking with copper (not yet bronze) being used to make plates and instruments (although finely worked flint tools also remained in favor). These Egyptians wove linen and wool and invented writing. Until fairly recently it was believed that Thinite constructions were made only with unfired bricks, as attempted by their tentative efforts to pave tombs. Excavations at Helwan, some eighteen miles south of Cairo, have brought to light First Dynasty tombs in the form of underground chambers whose walls consist of neatly cut blocks of white limestone. These initiatives paved the way for the exploit carried off by the great architect Imhotep a few centuries later: the construction of the first pyramid at Saqqara.

Many writings, few writers

Hieroglyphic writing was invented in the Predynastic period and used through to the Roman conquest. The word comes from the Greek *hieros*: sacred and *gluphein*: to engrave. Greek travelers observed that these inscriptions were found mainly in temples. They are also known as ideograms, from the Greek for form, *eidos*, since the object referred to is drawn: for example, five snakes will be represented by a snake drawing followed by five bars.

In order to express ideas or actions, the ideograms were given a phonetic value and were read in the manner of a rebus. For example, to transcribe the word "to establish", i.e., *semen*, one represented a folded cloth, named *se*, and part of a checkerboard, or *men*. Another example: the coronation name of Prince Tutankhamun was Nebkheperure. It was written using three hieroglyphs: a basket (*neb*), a scarab (*keper*) and the sun disc (*re*).

These meticulous, tasteful hieroglyphic inscriptions reflect the desire to make monuments in which the god, or the deceased, is surrounded by

beauty. These inscriptions are compositions in their own right, each one a painting or bas-relief in miniature.

Although we are aware of some moving legends and superb myths, the ancient Egyptians had no Homer, Sophocles or Anacreon. No doubt they were too religious to create secular literature.

Left: Example of hieroglyphic writing.
The names of the kings were written
in cartouches surmounted by solar symbols.
Right: The Temple at Karnak.

Ancient Egyptian religion

The religious beliefs, cosmogony and mythology of Pharaonic Egypt were already in place during the Predynastic period, ready to be perpetuated, amplified and, depending on political needs and events, transformed over the next three millennia. Unlike the Greeks with Mount Olympus, the Egyptians did not imagine their gods residing in a particular place: whether minor and local or supreme, their divinities resided wherever there was a temple dedicated to them: some in only one town, others in several. Each of the 42 nomes and each town had its own divine patron whose form was either human or animal. Sometimes, over the years, these gods were replaced by others, or a nome or town would adopt a second or third divinity, or merge a local guardian deity with some new object of worship.

Priests responsible for a given cult were expected to know all the god's avatars, metamorphoses and activities. Often, the priest's function would be determined by that of the god. For example, the high priest of Ptah was the master of the arts because Ptah was the god of artistic activities. The clergy devoted to the lion-headed goddess Sekhmet were doctors because Sekhmet could both bring on and stop epidemics.

A god's appearance and attributes, or even history, could vary from one town where it was worshipped to another. Egyptian mythology was not uniform in the way that Greek, Hittite or Assyrian mythology was. At Memphis, Ptah was held to be the creator of the other gods and organizer of the world. At On, on the other side of the Nile, it was thought that the Sun, Aten (or Re) was the divinity who created all things: hence the Greek name for the town: Heliopolis.

Below:
A member of the Italian archeological expedition at work in the tomb of Nefertari, wife of Ramesses II. Valley of the Queens, 1904.

Opposite: It is possible that the outlines of Djoser's pyramid at Saqqara are those of the core only, without the original plaques that would have made it look like the well-known pyramids at Giza.

Over these three millennia, certain gods declined in importance while other cults developed prodigiously. This was the case with Amun who, although not the god of Thebes (that function was held by Mut) took precedence over all the other gods after his protégé, the pharaoh Kamose, had expelled the Hyksos invaders from the Delta. Amun's clergy grew rich on royal favor, so much so that the high priest of Thebes ended up taking power and leading the country to division and ruin under the last pharaohs of the New Kingdom.

The Greek historian and traveler Herodotus recorded the numerous religious feasts celebrated by this people whom he considered the most pious of all nations. He describes in particular the procession of boats when the Nile burst its banks, that time of great ceremonies when the fields were flooded and it was impossible to till the soil for at least a third of the year; a time when only the cities of the Delta could be seen above the water level.

Herodotus has also left us a fairly clear description of each cult, centering on the animal attributed to its god: "For certain Egyptians, crocodiles are sacred whereas others treat them as enemies. Their sacred character is particularly recognized around Thebes and Lake Moeris. Each region chooses a crocodile and feeds it; the beast is tamed, is bedecked with glass paste and gold earrings with bracelets on its front legs, and is offered special food and victims. Every care is lavished on it while it is alive. Dead, it is embalmed and placed in a sacred tomb ...."

All of which explains the embalmed oxen and mummies of cats, ibises, jackals and other animals found in specially created necropolises.

The Old Kingdom

The Thinite kings brought the country out of prehistory. Narmer and his successors also forged Egypt's political structure, in which all eyes were on the divine figure of the sovereign, to such an extent that dates were reckoned from the beginning of each reign and not, as for the Maya or Babylonians, from a given historical event. A real nightmare for historians.

The sphinx at Giza, a portrait of King Chephren cut from the rock near the 4th Dynasty ruler's pyramid, is one of the oldest monuments in Egypt. More than a thousand years after it was made, the sphinx was restored by the pharaoh Thutmose IV, who himself lived some 3,500 years ago!

With Djoser, founder of the Third Dynasty, we enter both the Old Kingdom and the historical period, when hieroglyphs began to be used to transcribe texts, give form to thought and codify social and religious names. They reveal to us the names of the princes and their most meritorious servants, such as Imhotep, who designed the Step Pyramid at Saqqara for Djoser. But such explicit references are very much the exception.

The builders and the artists commissioned to decorate the residences of the deceased worked together, anonymously, without enjoying the esteem accorded to their counterparts in Greece, where even potters signed their works.

As the inventor of the stepped, pyramidal stone mausoleum (in fact, the construction at Saqqara would well be merely the core, shorn of its original outer plaques), Imhotep attained a glory as enduring as Pharaonic civilization itself: honored, revered as a precursor, he eventually had his own cult, like a divinity, being considered the patron of architects and scientists. Thus, before taking up their quills, scribes would perform a libation in honor of him, and recent excavations at Saqqara, where there is a chapel dedicated to the master architect, brought to light underground chambers containing numerous ibis mummies: the bird is the attribute of the god Thoth, who is the patron of scribes and men of science.

The same Imhotep could well have been the builder of the white wall protecting Memphis, the Egyptian capital throughout the Old Kingdom period.

Djoser's successors were the sovereigns of the Fourth Dynasty, who built the three famous pyramids at Giza, whose architects are unknown to us. Herodotus writes at length about the kings Cheops (Khufu), Chephren (Khafre) and his son Mycerinus (Menkaure). Cheops' ignoble behavior in forcing his daughter to prostitute herself so as to obtain extra revenue, is not just something Herodotus made up: rumors to this effect are already mentioned on a papyrus from the New Kingdom and these rumors had grown so strong by the Greek's time that his guides

The god Thoth. Wall painting in the tomb of Queen Tawsert (extended by the pharaoh Sethnakht, 1185-1182 BC). Valley of the Kings. New Kingdom. 19th Dynasty.

told him that the wretched princess, in her desire to make her abasement known, "implored each of her visitors to leave her a stone. With these stones was built the biggest of all the pyramids."

Such fables show that as far back as the 4th century BC, tourists were already being taken in by tall stories told by locals seeking to embroider on a truth that was in no need of embellishment. They also underline the extraordinary age of these monuments at Giza, since almost as many centuries had passed since their construction and Herodotus' visit as between his account of his travels and the publication of this book.

In fact, the growth of royal power was accompanied by the development of a turbulent feudal nobility and of a class of higher public servants with extravagant prerogatives. The governors of the nomes (Herodotus calls them nomarchs) were constantly tending to break free of the royal authority in Memphis, whose power waned seriously during the Sixth Dynasty.

The country also suffered from Semite invasions. Under the Ninth and Tenth Dynasties, the king's authority was reduced to only Middle and Upper Egypt, over which he reigned from Heliopolis and the Fayium. The Delta was divided up into a great number of principalities. This was the First Intermediate Period, which lasted from about 2400 to 2100 BC. It was the Eleventh Dynasty, from Thebes, that rebuilt Egyptian unity. The energetic kings Antef and Mentuhotep made Amun their main god. Their successors, the Amenemhats and Sesostrises of the Twelfth Dynasty, who established their residence at Lisht, near the Fayium, merged Amun and the sun god Re, thus conciliating the powerful clergy of Heliopolis. The god now worshipped was Amun-Re!

The famous stone falcon at Edfu. This evocation of the god Horus wears the double crown, with the low crown for Lower Egypt and the high one (inserted inside it) for Upper Egypt.

The Middle Kingdom

The Eleventh Dynasty ushers in the Middle Kingdom. To limit the ambitions of his feudal lords, the king now granted favors on the basis merit. This egalitarianism was also evident in religion, where the development of the Osiris cult offered the hope of eternal life to all (and not just to the powerful and the princely), on condition that they

Queen Nefertiti, wife of the pharaoh Amenhotpe IV (Akhenaten). Polychrome bust found at Tell El-Amarna. New Kingdom. Staatliche Aegyptisches Museum, Berlin.

performed the rites reenacting the god's death at the hands of the evil Seth and his resurrection after Isis' quest for him, as related in the well-known myth.

But this period of prosperity and wise governance did not last forever. The kings of the Thirteenth and Fourteenth dynasties were weak and the inhabitants of present-day Palestine, mixed with peoples displaced by the movements of the Indo-Europeans in today's Turkey, started to make incursions into the Delta. These "foreign kings" (Hyksos) put down solid foundations. The guardian deity of their chosen capital, Avaris (Tanis) was Seth, who in some ways resembled their god Baal. The Second Intermediate Period (from circa 1800 to 1600 BC) now began. The Hyksos proclaimed themselves king of Egypt and, for greater security, contracted alliances with the African monarchs of Kush in Upper Nubia. The princes of Thebes were their vassals even though, unlike Memphis, their city was not occupied. The Fifteenth and Sixteenth dynasties had Hyksos sovereigns, but they were soon challenged, and eventually driven out, by the princes of Thebes. Kamose, founder of the Eighteenth Dynasty, cut off communications between the king of Avaris and his ally in Kush, entered the Delta and pursued his enemy all the way to Palestine, reaching the Euphrates. Thus began the New Kingdom.

The New Kingdom

One might think that the supposed divinity of an Egyptian king would make it impossible for a commoner to accede to the throne. But that would be to underestimate the mystery surrounding the gods, as well as their omnipotence. Witness the wife of a mere scribe who, with the help of several divinities, gave birth to magnificent children who came into the world with their members "covered with gold" and "genuine lapislazuli." These three miraculous infants succeeded one another on the throne, bringing the Fourth Dynasty to an end. Who could contest their status as "semi-divinities," when the priesthood itself adamantly confirmed it? Similar situations occurred during the New Kingdom as, for example, the general Horemheb seized the throne with the blessing of the powerful priests of Amun. He quickly set about having the names of his predecessors removed and having his own engraved in their place. As for his own successor, Ramesses I, the chief of his guard, this founder of the 19th Dynasty was accepted without demur by the people as the "son of Re."

There were stranger occurrences. Not long before the reign of Horemheb the double red and white crown was worn by Queen Hatshepsut (no one chooses their name), who used to dress as a man and brandish her weapons from a chariot. She left posterity with a quite exceptional funerary temple which can be admired at Deir el-Bahri.

Pharaonic architecture

Countless temples and sanctuaries were built and modified to honor Egypt's numerous divinities.

The Egyptians invented the stone column in the middle of the second millennium BC (2,000 years before the construction of the Parthenon). There were three orders for the capitals, respectively using the leaf shapes of the lotus (the symbol of Upper Egypt), papyrus (papryus which grew in the Nile Delta, though not any more) and palm.

These precisely proportioned floral columns (with a height: diameter ratio of 7 to 1) were carved from a single piece of stone and could be as much as 10 meters high (see photograph opposite).

The kings of the Old Kingdom built their tombs in the form of pyramids, with small temples placed nearby for performance of the funerary cult required by their divine nature.

In the New Kingdom, kings' temples and tombs were often built underground, marked by grand facades with gigantic statues of gods or kings. Egyptian artists were not gifted individuals working in close partnership with a patron: they were worshippers of a living god, or respectful servants of a prince or minister basking in the aura of the pharaoh.

Temples and tombs were built with fervent devotion. They were collective creations inspired by the belief in eternal life. The materials chosen therefore had to be as strong as possible, to ensure that the dead would continue to enjoy all possible comfort. The Egyptians' faith was self-fulfilling: Djoser, Ramesses and even their courtiers live on, better known to many of us than our own great grandparents, whose burial place and even name we may have forgotten.

Its very pure design was the work of Senenmut, the rather obscure favorite or perhaps husband of the warlike sovereign.

The Theban dynasts, who were proud of having driven out the Hyksos and raised Egyptian power to new heights, were strong personalities and great warriors but also builders. It was they who decided to build their tombs and those of their wives and daughters in the arid cliffs of the Nile's east bank. Hence the building in the Valley of the Kings and Valley of the Queens. The former was where the tomb of the adolescent Tutankhamun, who died in around 1342 BC, was discovered in 1922. The underground chambers opened in front of amazed witnesses were full of riches and works of art of incomparable beauty (to be admired, nowadays, in the Egyptian Museum, Cairo).

Ironically enough, given his brief reign and apparent absence of noteworthy deeds, Tutankhamun is the best known of all pharaohs. He was the close relative, perhaps brother-in-law, of another sovereign whose mystical leanings are well known to art lovers and history enthusiasts: Amenhotpe IV (Amenophis). This ruler incurred the wrath of the clergy of Amun-Re by dedicating an exclusive cult to the sun-disc, Aten, the creator of all things. Not only did he seek to unburden his people of the need to worship the numerous divinities to whom so many sacrifices had to be made (these were ruinously costly for the more modest members of the population), but he also changed his name to Akhenaten and founded a new capital, Akhetaten, on the site of today's El Amarna. That is where superb reliefs were found showing the king receiving the benefits of the sun in the company of his wife, the famous Nefertiti. Her brightly-painted portrait, held in Berlin, is well known (see p. 230). However, the museum in Cairo has an unfinished sculpture which conveys even more poignantly the beauty of this woman who, against the usual rules, was not of royal blood, nor even the sister or niece of her royal husband.

No sooner was Akhenaten dead and buried than his successor, Tutankhatun, repudiated the new religion. Taking up the more orthodox name of Tutankhamun, he returned to Thebes. Now, although the

Opposite: The body of Queen Nefertiti, consort of Amenhotpe IV Akhenaten. Circa 1365-1349 BC. Under this mystically inclined pharaoh, the canons of Egyptian sculpture were strangely modified. After his death, the clergy removed all trace of the monotheism he had sought to institute. 18th Dynasty. Red quartzite. H. 11$^{1/2}$". Musée du Louvre, Paris.

Following pages: In order to save it from being submerged by the newly created Lake Nasser, the temple at Abu Simbel, built for Ramesses II, was completely dismantled and rebuilt on the cliff that had overlooked it for thousands of years.

Amunite clergy had never suffered persecution, they set about stamping out Akhenaten's heresy. Was the splendor of Tutankhamun's burial a reward for the young king's conversion? Perhaps all the other kings of the 18th dynasty were endowed with equally rich grave goods and solid gold sarcophagi. We certainly know that their tombs were visited by robbers not long after the funeral, and that, as their traces reveal, these thieves knew exactly where to look. Tutankhamun's tomb was planned with unusual care, the entry to the underground chambers being hidden under several feet of gravel so that the young pharaoh slept on undisturbed until he was discovered by a particularly observant English scholar.

Few other rulers enjoyed such rest. Certainly not Ramesses II. He may have littered the country with commemorative statues, chapels and huge buildings such as the Ramesseum, a temple dedicated to the majesty of his divine self (something no other pharaoh had ever imagined having built during his lifetime), but his remains were nonetheless piled up with those of his predecessors in a hiding place when, seeing the devastation of his tomb by professional robbers, the priests decided that, if they could not save their treasure, they would at least save the mummies of their former rulers.

The bas-reliefs and frescoes of the New Kingdom, the refinement of the jewelry and splendor of the objects, as revealed by Tutankhamun's tomb (beds, chests inlaid with precious stones, engraved and marquetry-work chairs and throne), will seem even more amazing if we recall that these wonders were made before the legendary siege of Troy, at a time when metalworking was in its infancy (in Tutankhamun's tomb, the only object in this then rare metal to be found amidst all the gold objects and sculpted wood was a small amulet).

The last pharaohs

When, in the 12th century BC, Ramesses III drove out the "Sea Peoples," he proved himself a worthy heir of his princely predecessors

Memphis. Colossus of Ramesses II.

on the throne of the two Egypts. Egyptian chronicles record the names of some of these Indo-European invaders who pushed down from the Aegean basin. They have a familiar ring: the P'l's't, for example, eventually settled in the neighboring lands now named after them: Palestine. The "land of the two kingdoms" was, in the second millennium BC, a rich place indeed. But while the Ramesside Dynasties seem to have taken Pharaonic power to new heights, royal power was nonetheless threatened by the growing authority of the clergy. Based in Thebes, the high priest of Amun could thus award land and positions, although his powers were almost nonexistent in the Delta, this being under the authority of quasi-autonomous princes.

The dominant figure at the beginning of the Third Intermediate Period, which began with the end of the New Kingdom in 1085 BC, was the descendant of Libyan mercenaries, those North Africans known as "Mashouash" whose physique was indistinguishable from that of the

Egyptians. Over the centuries, these foreigners became completely Egyptianized. It was one of their commandeers, the "chief of the Ma" (an abbreviation of Mashouash), who would seize the double crown worn by the last kings of Tanis to become Shoshenq I. He built his capital at Bubastis and it was under his reign and that of his successors that Pharaonic power was reasserted in the Delta, in contrast with the decadence at Thebes due to the excesses in the cult of Amen. But while royal power held firm, the multitude of feudal lords throughout the Delta held the potential for serious problems in the future. Still, the Shoshenq were rich: their magnificent, solid silver sarcophagi indicate the existence of profitable trading relations in the Mediterranean (there were no silver mines in Egypt). Shoshenq I was a prudent ruler. Thus he was careful not to manifest any interest in the gold of Solomon who reigned in splendor, and with a powerful army, over the neighboring

Hebrew kingdom (973-936 BC). However, after Solomon's death, and the moment his son's succession was challenged by the insurrection of Jeroboam, he marched on Jerusalem and, if we are to believe the boasts recorded on a funerary monument, returned to Egypt with Solomon's famous golden shields.

In spite of such exploits, the Twenty-Second Dynasty founded by Shoshenq disappeared with the fragmentation of royal power. The princes of Tanis, Bubastis, Hermopolis and other cities began wearing around their brows the uraeus, the insignia of supreme power, while lesser princes declared independence, even if they did not proclaim themselves king. In Nubia, former Libyan mercenaries brought in by the Ramesses to guard the southern frontier ruled from Napata and combined their occupation with the function of high priest of Amun, flouting the pontiff at Thebes. At the first opportunity they dashed south and set up the Twenty-Fifth Dynasty in around 715 BC. However, there was now a new factor to be reckoned with: the immense power of the Assyrians. In 670, their ruler Esarhaddon seized the Delta unopposed. The princes of the towns and the nobility all rallied to the invader (among them, the kings of Sais, which would have a long history of closeness to Assyria). It was left to Psammetichus, founder of the "Saite" 25th Dynasty (named after its capital, Sais) to reunite Egypt in circa 665 BC. The decline of the cult of Amun and the restoration to its former grandeur of Memphis (home of the cult of Ptah and Osiris) helped Psammetichus I to overcome the rebellion of the feudal lords. He reduced their powers and reorganized the country's administration and system of justice in accordance with Old Kingdom models.

This period saw a remarkable fascination with the Old Kingdom style, which infuses all the highly

Bronze cat, effigy of Basteet, the guardian deity of the Delta town of Bubastis. This work exemplifies the realism of Saite art during the 6th century. H. 10$^{5/16}$". Musée Barbier-Mueller, Geneva.

realistic monuments and sculptures of the Saites.

In the 6th century the Delta was frequented by large numbers of Greek traders and Greek was the language of the pharaoh's army because of all its mercenaries. It also became the language of trade and, as such, was taught in schools. King Nechao officially linked the cult of Zeus with that of Horus, the guardian of the pharaohs. As for the Greeks, who were emerging from the Archaic period like a butterfly from its chrysalis, they were full of admiration for Egyptian civilization. Psammetichus was even asked to set the rules of the Olympic Games. The last Saite king, Amasis, was a general, a former mercenary who had been known as a thief in his youth. On coming to the throne, he was the first ruler to abandon the official title and, instead of "son of Re," call himself simply King of Upper and Lower Egypt. The Greeks paid homage to this reforming sovereign by placing him alongside his predecessor Bocchoris and Darius as one of the great lawmakers. Amasis died in 525 BC, at the moment when Greece was about to take on the power of Persia. Links between the two countries had grown slack. Disaster loomed. The last Saite king was defeated and Egypt became part of the Persian empire. In 518 BC, Darius passed himself off as the heir to the pharaohs, styling himself "image of Re."

After a few uprisings and one final Saite revival, Nectanebo was the last true successor of Narmer, who had reigned 3,000 years earlier.

He was defeated by Artaxerxes III and Egypt remained under the domination of the Persians until the latter's defeat by Alexander the Great. At Alexander's death, Egypt came under the authority of a Macedonian general, Ptolemy, the first in a line of rulers who soon put their Greek origins behind them.

The history of Pharaonic Egypt comes to an end with the suicide of Cleopatra, one of Ptolemy's heirs, thirty years before the beginning of the Christian era. Who knows what would have happened if Julius Caesar had survived and the son the Egyptian queen had with him, Caesarion, had become the successor of the Ptolemies, as seemed to be the Roman general's wish. With Caesar dead,

Painted in encaustic on a wooden panel, this portrait was placed over the wrapped body of the deceased during the Romano-Egyptian period. Most of these paintings were found in the oasis at the Faiyum. H. 20½" (with shroud), 13" (panel). Musée Barbier-Mueller, Geneva.

Cleopatra, heiress to the pharaohs, attempted to shore up her power, but she came up against a stronger force: her plans were at odds with the designs of the future first Roman emperor, Octavian (Augustus). Her fate was sealed. Pharaonic Egypt would become Roman—worse, not even a province; merely the personal property of Augustus.

Circa 5000 BC – Climatic changes encourage autochthonous populations to settle on the banks of the Nile, especially in the highly fertile Delta. Archeologists have defined several distinct periods of this Predynastic era ending in around 3200.

Circa 3200 – Thinite period. Narmer, the probable founder of the first dynasty, unifies the country which had previously been ruled by two different sovereigns as Upper and Lower Egypt. A schist paddle shows the falcon-god Horus, his guardian deity, bringing to him the inhabitants of the Delta as prisoners. The 1st and 2nd dynasties produced engraved stelae with the first hieroglyphs but, apart from underground tombs, no stone monuments.

Circa 2800 – Old Kingdom. King Djoser founds the 3rd Dynasty with Memphis as capital. The architect builds for him the first pyramid at Saqqara. The kings of the 4th Dynasty build the three pyramids at Giza. In the 6th Dynasty royal power is weakened by the nobility. The governors of the nomes seek political freedom.

2400-2100 – (approximate dates) First Intermediate Period. The power of the kings of the 9th and 10th dynasties is restricted to Middle and Upper Egypt. The princes of the Delta no longer obey.

Circa 2150 – The princes of Thebes restore monarchic power and found the 11th Dynasty. This is the Midde Kingdom. Under the Antefs and Montuhoteps the capital is at Thebes. The 12th Dynasty, whose best known kings are the Sesostris, transfers the capital to Lisht. Conquests in Palestine and Nubia. Effort towards greater social equality. This period of prosperity ends with the invasion of the Semitic nomads.

Circa 1780 – Invasion of the Hyksos (the "foreign kings") who make Avaris their capital and control all Lower Egypt as far as Thebes. This is the Second Intermediate Period.

1580 – Having retreated to Thebes, the Egyptian kings drive out the Hyksos and inaugurate the New Kingdom. The reins of the 18th Dynasty (with the Amenhotpe and the heretic king Akhenaten, who seeks to replace the countless gods with a single cult of the solar disc as creator of all life) and the 19th Dynasty (with the great conquerors Sety I, Ramesses II and Ramesses III) can be considered as the golden age of Pharaonic Egypt. The riches of Tutankhamun's tomb give an idea of the creative ferment of this period. The capital remains at Thebes. Nubia is conquered and the royal troops advance as far as

Mesopotamia. The end of the New Kingdom sees Ramesses' victory over the "Sea Peoples." This radically changes the political and ethnic situation in the Near East.

1085 – Beginning of the Third Intermediate Period under the 20th and 21st, or "Tanite" dynasties, several of whose royal tombs have been discovered intact. The authority of the pharaoh is threatened. Shoshenq, the chief of the Lybian mercenaries, takes advantage of the situation and proclaims himself king and founder of the 22nd Dynasty in around 950. However, Thebes remains under the power of the all-important high priest of the god Amun. In the Delta, the great feudal lords finally gain independence.

Circa 750 – Invasion of Upper Egypt by the kings of Napata in Nubia, who proclaim themselves pharaohs. These Nubian monarchs and former vassals of the Egyptian kings are the descendants of Libyan mercenaries sent south to fight off the Black Nubians, with whom they eventually mixed. When they are eventually driven out of Thebes, they take the Egyptian customs that they maintain for long years in their new capital of Meroe.

Circa 670 – The Assyrians invade the Delta and local princes rally to their cause. Thebes is sacked. Thus begins the Late Era.

Circa 665 – Psammetichus I, King of Sais (a descendant of the faithful allies of Assyria) drives the Assyrians out of the Delta and the Assyrians out of Upper Egypt with the help of mercenary forces that include Greek soldiers. This Saite period of artistic renewal ends with the conquest of Egypt by the Persian king Cambyses.

525-404 – First period of Persian domination, marked by numerous revolts of the Egyptian princes.

404-333 – Last Egyptian dynastic period. The Persians are driven out. 28th-30th dynasties.

333-330 – Death of Alexander the Great after the foundation of Alexandria. His generals carve up his empire, with Egypt going to Ptolemy. The Greek Lagide dynasty (Ptolemy is the son of Lagos) reigns without interruption throughout the Ptolemaic period and its monarchs adopt local traditions, having themselves crowned and living as the heirs to the pharaohs.

66 – Rome insists on the allegiance of the Ptolemies. Cleopatra, the last descendant of Alexander's general, seduces Caesar and has a son by him, Caesarion. She then marries Antony who is defeated by Octavian (the future Augustus) in the war for Caesar's succession. Cleopatra commits suicide.

THE ACHAEMENID EMPIRE OF PERSIA

The Achaemenid sovereigns of Persia employed the finest Assyrian, Egyptian and Greek craftsmen to build the palaces that would stand as monuments to their grandeur. Still, their lavishness made little impression on the 26 year-old hero Alexander the Great, that descendant of tough Macedonian warriors who put an end to their power. Seeing the gold plates piled up in the camp of his vanquished adversary, Darius, he turned to a fellow soldier and asked: "Do you think that this is enough to make a king?"

Historically, the Iranians appeared at the beginning of the first millennium BC, in other words, pretty much at the moment when iron was replacing bronze as the material for making weapons and tools. Linguistically, the Medes and the Persians belonged to the great Indo-European family and were related to the Scythians and Cimmerians, their allies against the powerful Semitic kingdom of Assyria. In 825 BC, the Medes were present in the region of Lake Urmia. In 834 BC, the land of Parsua is mentioned in the annals of the Assyrian ruler Salmansar III. But that was only a phase. The Persians were on the way to their definitive habitat, southeast of Susa, the capital of Elam, another country at war with Assyria. There they carved out for themselves the principality of Parsumash, adding to it today's Fars (Parsa). Meanwhile, the Medes had taken Niniveh after triumphing over the Scythians. They had founded a splendid capital, Ecbatana, but their enjoyment of the vast realm they had created was short-lived. Their king married his daughter to the Persian king Cambyses, a descendant of

View of the
apadana at
Persepolis, with the
remaining columns.

Achaemenes, and the son born of their union, Cyrus the Great, won a magnificent victory over his grandfather, uniting the Medes and Persians under his authority in 550 BC. The Achaemenid dynasty would found the world's first great empire, stretching from India to Greece. While continental Greece put up a heroic fight (we have all heard of the battles of Marathon and Salamis, which put paid to Achaemenid ambitions in the area) and avoided the fate of Egypt, its Ionian neighbors (in present-day Turkey) were subjugated.

Even at the height of their power, when the riches gathered from their thirty-two subject peoples afforded a life of incredible luxury, these former nomads never forgot their origins. The historian Herodotus tells us that young Persians were trained in three disciplines: riding, archery and always telling the truth. Respect for ancestral traditions was also manifest in their style of clothing. As can be seen in the famous bas-reliefs that decorated the Achaemenid palaces, the Persians were immediately distinguishable from the Medes and other peoples.

Outline chronology

Circa 1000 BC – The Iranians, Indo-Europeans from the north, arrive on the Persian plateau. Nomads occupy the mountain regions southeast of the Caspian Sea (the so-called Amlash or Marlik culture) and the Zagros Mountains in Luristan. These tribes of shepherds create cast bronze works using the lost wax technique and revealing a variety of influences (Scythian, Assyrian, etc.).

9TH CENTURY BC – The land of Parsa is mentioned in the Assyrian annals of Salmansar III in 834. It is located to the south of Lake Urmia. The Medes are also mentioned: they live to west of the Persians.

8TH CENTURY BC – This is the period of the Persian migration. They eventually settle south-west of Susa, in Elam. At the end of the century, Ecbatana (today's Hamadan) is founded by the Medes. The king of the Persians is Achaemenes, the eponymous founder of the Achaemenid dynasty whose last representatives were defeated by Alexander the Great. Architecture is limited to tombs lined with slabs of stone.

7TH CENTURY BC – Cambyses marries the daughter of Astyages, the last king of the Medes. They have a son, Cyrus II, "the Great," who will later defeat his grandfather Astyages and unite the Median and Persian kingdoms. He and his grandson, Darius I, will conquer Babylon, Egypt, Asia Minor (present-day Turkey), several Greek cities and a part of India. Pasargadae is the capital of the empire under Cyrus the Great. He builts the first Achaemenid palace with vast halls and numerous columns and doorways flanked by winged bulls. Darius I chooses Susa as his residence and founds Persepolis.

5TH CENTURY BC – In 409 the Persian Wars set the powerful Persian emperor against the Greek cities. Xerxes I is defeated by the Greeks at Salamis. But he also conquers Egypt and extends the palace at Persepolis. Under

Below:
Vase in the form of a zebu. Marlik. Circa 1000-900 BC. H. 13¹/²". Musée Barbier-Mueller, Geneva.

Opposite: Object, function undefined. Bronze with repoussé decoration. Iran. Luristan. 750-650 BC. W. 9". Musée Barbier-Mueller, Geneva.

Artaxerxes I, Babylon becomes the fourth capital of the Persians and under Darius II, at the end of the century, Egypt throws off the Achaemenid yoke.

4TH CENTURY BC – Artaxerxes rebuilds the apadana at Susa built by Darius I. This is the period of the enameled brick friezes. Under Artaxerxes III, Egypt is reconquered in 341, but this is the swan song of the brilliant Achaemenid dynasty. In 335 the throne falls to Darius III. In 334 the vast Persian empire is invaded by the king of Macedon, Alexander, who dominates the entire Greek world. In 330 Darius is defeated and killed and Persepolis is in flames. When the young Alexander the Great dies in Babylon in 323, the kingdom of the Achaemenids is divided up and shared out between his generals. The Greek Seleucos is given the redoubtable honor of having to establish himself as successor of Xerxes and Darius. Only in Asia Minor (present-day Turkey) do the former subjects of the Persian kings really adopt Hellenic culture as a coherent whole.

3RD CENTURY BC – A nomadic Iranian tribe, the Parthians, oppose the Seleucids and found a new Persian empire in circa 250 BC. They are followed by the Sassanids, the last authentically Iranian dynasty, who will be swept away by the expansion of Islam in around 650 AD.

The archer's head shown here (p. 249) no doubt comes from Persepolis, where intrepid travelers began collecting "souvenirs" in the 19th century. The fragment shows the fluted diadem worn in imitation of a feather crown. No doubt this was a throwback to the headdress worn by the ancestors of the Persians, the nomads with their herds who celebrated their wild rituals in the steppes beyond Caucasia.

From nomads' tents to Achaemenid palaces

No sooner had they settled in Iran than the Persians began covetously eyeing the surrounding kingdoms. Nearby was Elam. To the west lay Babylon and its rival Nineveh, capital of the Assyrian state. Towards Lake Van, in what is today Turkish Armenia, the kingdom of Urartu was the only culture to use rough-hewn blocks of stone for large-scale constructions. The technique had been borrowed from the Hittites of Anatolia, who had been wiped off the political map of the Near East by a Nordic invasion in the 13th century.

Urartean architecture laid the emphasis on alternating black and white blocks of stone. These alternating colors are also found in Ionia. This tradition has a profound influence on Persian architecture, which was characterized by the use of vast halls whose roofs were held up by forests of columns. The ruins at Persepolis give us a very precise idea of these majestic buildings. It has been suggested that this design was a transposition and evocation of the tents used for so long by the nomads, which were supported on the inside by large numbers of stakes. After all, as recently as the early 20th century Iranian lords were still receiving their guests in vast tents. But whatever the reality, it is clear that in the first palaces, for example the one built by Cyrus the Great at Pasargadae after the foundation of the Medo-Persian empire, the stone columns cohabited with square wooden columns resting on similarly square bases of black and white stone. In this first Persian capital, whose construction dates from 500 BC, we can already make out the features that would grow more marked in the palaces at Susa and Persepolis, and particularly the apadana, the audience chamber

reached by monumental stairs and entered through huge porticos that distinguished these buildings from the massive, bare facades of Elamite and Mesopotamian buildings. Other features were borrowed by Cyrus the Great's architects from foreign counterparts. The most majestic palace of the times were in Assyria.

One of the many inventions borrowed by the Persians were the large winged bulls with human heads that guarded their main entrances. However, the capitols (or imposts, to be precise) of the columns were a pure Persian invention. These consist of the forequarters of two bulls (see p. 259), lions or horses (griffins were also used later), between which a square space was made to fit the roof beam.

This was in effect the last step in the series of developments leading from those primitive structures in which forking branches served as supports for the trunks.

Later on, the Persians copied Babylonian techniques and introduced enameled paneling to decorate their walls, modeling these so as to

produce superb decorative schemes with bulls and lions (see the examples from Susa in the Louvre).

Persepolis and the feast of the New Year

The culmination of Persian imperial architecture was the gigantic palace-cum-town of Persepolis. This site was not pillaged until fairly recently and centuries of providential neglect left magnificent sculptures buried there, waiting to be rediscovered.

Darius I began work on construction almost before he had finished the palace at Susa, and without abandoning Pasargadae, the capital founded by Cyrus, but he did not live to see the work completed. The famous apadana with its monumental stairway was terminated by his successor, Xerxes.

Most of these buildings were meeting halls for the reception of delegations and embassies. Above all, they were designed as the setting for the great feast of the *No Ruz*. These New Year rituals marking the beginning of spring and were overtly intended to celebrate and seal the unity of the thirty-two disparate nations brought together under one authority by the Medo-Persian armies.

This was when representatives of all the main vassal principalities and subject peoples streamed in from all over the kingdom bearing magnificent gifts: precious metal vases, horses, arms and riches of all kinds.

This colorful procession was recorded for eternity on the bas-reliefs designed to magnify royal power and we can even distinguish the origin of each character thanks to their particular clothing: a round bonnet for Medes and a pointed one for Scythians (see p. 248-249).

The political organization of the Persian empire

The first two rulers forged the empire. The third, Darius I consolidated it and endowed it with an administrative structure, dividing it up into provinces (satrapies) governed by a satrap with the assistance of a treasurer and a military officer. All three officials were chosen

Bas-relief, typical of the rather stereotyped but majestic court style. Persepolis.

Achaemenid bas-relief still in place at Persepolis. 5th century. It revisits the old theme of the "hero with lion."

Achaemenid art

A letter written in the 5th century BC by the *satrap* (viceroy) of Egypt, then staying at Susa, and addressed to the intendant of his Egyptian properties, reads as follows: "As regards the sculptor named Hanzani … have him make a sculpture of a horse and its rider similar to the one he has already made for me …." This shows us that nobles did not just summon foreign artists (as guests or slaves?) to Persepolis, Susa or Pasargadae, but that they also had them make small objects for sites all around the empire. These circumstances make the existence of a marked "Achaemenid style" (even if did undeniably show the influence of Assyrian, Urartian or Scythian borrowings) that much more remarkable. Although the stone capitals in the form of double lions, bulls or griffins, as well as a number of bronze animals, do bear witness to the skill of Persian sculptors, sculpture in the round was generally neglected in favor of relief. This is because the decoration of the royal palace was dedicated to glorifying the sovereign and the profusion of servants around him had to be represented on the walls of the buildings where subjects came to bow down before him. The two reliefs shown here, one Assyrian and one Persian, show how the serial repetition of identical motifs induce a stiffness in Persian monumental art that was rendered even more tedious by the almost servile borrowing from Assyrian sculpture. The magnificent Assyrian relief on the right shows the "hero with lion" (a theme that goes back to the

Sumerian legend of Gilgamesh, the eastern precursor of Hercules). He is strangling the animal with his left hand while the big cat's rear claw is digging into his belly. In the figure to the left, the same theme is no doubt meant to symbolize royal power triumphing over the forces of evil. But the Persian hero, who is shown in profile, is holding up a pitiful lion whose legs are hanging down in a most unnatural way since, no doubt in order not to obscure the royal calf, they have been moved to the right in accordance with convention. Compared to the Assyrian work, the result is lifeless. Still, the severity of this judgment should not make us overlook the fact that the rather cold, stereotyped realism of these reliefs coexisted with the highly refined art of the bronze makers, sculptors and goldsmiths. The most admirable thing, though, is that while drawing on talented artists from countries all around, the Persians were still determined to create their own style. We know from Darius' charter, found at Susa, that the Greeks were employed to build the royal palace, but that their role was restricted to simply carving columns. And yet the Achaemenid sovereign was surely an admirer of the Greek art he had seen on the Ionian coast. In the end, while Egypt and Greece, and before them Assyria and Urartu, made an important contribution, the Persian genius was still strong enough to have bequeathed some of the most glorious monuments known to mankind. Spotting evocations and borrowings is a sport for specialists, not for those who will marvel at the ambition of such a people whose inspirational energy continues to thrill us after all these centuries.

Assyrian bas-relief from Khorsabad (8th century BC). Musée du Louvre, Paris.

uniquely from among the Medo-Persian nobility and were answerable for their acts to the "king of kings."

Roads were built to enable couriers to bring reports and orders with the required swiftness. And a complex taxation system enabled the rulers to exert sufficient fiscal leverage over the various populations who had the "good fortune" to have been united in the kingdom bequeathed by Aura Mazda to Cyrus and his successors.

Crippled by the very taxes that enabled the royal towns to attain such splendor, and by the pomp of the satraps, these peoples would have few qualms about siding with Alexander—just as the vassals of the Aztecs would rally to Cortez.

As for the army, Cyrus the Great lost no time endowing it with a structure based on the predominance of disciplined cavalry. This is quite remarkable if one bears in mind how little time had passed between the conquest of Assyria and the moment when the Iranians had left their nomadic life in the pasture lands.

In this army, mercenaries from every ethnic group were commanded by Median and Persian officers (Cyrus had put the two peoples on an equal footing). A Scythian or Bactrian soldier, say, had very little chance of rising in the ranks.

This system can be contrasted with the very different one set up by Alexander of Macedon after his victory. The young ruler even went so far as to upset his long-standing companions by entrusting yesterday's enemies with important responsibilities, and by marrying an Achaemenid princess.

Nevertheless, for all the greatness of Cyrus and Alexander, their empires were mosaics, with all the fragility that this implied. If their heterogeneity was a factor for great cultural richness, it was also the cause of their speedy disintegration.

Bull capitol.
The apadana,
Persepolis.

The historical context

The map here does not show the whole of the Achaemenid empire, which stretched all the way to India.

There are some states which, in spite of their considerable cultural and political importance, remain little known. One is Urartu, in Turkish Armenia. Founded in the region of Lake Van in the 9th century BC, at its apogee it stretched all the way to the Black Sea.

It was a great mining center and amassed great wealth from exporting raw metal.

Urartan bronzes have been found in certain Archaic Etruscan tombs. The art of this kingdom influenced the Assyrians and Scythians and, through them, the Persians. Urartu was conquered by the Medes at the beginning of the 6th century BC.

The mountain countries of Zagros and Guilan were home to fierce tribes and, until quite recently, it was considered dangerous to travel there unescorted.

Zagros was home to the "Luristan" culture and Guilan to the "Marlik" or "Amlash" culture, possibly created by a people referred to in ancient texts as the Mards. Here and there they produced magnificent bronze objects, often imitated by Achaemenid art, as well as highly inventive ceramics that the Persians did not copy (see p. 250-251).

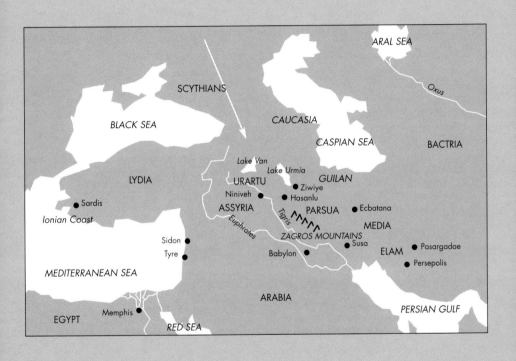

THE OLMECS
The Dawn of Mexican art

Some 28 centuries before Cortés and his soldiers laid waste the Aztec empire and, with it, the great cultural traditions of Mexico, a strange revolution took place in the fertile and insalubrious lands along the great Gulf that sweeps from today's North American border to the Yucatan peninsula, from the town of Veracruz to Villahermosa.

Modest agricultural villages were suddenly subjected to the authority of a minority whose power seems to have been founded on a superiority of a mystical nature.

Where did this class of leaders come from?

Were they new arrivals, or were they descended from the chiefs of local villages, one of which had perhaps achieved supremacy by inventing a new cult?

We cannot say. The most we can do is distinguish two ethnic types in the humans represented in the bas-reliefs and sculptures engendered by this intellectual revolution. One is fleshy, with flaring nostrils, the other tall and slim with fine noses and lips.

Whichever answer we opt for—the arrival of outstandingly gifted foreigners, or the local emergence of a family of prophets and hereditary princes—we are still no closer to understanding the origins of their desire and ability to make monuments of extraordinary size and beauty, doing so seemingly without preliminary trial and error.

Who were the Olmecs?

We do not know their true name. "Olmec" in fact derives from olmán,

Olmec colossal head from La Venta, displayed at the museum in Villahermosa. This basalt monolith is 8 feet high and weighs 25 tons. The face with its frowning lips and flared nostrils is topped by a protective cap similar to the one worn by ballgame players. This work was sculpted between 1000 and 800 BC. Photo by the author.

262

meaning "region of rubber" in Nahua (an Aztec language); it is therefore a term recorded by the Spaniards, arriving in Mexico 25 centuries after the sculptors of colossal heads disappeared from the scene, and we have no reason to believe that the villagers now living in that coastal region are the descendants of the people who built the temples at La Venta, San Lorenzo and elsewhere. Some theories have claimed that the Maya were the direct heirs of the Olmecs, seeing the latter as proto-Maya, but these are based on simplifications that are excessive to say the least. Several centuries separate the abandonment of the distinct Olmec sites in the Gulf region and the emergence of a flourishing Mayan civilization. During that time, Olmec inventions were transformed and developed. As Ignacio Bernal has written, it is not enough to say that the Olmecs were the "mother culture" of

Mesoamerica. The reality is that the Olmecs, Maya, Toltecs and Aztecs are different manifestations of a single civilization, as it was modulated over the centuries.

Rediscovery of the Olmecs

News of José Maria Melgar's discovery of the colossal head at Tres Zapotes in 1896 did not give rise to systematic archeological research, no more than did the 1926 publication of several monuments scattered around the same region, including another giant head at La Venta (p. 263). In 1938, when the American archeologist Matthew Stirling traveled to Tres Zapotes on horseback to see the head, he found it where Melgar left it, overgrown with tropical vegetation. Returning to Washington with his photographs, he obtained the support of the *National Geographic Magazine*, thus initiating a series of archeological campaigns in the course of which he visited the three main sites of the Olmec "heartland": Tres Zapotes, San Lorenzo (and environs) and La Venta. Discovery followed discovery. Stirling's work was continued and completed by his students and successors. In 1942 a round table was organized in Mexico to assess progress. In those days there was no technology for dating bones or wood, and the Maya specialists were not about to let their object of study lose their privileged position as inventors of the calendar and writing, as builders of the first pyramids and other cultural innovations that were picked up by more recent Mesoamerican cultures. The most these specialists would admit was that the Gulf region had been home to a remarkable and coherent civilization which had been contemporary with that of the Maya, not its predecessor. This view was indeed shared by several members of Stirling's team, including Drucker, his companion since the early days. The war between scholars dragged on into the 1950s, until the carbon 14 dating method put an end to the debate. The samples taken at San Lorenzo gave readings of some time around the 13th century BC: the Olmecs had sculpted their colossal heads more than a thousand years before the Maya erected their first stelae.

Olmec ceremonial sites

We are a long way from having an overall view of all the sacred sites scattered through this Atlantic or "metropolitan region." American scholars call this area the "heartland," much to the displeasure of their colleagues who would like to believe that Olmec culture emerged on the Pacific coast or in the center of the country. Some 40 sites have been discovered and have yielded over 200 magnificent monuments, plus numerous statuettes, masks, hardstone pendants and other small objects that rogue excavators or employees of the national petroleum company have fed to the international antiques market. Thanks to Stirling's work on La Venta and Michael Coe's on San Lorenzo, we now have a fairly good idea of what the Olmecs' "holy cities" were like. San Lorenzo was inhabited from the middle of the second millennium BC, but the titanic terracing work revealed by archeologists in 1966 began in around 1200 BC. An artificial plateau 1.3 miles long rises up 164 feet above the surrounding savanna. The ravines around it, like the plateau itself, are manmade. What for, we do not know. A carefully assembled system of stone drains runs through the entire site, rather like a Roman sewers, and includes a series of lagunas (reservoirs). The plateau is punctuated by mounds where temples or the dwellings of priests or other privileged figures once stood. Quite clearly, a complex like San Lorenzo could be built and its stone monuments raised only with a very large labor force. The priests in charge of its cults (who may have combined their sacred role with temporal power) must have wielded remarkable authority over the modest farming people who lived around the sacred plateau in order to get them to build on and ornament it in this way.

When San Lorenzo was abandoned, in around 900 BC, the site at La Venta, some 50 miles to the southeast, was at the height of its prosperity. This two and a half miles-long "island" emerging from the marshes was also raised and laid out as a result of terracing work, albeit on a lesser scale than at San Lorenzo. This began later on, in around 1000 BC But there again the sculptors and engineers evinced

Discovered at La Venta, this construction (a tomb?) formed by basalt columns is the only known example of this kind of architectural experiment. Photo by the author.

extraordinary skill. The series of colossal heads in basalt were placed there very early on, no doubt at the same time as the building of many of the large monuments, such as the "altars" whose function is still unknown. But while such heads and "altars" can be found elsewhere, what is unique to La Venta are the votive deposits buried deep under the surface, such as the large square blocks of serpentine (a rare green stone which had to be quarried from the mountains in the state of Guerrero), carefully arranged in a pattern and covered with successive layers of differently colored clays.

Above all, mixed up with bones that have crumbed to dust over the years (as in the tomb with the basalt columns), or buried in carefully prepared caches, charming pendants have been found, as well as figures made in serpentine or jadeite, or even in translucent blue or green jade which was probably imported from the Motagua Valley in Guatemala, as well as jewelry (earrings, pendants, labrets) patiently carved in the hardest of stones (without the aid of metal tools), the taste for which lasted through successive empires and invasions up until the arrival of the Spaniards.

No such exquisite ornaments or precious hardstone statuettes have been found at San Lorenzo, which might lead one to assume that such refined arts only developed after 900 BC However, finds at a recently discovered site of sacrificial offerings at Cerro Manati (near San Lorenzo) have included wooden figures with fine, typically Olmec faces and simply carved tortoises, as well as rubber balls, dated respectively 1200 and 1500 BC Not far from there a hardstone figure was also discovered. The total lack of written documents (whereas for the Maya we have the codexes, manuscripts collected by the Spaniards) makes it that much harder to get to grips with social integration. It would be a miracle if we were to discover monuments or temples bearing inscriptions or hieroglyphs, or (why not?) an Olmec-Maya stela that would enable us to correlate the dates of the Olmec calendar with those on the Maya calendar, whose correspondences with our own calendar have already been worked out.

Preceding pages: Left: Olmec art from Mexico. This serpentine pendant represents a head with a flattened, Negroid face similar to the colossal heads at La Venta and San Lorenzo. It dates from 1200-600 BC (Early to Middle Formative period). H. 2¼".
Right: Like the pendant, the small sculpture shown here was no doubt one of the offerings placed in caches. It dates from 1200-800 BC (early to Middle Formative period) and comes from the southern end of the Gulf of Mexico coast. It marks the blossoming of an art capable of endowing its small figures with a genuinely monumental quality. This seated serpentine figure may represent a ballgame player ready to return the ball with his elbow. The sacred ballgame was taken up by all the civilizations that followed in the wake of the Olmecs. H. 4". Both: Museu Barbier-Mueller Art Precolombi, Barcelona, Spain.

Terracotta bowl representing the jaguar-mouthed god. Early Formative period (1200-800 BC). H. 6¹ᐟ²". Museu Barbier-Mueller Art Precolombi, Barcelona.

Olmec architecture

We must try to imagine the platforms at San Lorenzo and La Venta as they were before the wind and diluvian tropical rains began to dissolve the packed earth and brick mounds, terraces and monumental stairways whose forms can still be made out here and there even today. Many of these mounds were foundations for temples which, for lack of solid, mineral construction materials were not strong enough to see through the centuries. Because of the lack of stone (the few basalt columns brought to La Venta remained an exception), the builders fell back on wood. The sculptors who painstakingly cut and decorated the bas-reliefs on the "altars" we know today cannot have had much difficulty squaring the tree trunks supplied in such abundance by the surrounding forest and building large-scale edifices. Nor should we doubt that these wooden temples contained numerous sculptures and even pieces of furniture, also in wood. In fact, we

273

The Preclassic era in Mexico

Between 1500 and the end of the 1st century BC, Mesoamerica went through what archeologists call the "Formative" and "Proto-" or "Early Classic" periods. The San Lorenzo site, which is older than the one at La Venta, developed during the "Early Formative" period, from 1300 to 900 BC, when it was devastated and destroyed. The La Venta culture began to take shape in around the year 1000 and died out in 400 during the Middle Formative period. The colossal heads were thus sculpted at the beginning of the La Venta culture and towards the end of San Lorenzo, since they express the same concept on both sites. This is also the case for monuments such as the "altars" or large-scale statues. At San Lorenzo excavations have brought to light fragments of pottery that are strikingly redolent of the "jaguar-" or "serpent-mouthed babies" found in the necropolises of Central Mexico. At Tlatilco, near Mexico City, these "jaguar babies" coexist with small figures and hollow terracotta sculptures that are not much bigger; these are specific to local populations, who also occasionally copied Olmec models. The Early Formative (pre-Classic) sites in the highlands were not rich in jade or hardstone sculptures. In fact, the art of the stoneworkers only developed later, during the Middle Formative period, as is borne out by the discovery of pieces at San Lorenzo and their absence at La Venta. This was the time when the need to find raw materials drove Olmec traders further and further outwards, carrying the style born in the Gulf area as far afield as Honduras and even Costa Rica, where Olmec jade ornaments have been found. Other Early Formative sites have been dated to this period at the end of the 2nd millennium BC, although the Olmec presence has not been conclusively proven. This is the case at Xochipala, in the State of Guerrero, where delicate terracotta figures have been found.

Counterclockwise from top left: "Pretty Lady" style terracotta female figure wearing a necklace. Early Formative or Middle Formative period (1150-550 BC), Tlatilco. H. 2¹ᐟ²". Baby with jaguar mouth. Hollow ceramic. State of Guerrero. The "babies" made in this region have red palms. 1200-800 BC. H. 12". Duck-shaped incised vase in terracotta. Las Bocas, Central Mexico. Olmec style. Early Formative period (1200-800 BC). H. 9¹ᐟ²". Terracotta statuette from the State of Guerrero, "Xochipala" culture. Early Formative period, 1500-1700 BC. H. 4¹ᐟ⁴".

can take our suppositions even further. Some of these monuments show men wearing monstrous masks representing divinities that the officiants were no doubt expected to personify. Only one of these wooden masks has been found, in the state of Guerrero. Terracotta objects are also rather scarce. For while it is true that the sites in central Mexico have yielded numerous examples attesting the refinement of the Olmecs, only fragments have been found in the heartland. These vestiges give us an idea of the unity of style, not only in the major temple complexes mentioned above, but also in the Olmec "colonies" or "counters" that were set up on the roads of the Altiplano taken by the caravans exporting copal, salt and rubber from the Atlantic coast, and that also imported jade, serpentine and obsidian for making religious objects and finery. This stylistic unity clearly reflects an equally significant unity in the belief systems: religion and style went hand in hand and reveal the personality of the Olmecs.

Olmec religion

All the "works of art" discussed here come from a religious context. It may be that sculptors and craftsmen lived alongside the priests and their families within the sanctuary walls, as they did among the Maya. One might also assume that the ritual ballgame was already in existence at this point. Preclassic (Early and Middle Formative) figures from the sites of Tlatilco and Xochipala, which date from the same period as the Olmec temple complexes, represent ball players wearing heavy belts and helmets. Why should we not believe that even in those ancient times the winners of the sacred game were considered as chosen by the gods? One of the leading experts on Olmec civilization has said: "I believe that all the ballgame players were politicians!" But which god presided over the games? The study of Olmec monuments suggests that there were several, perhaps many gods, and the singular appearance of some of them suggests that part of the Olmec pantheon was absorbed into the Mayan one through the intermediary of the Protoclassic civilizations that we as yet know

Wooden mask. State of Guerrero. H. 6¾". National Museum of Natural History, Washington DC, USA.

little about, subsequently finding their place in the pantheons of more recent Mexican civilizations, albeit not without the occasional change of function.

Did the Olmecs see themselves as offspring of the physical union of a woman and a jaguar? The theme of the "jaguar-faced baby" with its ferocious mouth drawing back at the corners to reveal, sometimes, protruding fangs, is found wherever Olmec influence has made itself felt. According to some specialists the "Olmec mouth" is that of a rattlesnake and the choice of the baby as a theme of representation is due to the propitiatory victim role played by young children. The recent discovery at the Manati site of wooden and serpentine sculptures, rubber balls and numerous tombs containing (usually) dismembered young babies, tends to suggest that the sacrifice of young children was linked to a cult.

Hardstone (serpentine) mask. It is not known whether these objects were placed on the face of the dead or worn during ceremonies (although, given their weight, this is unlikely). This mask is astonishingly lifelike. Atlantic coast, circa 800 BC. Museu Barbier-Mueller Art Precolombi, Barcelona.

The origins of the Olmec style

Several different theories have been put forward to explain the sudden emergence of the brilliant civilization created by the people whom, for lack of information as to the name they gave themselves, we know as the Olmecs. There is nothing in North or Central America to help us understand the accomplishment of these sculptors and engineers who transported huge blocks of basalt nearly 300 miles to make giant portraits of their chiefs—that being the interpretation given to the colossal heads exhumed at San Lorenzo, Tres Zapotes and La Venta.

So far the only large-scale Olmec sculptures to have been found outside the coastal region along the Gulf of Mexico are at Chalcatzingo, and these are only bas-reliefs cut into the rock.

Experts consequently believe that the Gulf region was the heartland of this style which then spread westwards all the way to the Pacific coast and southwards as far as Central America.

This expansion was brought about by the movements of merchants whose mission it was to bring back precious jade, magnetite and serpentine to the princes of La Venta and the other Gulf "cities," whose forests and marshland afforded none of these stones. Thus these rulers increased both their wealth and power, for it was by offering figures and jewels to the gods, placing them in carefully prepared hiding places, that they obtained divine benevolence for their people.

- ● Olmec or Olmec-influenced sites (post-Olmec)
- ■ Modern towns
- ▨ The Olmec "heartland"

Unofficial excavation, official spoliation

In the 1960s terracotta statuettes representing "jaguar-babies" and vases in a variety of forms began appearing on the antiques market. It was said that they came from Las Bocas, a little-known site southeast of Mexico City.

But what of the objects in jade and other hardstones that appeared in the stores of so many antique dealers at the end of the 1950s? They no doubt came from La Venta, where several "caches" had been found during digs by American experts. Their excavation work was prematurely terminated when the site was occupied by the national oil company, whose workers blithely displaced the main monuments, leaving local villagers to pillage whatever they could carry away.

In Guatemala, where the Olmec style can be found in the bulky figures with closed eyes made some thousand years after the Olmecs' colossal heads, the damage done by the last few decades of civil war is just as catastrophic. This political confusion is of course to the advantage of the local peasants as well as collectors and museums, but it has (understandably) prompted cries of protestation from archeologists, who are horrified to see that the bulldozers will have rendered some of the sites permanently "illegible."

This heavy statue with lowered eyelids comes from the post-Olmec civilization of Guatemala. Proto-Classic period (1st or 2nd century AD). H. 13". Formerly collection of Josef Mueller. Museu Barbier-Mueller Art Precolombi, Barcelona.

THE MAYA
Grandeur and Decadence

Why did poor Indians, simple corn farmers, suddenly put all their energy and ingenuity into erecting (without the use of metal tools) immense temples and prestigious monuments, then abandon everything and return to their fields, where their descendants live today with little thought of this forgotten glory?

Invasions or a local revolution have been advanced as possible explanations, but what is certain, in any case, is that the Maya question represents one of the most surprising chapters in the human adventure. While the mystery surrounding the Maya has been cleared up more or less, the vision of these stelae and grandiose temples, the surprise provoked by the appearance of this mirage of stone in the middle of the New World's tropical forest grows with each discovery.

From the Olmecs to the Maya of the Classic Period

When the Olmec civilization reached its zenith, between 500 and 800 BC, along the Gulf of Mexico and on the high central plateau, it exercised more than a cultural influence on distant peoples. Although the reality of a militarily backed colonization cannot be entirely ruled out, it is above all the presence of "commercial centers" under Olmec control that has come to light. These centers guaranteed a steady flow of jade, serpentine, obsidian and other materials that were unavailable in the marshy lands where the Olmec lived. Similarly, a great number of sculptures executed in the Olmec style have been found as far off as the shores of the Pacific. This characteristic style includes figures sporting animal mouths, protruding fangs

The Maya were architects of genius. Not even the voracious encroaching jungle could destroy monuments they left behind. Here, the famous site of Tikal in Guatemala.

Who are the Maya?

By analyzing the 26 Maya languages spoken today, experts have calculated that they must have separated from a common trunk around 2500 BC. The results of this method, which is known as "glottochronology," have been confirmed by recent archeological excavations.

In Belize (formerly British Honduras), Maya ruins show successive traces of uninterrupted occupation of the site prior to 2000 BC. In that period, platforms having some religious use, the forerunners of the Maya's pyramids, already existed. The floor was covered with stucco and the holes left by wood posts show that the constructions of the Maya's ancestors doubtless had the same shape as the huts of present-day natives. It was this layout that was adopted in the temples erected atop the Maya's pyramids.

From the above, we can deduce that the Maya were native inhabitants who assimilated cultural elements that originated with the Olmecs and were transmitted by the inhabitants of the Guatemalan Highlands (the civilizations of Izapa and Miraflores in particular). The fact that these innovations were actually borrowed diminishes neither their genius, nor the later accomplishments of the Maya in the first millennium AD; they merely offer an explanation of their distant source without enlightening us as to why the Maya suddenly abandoned mathematics, architecture, writing and astronomical observation to return to the land and a simple life of farming.

Indeed, another widespread error is that the Maya themselves have disappeared. After visiting Palenque, you need only follow the Usumacinta River upstream, in the Mexican state of Chiapas, and wander about a little and you will run into the most surprising of the Maya's direct descendants, the Lacandon Indians,

These three monuments show how Olmec culture influenced Maya art.
Left, an engraved Olmec jade ax from the 8th century BC.
Center, a stela from Kaminaljuyú from the 2nd century BC.
Right, a Maya jade plaque dating from AD 320.

and frowning lips. In the course of this cultural expansion, which began in the 4th century BC and continued for several centuries after, stelae were carved in the characteristic Olmec style throughout southern Mexico and northern Guatemala. One can see these pieces evolve and eventually give rise to the great relief sculptures of the classical age of Maya history, starting in the 3rd century AD. This intermediary period between the end of the Olmec civilization and the start of the Maya—still somewhat unclear to experts—is occasionally called the "Izapa Culture," from the name of an archeological site near the Pacific coast that boasts masonry pyramids, stone spheres and some fifty stelae without inscriptions which have been dated to between the 4th century BC and the 2nd century AD.

The political and social organization of the Maya

The Maya Classic Period starts in 250 AD and draws to a close toward 900 AD. Culturally, the beginnings of this civilization were fueled by the ties that the Proto-Classic principalities of the highlands, especially those in Kaminaljuyú (now a suburb of Guatemala City), maintained with the Maya towns of the central region, which rapidly grew to become powerful cities like Tikal. This city seems to have enjoyed close ties with Kaminaljuyú in

This cup carved from serpentine is an example of the "Izapa style," which prefigures Classic Maya art. Monuments decorated with similar motifs have also been discovered beyond the Pacific coast where the site of Izapa is located. Examples have been excavated along the Gulf of Mexico, in places where all the evidence suggests that they are a continuation of Olmec art. H. 3¹/²". Museu Barbier-Mueller Art Precolombi, Barcelona.

particular. When Tikal, for example, came to be dominated by the great northern city of Teotihuacán in the 5th century AD, Teotihuacán forms quickly began to appear in Maya pottery of the central region. Throughout the Classic period, the Maya city-states are more readily comparable with those of Mesopotamia during the neo-Sumerian period than with ancient Greek city-states, since democracy was altogether unknown in Mesoamerica. Deified after their death, Maya princes wielded considerable religious power during their life. The Maya's intellectual endeavors were wholly wrapped up in their beliefs. Astronomy, hieroglyphic writing, chronometry—every discipline revolved around religion, which was itself focused on the person of the sovereign and the reigning dynasty. The masses

Maya art reveals a recurrent macabre theme which is especially frequent during the late period, under the influence of the ritual sacrifices practiced in the high plateaus. The image on the left comes from a Maya vase (Mexico; Museu Barbier-Mueller Art Precolombi, Barcelona). On the right, a stela from Izapa.

of peasants and artisans, not to mention the vast numbers of slaves, spent their lives working toward the greater glory of their princes. And the gods, who protected these sovereigns, demanded ever greater sacrifices, including the forced labor needed for erecting the buildings and the monuments that we admire today. This mania for building on grandiose scales may in fact explain the demise of the sacred cities. According to one hypothesis, the masses, under constant pressure from their rulers, rose up and massacred them, then allowed the dense tropical forest to overrun the delicately carved temples and altars. These constructions, either platforms or pyramids, were built according to a simple layout which placed them along two, three, or four sides of a rectangular open space. From this formula, Maya city planners designed immense conglomerations in both the central region and the Yucatán, which was somewhat slower to develop.

Tikal, whose earliest stela has been dated to 292 (the oldest Maya monument), is estimated to have contained some 40,000 inhabitants at its peak. As for Copán in Honduras, the city once stretched over 75 acres. When the cities began to expand, pushing dwellings further and further from the center, the addition of ceremonial buildings was harmoniously

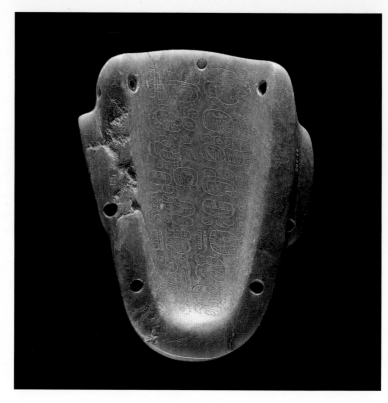

Fuchsite mask (front and reverse). Early Classic Maya. Circa 350 AD. H. 7³/⁴". On the inside, hieroglyphic inscriptions. Museu Barbier-Mueller Art Precolombi, Barcelona.

Preceding pages:
Left:
Wooden figure of a priest. Maya. H. 14". The Metropolitan Museum of Art, New York.
Right:
Terracotta face, fragment of an incense burner. 500-900 AD. H. 10". Museu Barbier-Mueller Art Precolombi, Barcelona.

integrated into the expanding design by preserving vistas and favoring an asymmetric layout, rather than aligning the new constructions along an avenue prolonging the initial small square. The well-known truncated pyramids were in fact the foundations or supports of temples. At first, these temples were built with light materials and imitated the common huts of the general population; later they were constructed with stone and decorated according to the local style. One or even several stairways led to the temple. Occasionally, the pyramids served as tombs, which once again recalls ancient Egypt, although the link is purely coincidental. Besides jade, other semiprecious stones were employed in highly prestigious grave goods, such as this other mask in fuchsite (a stone that resembles a very light green jade); the mask's reverse reveals a hieroglyphic inscription which has yet to be deciphered. Besides temples, Maya stone constructions include palaces, which for

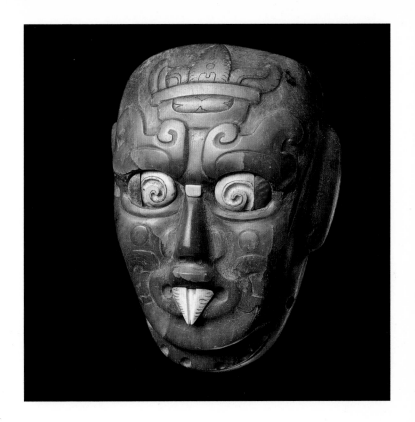

many years were thought to be temples or halls where priests would gather. In fact, it now seems quite likely that priests, as well as the members of the prince's family, did indeed live there permanently. In all of these constructions, an invention that is purely Mayan will strike the visitor, namely, the distinctive corbel vaulting used in doorways and corridors. This type of construction is a remarkable creation that was quite advanced for its time, appearing even before the start of the Classic Period, around 150 BC. The art of modeling clay and stucco was seconded by a special talent for working wood. The famous bas-relief panels displayed in the Museum der Kulturen, Basel and collected in Tikal, and the magnificent— and very rare—statue representing a mustached male figure with crossed arms conserved in New York's Metropolitan Museum, make one regret even more keenly that the humid climate of the tropical forest where the Maya lived was so destructive to wooden sculptures, textiles and feathered

Following pages:
The site of Chichén Itzá. Temple of the Warrior. Heads of the Feathered Serpent. 11th century AD. Maya-Toltec art.

Famous stone bas-relief at Xaxchilán, depicting a prince being presented with a jaguar mask (or head).

ornaments. Fortunately, numerous painted vases and pieces of polychrome pottery from the Classic Period have come down to us and can be admired in museums today. And finally, we have the incised earthenware on which mythological scenes are depicted—unless, that is, these illustrations are simple portraits of sovereigns. (But then we should bear in mind that these rulers were feared and revered like gods!).

The Mayan system of writing

The Maya covered their stelae and stone and wood lintels and their decorated vases and cups with small rounded figures that may be aligned either vertically or horizontally. These are in fact hieroglyphs (see p. 292) which make up a writing system comparable with the hieroglyphs of ancient Egypt. This discovery, which probably did not originate with the Maya, was nevertheless raised by them to a new level of perfection. In the same spirit, two calendars (lunar and solar) were used to record events

such as the stages of a certain reign. Here again we should recall that all
three monuments bearing the earliest dates were found outside the area
occupied by the Maya and were carved prior to the Classic Period. The
monuments in question are Stela II of Chiapa de Corzo (36 BC), Stela C
of Tres Zapotes (31 BC) and Stela I of El Baul in Guatemala (36 AD).
Although we are still far from being able to decipher the hieroglyphs
making up the many inscriptions that have been registered by
archeologists, we can read dates. In this we are quite fortunate to have
an event from our 16th century that was also recorded according to the
Mayan calendar. The Maya calculated their years from a "point zero"
that corresponds to 11 August 3114 BC in the Western calendar (we
have no idea what exact event, mythological or real, is supposed to have
occurred at that time!) Finally, it is believed that a glyph representing
"I made it," followed by the artist's name, has been recently identified.
Painters and sculptors apparently belonged to royal families.

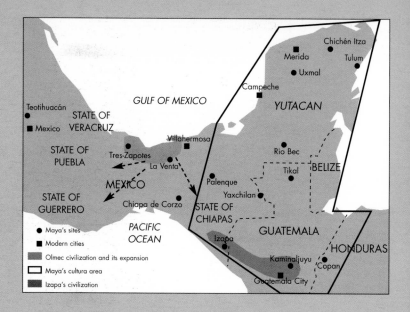

Concise chronology of the Maya *(dates according to Western calendar)*

300 BC-150 AD – Pre-Maya cultures are found in the lowlands, including the Chicanel culture, which is contemporaneous with the cultures of Miraflores in Kaminaljuyú and Izapa (the latter strongly rooted in Olmec culture). First stone temples, creation of miniature statues in jade and hardstones.

Circa 200 – The Maya's characteristic vaulting appears. No dated stelae found in Maya territory.

300 – First Maya stela, dating from 292, in Tikal.

400 – The entire region of the highlands under the domination of the northern city of Teotihuacán. Large dated stelae in the central region. Beginnings of polychrome pottery, stucco ornamentation and fresco painting.

475 – First dated stela found in Yucatán.

600 – The Teotihuacán city-state collapses. Middle Classic Period. No new construction for several decades.

642 – Erection of the Temple of the Sun in Palenque. The Late Classic period begins. Tikal also revives during this period, in the course of which a great number of temples and palaces are constructed in the central and northern regions.

900 – The central Maya cities are abandoned (the most recent stela at Tikal is dated 889).

End of the Classic period. Beginning of the Postclassic period.

987 – The Toltec conqueror Tolpitzin, dubbed the "feathered serpent," arrives in the Yucatán. He settles in Chichén Itzá.

1000 – The Mexican dynasty of the Xiu comes to power in Uxmal.

1460 – All of the Yucatán is divided among 16 principalities having Mexicano-Maya cultures.

1517 – Fernández de Córdoba discovers the Yucatán.

Calendar and dates

The passage of time was considered by the Maya to be a phenomenon that depended on the divine order of the universe. There is nothing exceptional about this concept; indeed, many mythologies oppose "gods of light" and "gods of darkness." In all known cases, a balance between creative and destructive supernatural forces must be struck, otherwise there would be a disruption of the cosmic order.

The Maya had several ways of measuring time. In the "Long Count Calendar," 20 years formed a *katun* and 20 *katun* made up a *baktun* (400 years); the indication of a date gives in the following order the number of *baktun*, *katun*, *tun* (years), *uinal* (months) and *kin* (days) that had elapsed since the "zero date," 3114 BC in the Western calendar.

The five consecutive numbers (e.g., 8.5.4.6.3) that are seen on monuments and various portable objects like the Leiden Plate enable us to situate certain events in time—a prince's accession to the throne or his death, for example. To her credit, in 1960 the archeologist Tatania Proskuriakoff grasped that the stelae of certain classical sites actually formed groups of monuments and had been erected to mark several events that had occurred during a specific reign.

Unfortunately, we cannot say with certainty that an archaic date like the one indicated on the stela at Tres Zapotes does indeed belong to the Maya's "Long Count." If the Olmecs were in fact the inventors of the system, it could well be that their "zero date" differed from the Maya. Our modern reading of a date would thus be thrown off accordingly.

The discovery of other Maya inscriptions dating from before the Classic period should shed light on this point.

End of a civilization

During the 9th century AD, the cities of the central region were definitively abandoned. In some, the stelae were attacked with hammers and mutilated. Elsewhere these monuments were left untouched, but the aristocratic caste disappeared and the creative miracle ceased to exist. Was this the outcome of a revolution, an epidemic, a major drought, a brutal invasion? In general, archeologists favor the first hypothesis. In the Yucatán, where the oldest stela dates to 475, the Classic Period ended in 987 with the arrival of Toltec invaders from northern Mexico, led by a famous hero whose illustrious name, Quetzalcóatl, was translated by the subjugated Maya as *Kukulcan*, that is, "feathered serpent." The Toltec-Maya culture, too, would know its moments of glory.

The centuries that followed were marked by internecine struggles, abandoned cities and changes of dynasties. When the conquistador Francisco de Montejo launched his assault on the Yucatán, he found only a scattering of principalities, although they still made life quite difficult for the Spanish invaders, practicing guerrilla warfare with great energy and courage. The Europeans would eventually conquer the region. Yet centuries later, in Tulum, on the Caribbean, and still later in Tayasal (present-day Flores, where the wandering Itza eventually settled), or in the isolated hills of Chiapas, Maya priests continued to recite their litanies.

Even today, here and there, medicine men pray to the god Chac during times of drought.

The writing system, however, has been lost, along with the traditions that made up the grandeur of the Maya.

Below:
Small terracotta head. Late Classic period, circa 900 AD. It is probably the accurate portrait of a Maya chief who reigned over a town. H. 3³⁄₈". Museu Barbier-Mueller Art Precolombi, Barcelona.

Opposite:
A modern Maya appealing to the Chacs, the rain gods, during a period of drought.

THE AZTECS
Children of the sun

In barely a century and a half, a small tribe of "Chichimec" (the term is synonymous with "barbarian") Indians from the arid regions around the present-day border between Mexico and the United States created a prodigious capital in the middle of a lake that is today surrounded by Mexico City and its outskirts, establishing a vast empire that stretched from the Atlantic coast to the shores of the Pacific.

At the foot of the steps leading up the pyramid of the *Templo Mayor* in Mexico City-Tenochtitlán stands a series of basalt Aztec statues. These were recovered during the excavations conducted by the Mexican archeologist Eduardo Matos Moctezuma in the 1980s. The pieces date from the 15th century and were taken to the Museum of the *Templo Mayor*. Casts now replace them at the site. Photo by the author.

We must try to conjure up this small tribe of barefooted wretches, the last to reach the Altiplano (Mexico's high central plateau), who claimed to have witnessed a scene described by their soothsayers—that of an eagle devouring a serpent while perched on a cactus—unfolding before their eyes on an insalubrious lagoon of Lake Texcoco. A village was founded at the site where the soothsayers' prediction came true. They were no doubt happy to receive this nod from the gods to settle in a marshy place that no one else seemed to covet. The newcomers' industrious, tenacious character suited the environment, even thrived there. It was this tough character that enabled them to build their "floating gardens," or chinampas, by sinking wickerwork platforms covered with earth and mud into the shallow water. This method yielded abundant harvests. At the same time, the tribe's chiefs worked hard to weave a network of alliances, which they would treacherously denounce at times if that happened to prove useful, and, little by little, succeeded in establishing their political supremacy over populations that actually outnumbered them.

The phenomenon is unique in the history of humanity and cannot be overstressed: in just 150 years, between 1350 and 1500, Tenochtitlán

Ecatepec

Tenayocán

TEXCOCO

Atzcapotzalco

TLACOPAN

Lake Texcoco

Aqueduct TENOCHTITLAN

Chapultepec

Ixtapalapán

Coyoacán

Colhuacán

Lake Xochimilco

Xochimilco

Chalco

Today, Mexico City occupies
the location of Lake Texcoco.

The origins of the Aztecs

The name "Chichimec," which was given to the peoples from the south
of what is today the United States who overran the Altiplano, corresponds
to "barbarians," the term the Greeks used to refer to the rather uncivili-
zed nomadic populations that engaged in marauding adventures outside
their northern provinces. In the 12th century AD, seven Nahua-speaking
tribes left their native land called Chicomoztoc ("the place where seven
caves are found"), razed Tula and annihilated the Toltec state, then settled in the region of Lake Texcoco. Each of these tribes founded its own
small capital, sometimes a mere village. The Colhua, for instance, were
grouped around Colhuacán, the Chalca around Chalco, the Acolhua
around Texcoco, the Tepanec around Atzapotzalco, etc.

The Aztecs, part of the Chichimecs as well, considered themselves the
forefathers of the seven tribes while also claiming a distinct origin. Their
homeland was supposedly Aztlán ("the place of the heron"), which they
apparently left in 1168 at the command of their tribal god Huitzilopochtli,

CHICHIMECS

Tzintzuntzan
Ruines de Tula
Castillo de Teayo
GULF OF MEXICO
Texcoco
Tlacopan
Tenochtitlán
TLAXCALA
Cempoala
Cuauhnahuac
Puebla
Veracruz
TARASC
KINGDOM
Teotitlán
del Camino
Coixtlahuaca
MIXTECS
Mitla
Monte Alban
PACIFIC OCEAN
SOCONUSCO

● Ancient sites
■ Modern cities
The Aztec Empire at the time of Cortés arrival

also known as Mexitl. Because of this divine command, they preferred the name Mexica ("adorers of Mexitl") to the name Azteca ("the people of Aztlán"). Given a cool reception by their fellow Chichimecs when they arrived in the Mexico valley, the Aztec were permitted to settle on Chapultepec (a hill that lies well within the limits of the present-day city) in 1256, only to be driven away from this area a half-century later.

Their own chronicles, moreover, indicate that their capital, Tenochtitlán, was founded in 1325, although this event probably only took place around 1380.

Without a king at the time, the Aztecs asked the inhabitants of Colhuacán, considered the heirs of the Toltec of Tula, to provide them with a prince. The first dynasty springing from this agreement had to recognize the suzerainty of the neighboring kingdom of Atzapotzalco, which was eventually subjugated by an Aztec general, the founder of the second dynasty and father of Montezuma I.

The great epic of the Mexica had begun...

(the name of the village on the lagoon) was made into a metropolis of several hundred thousand inhabitants that was linked to terra firma by a number of solid dikes and supplied with fresh water by an aqueduct, the water of the lake being brackish. This city boasted several temples decorated with numerous sculptures which recent excavations have brought to light. Nothing better underscores this stupefying development than the wonder and admiration that run through the stories told by Cortés' companions. They claim that no metropolis in Europe could rival this Aztec city whose rooftops, in their eyes, sparkled beneath the moon as if they had been fashioned from pure silver.

Warriors and merchants

Many conquering peoples only set store by the valor of their combatants, their fighters. Not the Aztecs. Although the aristocracy was indeed made up mainly of warriors, Aztec merchants enjoyed important privileges. The class of pochteca constituted a veritable caste that was highly closed to outsiders. The common people, or macehvatlin, could rise in society to join the ranks of notables (tecuhtli) if they showed daring in the incessant battles that were waged in order to take prisoners, who would serve as future victims of sacrifices offered to the gods; on the other hand, only the sons of traders could assume their fathers' duties, which were extremely well rewarded. The Aztec sovereigns, or *tlatoani* ("he who speaks"), took serious measures to insure the protection of *pochteca* traveling far from home to procure exotic materials. To this end, garrisons were maintained along the most heavily traveled routes and although the merchants themselves were armed, escorts of soldiers could be detailed to them if the situation warranted it. Likewise, it has been shown that the *pochteca*, whose clientele was found mostly among the aristocracy (commoners did not have the right to acquire non-indigenous products), also served as ambassadors and above all spies, in an empire far too vast for the Aztecs (who were less numerous than their vassals) to easily control. Indeed, all of Aztec history is made up of a long series of raids launched against neighboring populations, following the annexation of the small cities of the Altiplano. Occasionally such raids were even conducted under cover of diplomatic treaties, like the Triple Alliance concluded with the cities of Tlacopán and Texcoco which was still in force when Cortés and the Spanish arrived.

Certain attacks would end with outright conquests, as was the case with the Mixtecs. Others, including those directed against neighboring peoples to the north like the Tarasque, ended in bloody defeat, although without serious consequences for the young empire, which had already managed to guarantee itself access to the Atlantic and the Pacific. We should not underestimate, however, the importance of a military defeat; the expeditions organized by the Aztec kings were not launched solely in order to enlarge the national territory. One could even argue that this ambition was fairly limited. What was sought was the payment of tributes, in precious objects of course, but especially in human beings, who were sacrificed in increasing numbers to quench the thirst of gods whose demands would eventually provoke certain vassals. It was the cooperation of these rebellious peoples with Cortés and the handful of men accompanying him that enabled the conquistador to succeed in his rather foolhardy undertaking.

Mythologies and "flower wars"

The Aztecs's god, Huitzilopochtli, had ordered his people to move south. In the context sketched out above, this god would always remain the Lord of War. The Aztecs later added a "young war god," the sinister Tezcalipoca, who was supposed to have chased the good Quetzalcóatl from Tula. The Aztecs, a rather practical people who were careful to ensure every possible form of protection, annexed the divinities that were already worshiped by their predecessors on the Altiplano. This explains the double sanctuary built atop the pyramid of the Great Temple of Tenochtitlán. One was dedicated to Tlaloc, a very ancient rain god, the other to Huitzilopochtli, the only divinity that could claim a pure Aztec origin amidst a pantheon filled with very specialized gods and goddesses.

It is likely that the Aztecs adopted everything having a connection with an agrarian religion for they, like other Chichimecs, practiced a cult of the sun

Following pages:
Left:
Depiction of Texcoco's main pyramid with two temples at its summit. Two stairs lead to the sanctuaries, which are surmounted by a high covering. The decorative pattern of vertical lines symbolizes Tlaloc, the rain god, and the skulls mark the temple of Huitzilopochtli, the sun god, a divinity that thirsted for sacrificial blood. This drawing comes from the *Codex Ixtlilxochitl* and dates from the earliest years of the conquest. Bibliothèque Nationale de France, Paris.

Right:
Effigy of the goddess of water and fertility, Chalchihuitlicue, the female equivalent of the great god Tlaloc. H. 16″. Musée Barbier-Mueller, Geneva.

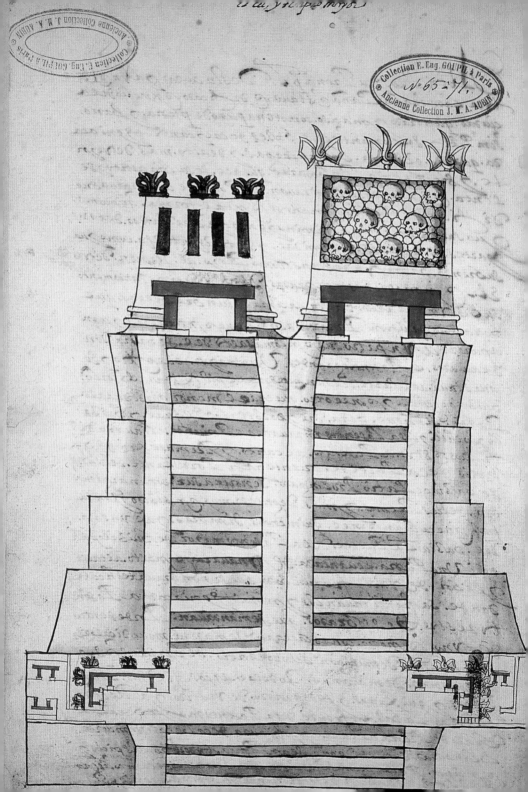

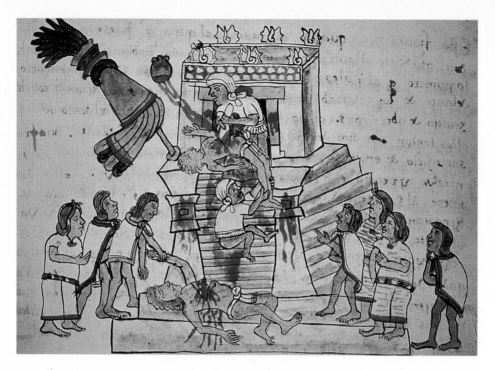

that led to a veritable mass slaughter of human victims. We know that prisoners of war, slaves and infants offered up by their consenting families were laid upon an altar and a priest, plunging into their chest an obsidian or flint knife, would tear out the beating heart of the unfortunate victim and toss it into a large stone basin shaped like some animal. This receptacle was sometimes shaped like the eagle from which it took its name (the bird was responsible for carrying the blood-drenched offerings to the heavens), sometimes like a jaguar, like the fabulous monument that greets visitors from the threshold of the Aztec gallery in Mexico City's National Museum of Anthropology.

Let's take a moment, however, to ponder this surprising work of art. Why is this gigantic receptacle, this *cuauhxicalli* (*cuauh* meaning "eagle"), shaped like a feline rather than a bird of prey? The question is a useful one, allowing us to examine the complexity of pre-Columbian symbolism. The jaguar was considered a "nocturnal" animal, linked with the setting sun. In all likelihood, the jaguar was responsible for bringing to the dying

star the human blood on which it fed in order to be reborn the following day. That explains the endless tragic obligation to obtain a sufficient number of victims to guarantee the perpetuation of a cosmic movement subject to the goodwill of bloodthirsty gods.

Things were taken to such an extreme that secret treaties were concluded between the Aztec sovereigns and the rulers of smaller kingdoms that had been conquered (the most widely known is that of the Tlaxcala) in which the same sacrifices were practiced. In skirmishes that were organized like ballets, soldiers from the two camps would face off solely for the purpose of taking prisoners, the number of which was fixed from the start. This tradition, known as the "flower wars," sparked no protests since a soldier who was sacrificed on an enemy altar believed he was called to become a companion of the sun and transformed into a star, a glorious fate if ever there was one.

The Aztec kings

Who has not heard of Motecuh-Zoma, or Montezuma, the second king of this name, who erroneously believed that the white, bearded strangers who arrived by sea in 1519 (a "reed year") were the companions of the hero Quetzalcóatl, also thought to have been white and bearded, and who had disappeared long ago, promising to return in a "reed" year"? The error certainly proved a costly one!

During the reign of Montezuma's ancestor, the great tlatoani Ahuitzotl (1486- 1502), the Aztec Empire was made up of 38 provinces (the list has come down to us!) which paid enormous tributes in cotton, feathers of rare birds, cacao, jade and gold. The Mixtec craftsmen settled in Tenochtitlán transformed these materials into extraordinarily refined ornaments and jewelry. The Spanish chroniclers cannot conceal their amazement when they pass through the outskirts of Tlatelolco. The market square was "twice as large as the town of Salamanca," the shops filled with strange fruits, jaguar and ocelot furs and sellers of animals for slaughter (dogs and turkey especially).

Of course this was not the El Dorado that Pizarro was to seek in South

Preceding pages: Interior of the extraordinary temple of Malinalco, showing the jaguar and eagles linked with the bloody sun cult. The entire construction is carved from rock.

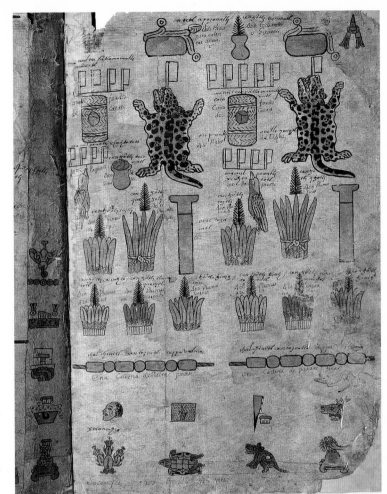

The Table of the Tributes found in the *Codex Mendoza* (1541-42) lists the foodstuffs and objects that each province of the Aztec Empire had to provide the sovereign. Drawn up at the dawn of the colonial period, the document details the products and the quantities required for each category: jaguar skins, the decorated feathers of tropical birds, cacao, etc. The National Museum of Anthropology, Mexico City.

America 20 years later—and the feathered crown that Montezuma offered Cortés (miraculously, the piece has been conserved in the Vienna Museum!) pleased Charles V less than a few sacks bursting with gold nuggets. Yet the head of the Spanish Empire had just seen a most magnificent metaphorical feather added to his cap. However, this success came at a terrible cost: the destruction of a civilization which, while its longevity was of course far from guaranteed, could have served the Mexicans as a springboard for achieving what the Franks and the Goths had accomplished in Europe upon the scattered shards of the Roman Empire.

Teotihuacán, 1,000 years before the Aztecs

Founded and flourishing around the time of Rome under the Antonines, and already razed once around AD 750, Teotihuacán (not far from present-day Mexico City) was probably the largest city of antiquity on any of the continents. The city covered some twenty square miles and extended out on either side of a complex of enormous temples where today one can see the pyramids of the Moon and the Sun, located along a sacred two and a half-miles walk. The Aztec stood gaping before these monuments which they were convinced no mortal was capable of building; hence their name for the ghost city, "the place where the gods were born" (there are other possible translations). The earliest construction must have begun at the start of the 1st century AD. Around 400, the city became an empire and its culture came to dominate most of present-day Mexico. It is possible that a "colonization" was undertaken in the land of the Maya and that the foreigner who assumed power in 378 in Tikal (Guatemala) was in fact a native of Teotihuacán. What is remarkable in Teotihuacán is the development of a class of craftsmen among an agricultural people. Moreover, several of these artisan activities eventually resembled true industries, probably motivated by the demands of exportation. Over 600 workshops, organized by neighborhood, have been excavated from the ruins of the great city. Such a production must have made it necessary to open certain trade routes in order to import a steady supply of raw materials; in exchange, various products were exported, including obsidian, a kind of volcanic glass that was used to fashion cutting tools.

Teotihuacán was surely the largest city of antiquity. The city encompassed some 20 square miles, extending from both sides of a complex of enormous temples. The Pyramid of the Sun, standing 213 feet high, covers 12.3 acres. Photo by the author.

Atop the Pyramid of Tlahuizcalpantehcutli in Tula, these large basalt Toltec Atlantean columns probably supported the sanctuary's roof (10th century). They had been dismantled and buried at the foot of the pyramid. Two cylindrical columns in the shape of the Feathered Serpent formed the temple's entrance. Photo by the author.

The Toltecs, 500 years before the Aztecs

Around 750, Teotihuacán, the great city on the Altiplano, was razed by an invasion of barbarians from the north,

The invaders included the Toltec, who spoke Nahua, a language from the Uto-Aztec family of tongues, common to all the "Chichimecs." They made their capital in Tula, which stood not far from Teotihuacán. According to Aztec chronicles, Tula was founded in 856, a date that should probably be moved forward slightly. Ten kings apparently succeeded one another up to 1168, when new invasions from the north led to the annihilation of the Toltec civilization.

These ten sovereigns, who also served as the city's high priests, included a figure who gave rise to a legend that the Aztecs, distant successors to the Toltec, were to put unshakable faith in. The sovereign was called Ce Acatl Topilzin, but he was better known by his divine designation

Cortés, conqueror of the Aztecs

The fall of Cholula, drawing from the *Llenzo de Tlaxcala*, a post-Aztec manuscript that is only known in various copies. At the lower right, Cortés, and behind him, Doña Marina pointing to some target. Bodleian Library, Oxford, Great Britain.

For some time, the legend of a Christopher Columbus "restoring America to humanity," in French writer Paul Claudel's grandiloquent expression, has been laid to rest. It is indeed true that the Genoese explorer was never even aware of the brilliant empires that his Spanish patrons were to overthrow in Mexico and later Peru. Nor did he ever learn of the bloody rites that honest Christians would put an end to—by carrying out widespread massacres, killing both sacrificer and sacrificed, and razing temples and toppling "idols" whose splendor and importance were to be rediscovered only in the last few hundred years or more. In 1504, all of these El Dorados were still unknown. That year a young man of some 20 years, Hernando Cortés, chose to leave Spain and make his way to the Greater Antilles. He first settled in Hispaniola, then took part in the conquest of Cuba in 1511. There he ran into serious trouble with Governor Velázquez, came close to being hanged, and never once distinguished himself in some act of daring or other. Given his utter lack of experience at sea, moreover, there is no apparent explanation for why his recent enemy, Velázquez, would trust him with the command of a small flotilla in 1518. His mission was "to discover and trade," not colonize. Velázquez was in fact biding his time, waiting to be freed of the authority of Columbus' son, Diego, the hereditary Admiral of the Indies, in order to carve up new

domains for himself. Cortés, scarcely any more loyal than the governor, hastened to found a town, Veracruz, along the Mexican coast near Cempoala. A few men were designated as the town's authorities, officially met and appointed a captain general, Cortés himself! At the same time, the emperor of the Aztecs, Montezuma II, was receiving word of these strangers to whom the princes ruling over his vassals, seemed overly devoted; he sent the exotic travelers an ambassador laden with gold and precious objects. In this way Montezuma hoped to keep the Spanish away from his capital, Tenochtitlán. For Cortés, however, the conquest of this city in the name of Charles V was the only way to palliate his insubordination. On 8 November 1519 he entered the Aztec city, having taken the precaution of dispatching across the Atlantic two of his friends to plead his cause. For two years Cortés would have to combat the "Indians" as much as Velázquez' partisans, before attaining the goal he had set himself. Montezuma was soon dead, a second king followed him to the grave, and in the end the courage and valor of the last tlatoani, Cuauhtemoc, could not compensate for the superiority of the Spaniards' arms, against which the Aztec were able to muster only clubs and lances. In April 1521 all resistance ceased. Cortés ordered Tenochtitlán to be razed. Reconstruction of the city as the capital of New Spain began in early 1522... Tenochtitlán was on its way to becoming the future Mexico City.

SPLENDORS OF PRE-HISPANIC PERU

Few regions of our planet have seen so many prestigious civilizations blossom as the north and center of the Andes, and especially Peru. For centuries, excavations of burial sites have brought to light textiles boasting magnificent decorative patterns, sculptured pottery, surprising jewelry. How is it that such brilliant civilizations, in which the most advanced metalworking techniques (except for iron) were well known, had only stone tools at their disposal, metal being limited to cult objects and adornment?

This is not the least of the contradictions that the Andean empires present.

In 1527, Darien, present-day Panama, had already been colonized by the Spanish. It was there that Francisco Pizarro and a few companions resolved to conquer the fabled country of El Dorado (whose king lived in a palace paved with gold and surrounded by walls of gold bricks). They determined to tap these riches to fill Charles V's coffers, but not without helping themselves copiously to the flow in passing.

While no one ever discovered the imaginary potentate's palace of solid gold, need we recall here that the conquerors did demand and obtain huge ransoms from the Indian princes that they captured? The inhabitants of Central America, as in Columbia and Peru, revealed a pronounced taste for ornaments fashioned from precious metals, unlike the Olmecs or the Maya of Mexico and Guatemala, who preferred pieces created from jade and hardstone.

When Pizarro set sail, he had no idea that there was such a thing as

Machu Picchu, an archeological site in the Peruvian Andes. The pre-Inca citadel was discovered in 1911 by Hiram A. Bingham.

the Inca Empire, comprising present-day Peru in its entirety and a good part of Ecuador, Bolivia, and northern Chile. Unfortunately for the Incas, and fortunately for the Spanish, several factors at the time served to destabilize the young, gigantic Andean state. First, there was the difficulty of trying to maintain peace among a multitude of tribes and princedoms strung out from valley to valley, over thousands of miles. Second, there were the ravages of an unheard-of epidemic then sweeping through the population; the disease was quite probably smallpox, introduced by the Europeans in Panama and which spread as far as Ecuador, where the White Man had never set foot. Finally, a fratricidal war pitted the son and legitimate successor of Emperor Huayna Capac, who had died in Quito (a victim of the epidemic devastating the area in 1527), against his half-brother Atahualpa. Five years passed. In 1532, soon after Atahualpa received word of the defeat and death of his rival, he was himself taken prisoner by the Spanish in Cajamarca. The empire itself was to fall apart very shortly thereafter. The centuries-old traditions of the Andes, which the Incas were the last to practice, had come to an end.

Geography and history of the Andes

The Cordilleras of the Andes runs along the length of South America, most often as two parallel chains of mountains, from the Caribbean to Cape Horn. Average elevation is 9,800 feet, with summits rising from 13,120 to 22,200 feet for the highest peak. This natural rampart isolates the narrow plain bordering the Pacific from the Amazon basin and, further south, the Argentine pampas. The whole of the Peruvian coast is broken up into short valleys transformed into oases by the flood of meltwater following the thaw of the Andes' snows. The absence of a system of writing and texts deprives us of any information touching on the political events that may have accompanied the successive waves diffusing certain local civilizations. These probably spilled over from their local valleys and spread religious beliefs, technological inventions, and styles of sacred and funerary art.

This terracotta figure from Ecuador is one of the earliest works of art from the Americas, if we exclude certain rock paintings. The piece belongs to "Valdivia culture," which dates from the 3rd millennium BC. It is believed that the art of making pottery in the New World originated in Valdivia. H. 3$^{1/2}$". Museu Barbier-Mueller Art Precolombi, Barcelona.

The Spanish were able to observe in detail the methodical colonization of the Incas, which was based upon a sophisticated bureaucratic apparatus and their military might; the system is depicted in several Spanish chronicles from the 16th century. On the other hand, we have no clear idea of whether the spread of iconographic themes peculiar to the styles that we call Chavín or Nazca (from the name of the localities or valleys where such styles were identified) is the result of a conquest, peaceful exchanges, commercial contacts, or even the activity of traveling priests who, acting like our own missionaries, wished to convert foreign sovereigns to their faith. Each year new discoveries modify the rich picture of a past that is almost unique in the world. The history of Andean civilizations begins with the production of modest stone tools around 20000 BC. Sixteen thousand years later, shortly before the appearance of pottery and hammered gold, beautiful textiles with animal motifs that already show a clear Andean character were being produced in northern Peru (Huaca Prieta). While the art of fashioning earthenware objects seems to be unknown in Peru at this early date, pottery was practiced in Valdivia in Ecuador which has yielded figurines that doubtless represent divinities of some sort. At present, save for a few wall paintings, these are the earliest "works of art" from the Americas.

Opposite:
The main divinity of Chavín de Huantar is a half-human, half-feline creature. *El Lanzon*, the great carved monolith planted in the middle of the Old Temple, is probably the oldest existing image of this god.

Following pages:
Left: A small Chavín receptacle for quicklime (early 1st millennium BC). H. 2⁵ᐟ¹⁶″.
Right: Another, larger Chavín stone mortar representing a feline standing on its four feet. Same period. H. 3¹ᐟ⁴″. These mortars were used to mash coca leaves. Both: Museu Barbier-Mueller Art Precolombi, Barcelona.

Chavín: the early horizon

We owe the identification in 1929 of the Chavín culture to the archaeologist Julio Tello, a native Indian of the Andes. The culture takes its name from Chavín de Huantar, the site where the most important and, stylistically, the most characteristic temples and stone monuments have been found. The style spread, eventually reaching Peru's northern regions, center (the Ancón culture) and the south, where Chavín motifs are found in Paracas. These religious themes spring from a sacred bestiary in which a mythical feline that was occasionally depicted with wings was gradually transformed into a human figure boasting a feline maw with protruding tusks, feet shaped

like an eagle's claws, and individual locks of hair which are in fact more or less simplified serpents, the same serpents found on the head of a painted figure on a bowl from Paracas. When confronted with some of these images, one cannot help but think of the jaguar god of the Olmecs in Mexico, given that the two civilizations are contemporaneous.

At this time, in the middle of the second millennium BC, farming had reached a high level of development in the Andes as well as Mesoamerica. Farmers raising corn (among other sources of food) banded together in villages; these communities saw the influence of their priests invade their daily existence, dictating every aspect of the inhabitants' lives, while religious sentiments became more complex and numerous "specialized" or secondary divinities appeared.

Black- or gray-slip pottery attained a high level of excellence; at this time the "stirrup-spout" vessel was also introduced and would survive until the Spanish conquest.

Along with these early vestiges of an Andean monumental stone architecture, we should say a word about the beautiful monochrome textiles that the "Chavín horizon" has left us, on which were painted the usual figures with feline maws. Finally, from the very start of this complex culture, in the mid-second millennium BC, the art of hammering gold was practiced using a technique that must have sprung up in southern Peru.

The Paracas culture

The arid region lying below the Cañete River, in particular between Paracas and Ica, has yielded a number of surprisingly rich burial sites. The earliest of these tombs are sunk into the ground like a well, hence their name, cavernas. The Paracas Cavernas phase began in the first half of the 1st millennium BC and was greatly influenced by the Chavín style. The

Opposite and above: Two Chavín Cupisnique terracotta vessels illustrating the birth of a form that would endure until the conquest, i.e., the stirrup-spout vessel. Above: H. 11¼"; opposite: H. 9". Both: Museu Barbier-Mueller Art Precolombi, Barcelona.

textiles from this phase show rather modest decoration, although certain pieces of pottery are remarkable for their colorful ornamental patterns (polychromy would always remain one of the outstanding traits of southern Peruvian cultures). Pottery was decorated by using pigments mixed with resinous fixatives which were applied after firing. The process was also employed in northern Peru, notably in the Chavínoid culture of Jequetepeque.

In the second half of the 2nd millennium, the *Cavernas* phase evolved. From this period on, Paracas tombs became veritable underground villages, vast burial sites with stairways leading down to interconnecting chambers, which gives the period its name, the Paracas Necropolis phase. This period has become famous for the truly sumptuous textiles in which mummified persons of high rank were wrapped. These moving, refined offerings, woven and over-embroidered with brightly colored mythological motifs upon a dark background, were preserved by the extremely dry conditions of the coastal desert which enabled the fragile cloth to come down to us intact, just like the textiles of the Nazca culture which succeeded Paracas (see illustration opposite).

Regional cultures

In the early years of the Common Era, the formative period that was the "Chavín horizon," along with the two southern Peruvian phases of Paracas, gave way to regional cultural developments. I shall limit my remarks to three of these, which wholly deserve the term "civilizations." They are the culture of the northern coastal region of the Mochicas (from the word for the language spoken in the Moche valley when the Spanish arrived); in the center, the culture of Recuay, from the name of a village not far from Chavín de Huantar (in the highlands, therefore); and, in the south, the culture that takes its name from the small Nazca River and the valley of the same name near Ica. I shall begin with the last-mentioned culture. We have seen that the Paracas Necropolis phase lasted several centuries, becoming a "proto-Nazca" culture. Here, as in Paracas, there is the same lack of stone statuary and the same abundance of both pottery and textiles (which combine cotton and wool, and the techniques of weaving, crochet, tapestry and embroidery). In terms of ceramics, we find an extravagant quantity of funerary pottery, and for this reason Nazca is one of the most popular and best known cultures of pre-Columbian America. The earliest vessels are decorated with rather simple naturalist motifs executed in sober colors that were fixed during firing. This style would evolve towards exuberant compositions covering the entire surface of the receptacle which was readily fitted with a double neck connected by a handle. The designs are outlined in black, while the palette of colors is limited to ocher, brown, yellow and white. Finally, the animal and anthropomorphic motifs were

Above: Wool cloak. Nazca culture, which grew out of and prolonged the Paracas culture (2nd to 6th century AD). 4' x 28³/⁴". Museu Barbier-Mueller Art Precolombi, Barcelona.

Following pages: The meaning of the immense line drawings on the Nazca desert pampas remains shrouded in mystery. These "tracks" are occasionally accompanied by realistic representations of animals. It is these figurative depictions that enable us to attribute the geoglyphs to the Nazca.

increasingly broken up until they became practically unidentifiable. Around the 6th century AD, the Nazca culture was in decline. Shortly before disappearing altogether and leaving its towns and villages, built from mud, to crumble to dust, this culture experienced a strange outburst of creativity. Immense networks of lines were carved in the desert floor at considerable cost to the society in labor and time. Certain gigantic engravings represent animals, trees or plants of a dimension that can only be properly viewed from an airplane. These cyclopean undertakings were, it seems, linked to astronomic observations and apparently served agricultural needs as reference points and a basis for various calculations.

At this time, the brilliant Mochica culture appears almost directly north of the coastal region and nearly 600 miles from the Nazca valley. Mochica grew out of several Chavínoid cultures in the region, including Cupisnique. The Mochica culture was to perfect the stirrup-spout, transforming these receptacles into admirable sculptures in the round. The Mochica repertory seems almost inexhaustible in

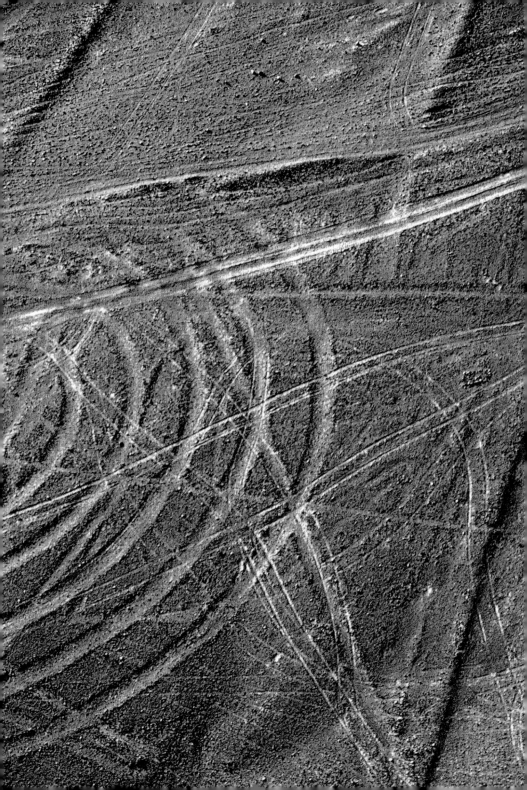

representing scenes of daily life (but then, aren't these evocations of mythological events?) These pieces depict sexual acts that would defy the imagination of the Kamasutra as well as hunting parties and figures tending gardens. The themes are also treated in paint, a brown pigment over a cream background; when paint is used, the sides of the vessels are smooth to accommodate, unfolding around the piece, a drawing as precise as it is lifelike.

We do not know whether the Mochica formed a veritable empire or a confederation of chiefdoms like Grand Chimú, 1,000 years later, in the same valleys surrounding present-day Trujillo. On the other hand, a recent and fortuitous discovery has confirmed the sumptuousness and complexity of the Mochican funerary art previously only glimpsed in the ornaments that have come to light over the years from looted tombs. The practice of pillaging these burial sites is in fact a kind of profession that has been passed down from father to son for centuries. In 1988, *huaqueros* (professional pillagers) discovered in the valley of Moche a complex of burial sepulchers whose contents proved so rich that the secret could not be kept.

Peruvian scientists were able to intervene before the main tomb had been found.

The Lord of Sipan (king or priest?) had been laid out there over 15 centuries before, his corpse covered in silver and gold jewelry mounted with turquoise and shells. Near him lay his familiars, wives and servants, sacrificed in order to serve as his companions in the Hereafter (see pp. 340-41). The Mochica proved to be brilliant smiths working in silver, gold and other metals, and talented modelers of clay, but showed no interest in carving stone or putting it to use in their architecture. They built tiered pyramidal temples with a rectangular design.

Below:
This Mochica vessel shows an instance of sodomy, perhaps evoking an effort to control births. The piece dates from the early centuries of the Common Era. H. 7³⁄⁴". Museu Barbier-Mueller Art Precolombi, Barcelona.

Opposite:
Terracotta vessel portraits are among the finest pieces of Mochica pottery. The depiction of this male head is unusually realistic. 200-700 AD. H. 9¹⁄²". Museu Barbier-Mueller Art Precolombi, Barcelona.

One of the most important of these can still be seen, albeit in a very rundown state, at the mouth of the Moche. It has been estimated that this pyramid was originally 314 yards long, 148 yards wide and 158 feet high. Some 50 million bricks made of mud mixed with straw and dried in the sun were used in its construction.

The third culture examined here, the so-called "Recuay" culture, introduced a new feature, namely funerary chambers made from large stone slabs that were carefully dressed and fitted together.

Unlike the Nazca and Mochica civilizations, Recuay was not a typically coastal complex, nor one located solely in the highlands. It is in fact found at various sites in central Peru.

Recuay pottery abounds in the most diverse themes (scenes showing figures in a temple, divinities flanked by animals modeled in relief, etc.). The vessels often have a square shape and present two bodies, two receptacles connected by a double spout—unless these are actually anthropomorphic urns! The true originality of the Recuay culture lies in its creation of rather large stone sculptures, some of which appear to represent armed military chiefs.

This object bears striking witness to the skill of Mochica smiths. The feline head is fashioned from a sheet of metal consisting of a copper-gold alloy, while the teeth and tongue, like the eyes, are made from shells. AD 100-200. H. 7". Museu Barbier-Mueller Art Precolombi, Barcelona.

The Huari empire and regional states

Around 600 AD, the "regional cultures," including those we have just mentioned, were rapidly subjected to pressure from another powerful culture, probably an empire prefiguring the Inca one. A highly uniform lifestyle was now imposed on large numbers of valleys, no doubt along with new religious

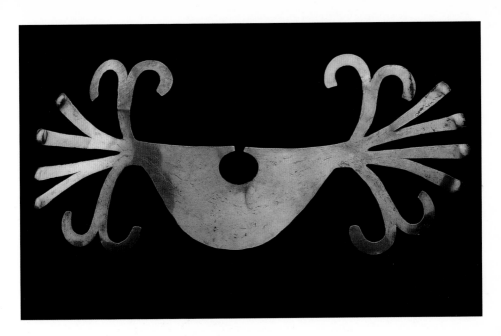

beliefs. At the same time, the use of polychrome pottery spread everywhere. The style recalls Nazca pottery, although occasionally we see the double receptacle of Recuay (which would continue in use even among the Incas). Textiles were also produced. These appear to be inspired by the textiles of Tiahuanaco and their animal figures, whose traits are simplified to the point of suggesting geometrical motifs.

As can be seen from local developments in sacred art and funerary ritual, the unification of Peru during the Huari period did not put an end to ancient regional traditions. Around 1000, when Huari power began to decline, the pictorial trends in the south and sculptural ones in the north gave rise to the styles of the "regional states." From that time until the Spanish conquest, in the course of some five centuries, pre-Columbian Peru was to shine with its last, dying lights...

But what fireworks they were!

Hardly had the Huari Empire loosened its hold on the Moche valley itself than the chiefdoms united, finally recognizing the authority of a local prince. The kingdom, or more accurately the confederation

Below: Solid-silver Inca figurine. Region of Cuzco. Circa 1500. H. 3". Museu Barbier-Mueller Art Precolombi, Barcelona.

Opposite: Stone statue evincing the typical style of Recuay, which is contemporary with the Middle and Late Mochica style (100-700 AD). H. 28³/₄". Museu Barbier-Mueller Art Precolombi, Barcelona.

of Grand Chimú was born. At the time of the Inca conquest in the 15th century, the confederation had extended its authority to the limits of present-day Lima in the south, and the border with Ecuador in the north. Numerous towns were founded in the most densely populated valleys. Systems of canals and aqueducts were built, thus stimulating agriculture.

The king of kings, Chimú, also raised a capital, Chan Chan ("Sun-Sun"), which stretched over eight square miles. Built from earth mixed with straw, Chan Chan is still an impressive site today, despite the half dozen catastrophes (earthquakes and rare—but torrential—rainstorms) that have been recorded over the last four centuries.

By the time Pizarro arrived, obviously the economy of Grand Chimú, which had become a simple Inca province in the meantime, had declined. The Chimú monarch, whose forefathers had reigned over an immense domain, was now but one prince among many.

The empire of the Incas

When the small kingdom that had its capital in Cuzco began to expand beyond its borders and its policy of annexation started to bear fruit, the new empire took the name of Tahuantinsuyu, meaning "the four directions" (or the four points of the compass). The empire was divided into four satrapies by two imaginary lines that crossed in the capital. The title of "Inca" referred to the emperor and the male members of the imperial family. The chronicler Garcilaso de La Vega, born in 1539, the son of a Peruvian princess and a Spanish gentleman, is quite clear in this regard. Thus, the expression "Empire of the Incas" is preferable to the "Inca Empire," although the adjective is frequently and handily employed. It is thought that originally the Cuzco kingdom comprised a small group of immigrants who had left the Amazon plains. Their language was not the *Quechua* spoken by the Andean tribes with whom they eventually fused and whose tongue they came to adopt and, eventually, impose on the populations of their empire. Around the 13th century, the title of *sinchi*, or "war chief," was

Opposite:
Detail of a stone wall in a fortress dating from the imperial Inca period. This is the first time that Andean architecture attained this degree of combined monumentality and technical excellence.

Preceding pages:
Left: Detail of a Huari tunic. 6th-10th century. 42 x 42".
Right: Detail of the upper section of a rudder from a possibly ceremonial or votive hardwood boat, from the region of Ica, a coastal area of southern Peru (1100-1500). H. 6'. Both: Museu Barbier-Mueller Art Precolombi, Barcelona.

the term applied to the sovereigns of Cuzco. The first of these sovereigns, a semi-legendary figure, was called Manco Capac. For two centuries, his descendants were only able to extend their authority to the immediate limits of their city. Then two Inca chiefs, Pacha Cutec and Tupac Yupanqui, gave proof of their organizational mettle. A network of roads paved with stones was built, crossing gorges and ravines with bridges. Throughout the growing empire shops provided patrols of soldiers and merchants with food and rest and ensured the safe transport of goods on their way to Cuzco.

The cult of Inti, the dynastic sun god, became the religion of the empire, although local gods were neither banished nor prohibited. Had such an absence of dogmatism already marked the empires and states before the Incas? Would that explain the apparently ready and repeated adoption of mythological themes, their spread and their

fusion? The supposition is certainly tempting in any case!

One of Pizarro's companions wrote this about Cuzco, "The city of this country's sovereigns is so beautiful that it is worthy of standing in Spain. It is filled with palaces and the poor are unknown there."

Garcilaso de La Vega, mentioned earlier, refers to the four master builders who oversaw work on the fortress of Sacsahuana in Cuzco. This construction is famous for the perfection of its gigantic blocks of dressed granite, which, as Garcilaso proudly underscores, were precisely fitted without the use of iron or steel tools.

The same chronicler, who at the age of 20 left his native Peru never to return, nostalgically describes the royal gardens filled with plants, fruit and flowers of silver and gold. He praises the luxury that surrounded the sovereigns, the multitude of servants, which would have turned the most opulent of monarchs in Europe or the East several shades of

green. Of course Garcilaso was born after Pizarro's men had laid waste to the splendors of Cuzco. His uncles on his mother's side, however, members of the royal family, had known this blessed golden age. They claimed that immense riches had been hastily concealed upon news of their last emperor's death and that even the children of those who had hidden this trove no longer knew where to find it, unless they happened upon it, just as the grave of the Mochica prince of Sipan has recently come to light...

So, perhaps El Dorado existed after all. Perhaps one day part of a cliff will collapse and reveal to an astonished world the treasure that Pizarro never managed to seize, despite all his daring and greed.

Above:
Veined-stone bowl with serpents carved in relief (D. 9¹ᐟ²")
and two small alpaca-shaped stone mortars for mashing coca.
Imperial Inca art, circa 1500. W. 4¹ᐟ²".
Opposite:
This massive horizontal piece of wood surmounted by a carved idol
may have been a kind of marker planted at a burial site.
It might also be an idol from some temple.
Often employed during this period, the color red clearly had some
symbolic significance linked with religious and funerary rituals.
Chimú culture, 12th-15th century AD. H. 43".
Both: Museu Barbier-Mueller Art Precolombi, Barcelona.
Formerly the Berlin-Dahlem Museum, and (for the stone bowl) Charles Ratton collections.

Two drawings
of angels
with human or
raptor heads.

Winged spirits

Andean iconography revolves around a number themes that are probably
derived from myths which, unfortunately, never had their Homer or Virgil,
even if some of them were indeed recorded by the Spanish chroniclers of
the conquest period.

Among the themes transmitted from one people to another, from century to century, with the greatest persistence, we find a figure depicted in
profile and holding a vertical staff before him.

The "God of the Staffs" (above, left) sports a long serpent-headed coiffu-
re and raptor beak and holds a reptile-staff. The depiction here is a bas-
relief found in the great temple of Chavín de Huantar and dates from the
late 2nd millennium BC. One thousand years later the same mythical figure appears in Tiahuanaco, the great Bolivian city near Lake Titicaca (above,
right). Even with the heavy addition of decorative elements to the design,
it is indeed the god of Chavín that appears here. The Andean themes show

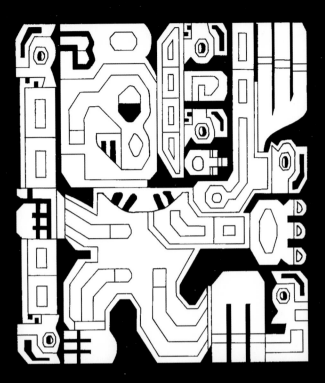

extraordinary longevity. But how can we know whether they were conserved intact over the 2,000 years that passed between their invention and the last avatars of these divinities (such as the God of the Staffs) whose metamorphoses are quite apparent? The Chimú, for example, firmly believed that, after death, the founder of their royal dynasty suddenly took flight on wings that had grown from his back.

Yet the winged figures are found in Peru well before this legend could have been conveniently invented to justify the divine nature of its sovereigns, as heirs of the mythical aeronaut.

It is also possible that the fable was borrowed from the Mochica, who lived in the same region as the Chimú, albeit separated from them by a good number of centuries.

In the end we shall probably have to content ourselves with mere conjecture, given the lack of information on these peoples, who possessed no system of writing and left no sacred texts.

ISHI, THE CALIFORNIAN INDIAN

The appearance in Sacramento Valley, shortly before World War I, of the last representative of the Yahi, a minuscule tribe that was thought to have disappeared long before, changed our understanding of prehistoric Indians. Between this "savage," who was surprised by everything yet feared nothing, and three scholars from the Museum of San Francisco a touching friendship was born.

A mutual appreciation and affection touched with a hint of reserve and modesty made possible a fruitful collaboration in which this Native American, whose mother tongue was eventually decrypted, provided a wealth of information. Yet despite his goodwill, he would never speak of his religion or reveal his own name, which only his fellow Yahi were allowed to pronounce. He came to be known as Ishi, which means "man" in his tongue.

Few human beings indeed had more of a right to be called "man" than Ishi. Dexterity, intelligence, humor and generosity coupled with a keen sense of economy, plus dignity—these qualities of the species he had in abundance. Yet he suffered from none of the faults that ambition, money, or jealousy give rise to. He had accepted with fatalism the systematic destruction of his people by settlers and ranch owners that had begun in 1849. He conceived no bitterness, felt no need to avenge the deaths of his relations and fellow Yahi, who had been killed during raids mounted under the pretense that the proximity of "savages" was a threat and in the name of the principle "the only good Indian [was] a dead Indian."

Ishi in 1911. Just discovered, he is on the point of being led away to the Oroville prison. His hair is short because he burned it as a token of going into mourning.

It was in 1908 that a prospecting party for a damn construction project happened upon the camp where the last four representatives of the Yahi people had concealed themselves, i.e., Ishi, his old mother, sister and an uncle or elderly cousin.

The technicians were accompanied by local cowhands who made off with the few wretched possessions of these men and women who had fled to the chaparral, the Californian brush filled with nettles and so dense no one ventured there for fear of treading on a rattlesnake.

Oddly enough, several of the objects that were plundered at this first encounter were later donated to the museum in San Francisco where they are conserved today in the Ishi Collection.

The two older Yahi died soon after. Ishi's sister also disappeared, swept away, it is believed, by the torrent she was trying to ford. Ishi was alone in the world.

Three years later, unable to go on, emaciated, weakened, he burned his hair, a sign of mourning for the Yahi, and lay down along a cow fence; ranches had since grown more numerous, slaughterhouses had been built, and villages of pioneers could be found on all the lands where the Indians had once hunted, leaving Ishi with the chaparral and a few shreds of original forest growing on the slopes of Lassen Peak, which rises over 9,900 feet.

Dogs discovered the dying man. Rather perplexed, white men arrived. The year was 1911 and no one feared the country's original inhabitants now. Ishi was taken to the sheriff of the small town of Oroville, where he was put in jail to protect him from the intrusive curiosity of the town's citizens... Ishi, on the other hand, clearly thought that the white men planned to put him to death.

Following an exchange of telegrams with the Bureau of Indian Affairs, federal authorities permitted the "savage" to be placed in the care of Kroeber and Waterman, a pair of anthropologists employed by the Museum of San Francisco. Waterman traveled as quickly as possible to Oroville. His friendly attitude eventually overcame the fears of the museum's future "guest," who promptly agreed to board a train, that

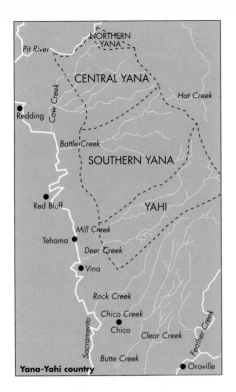

Yana-Yahi country

California Map of Native American languages

strange vehicle once glimpsed from afar and which the members of
his tribe had claimed was a dragon in the service of the white man.
Thus began Ishi's second life, which we shall hear more of further
on in this chapter.

The Yana and Yahi Indians of the Upper Sacramento

California lies between two chains of mountains. One is rather low and
follows the shore, the Coast Range. The other, a series of high peaks,
is the aptly named Sierra Nevada, the "snow-covered range."
To simplify, the Sierra Nevada extends south from the Cascade Range
which ends at Lassen Peak. These two mountain ranges border a pair
of fertile valleys that run north to south one after the other, Sacramento
and San Joaquin, from the name of the two rivers that channel the
runoff from the Cascades and the Sierra Nevada.
Upstream the Sacramento is fed by fast-flowing creeks that are never

dry and which have cut deep canyons. Between the river and Lassen Peak there lived a small group of highland people, the Northern, Central and Southern Yana, together with the Yahi along Mill Creek. The area inhabited by the Yana measured less than 60 miles long, yet a Yana from the north would have had trouble understanding an inhabitant of the center, even if less than 30 miles separated their respective homes.

Known among their neighbors for their bravery in war, the Yana boasted none of the firearms that other Indians had procured for themselves from the Spanish. They possessed bows and arrows tipped with chipped stone, wood harpoons, knives fashioned from obsidian (a natural volcanic glass) and slings. They did not have horses and hunted deer as well as rabbit, more rarely bear which are difficult to kill with a mere stake. For these people living in the Stone Age, life was certainly hard but not too difficult—until they began to be driven from their homeland in the mid-19th century.

One rare fact worth noting, the Yana (as well as the Yahi) spoke two languages, one reserved for men, the other for women. Each sex mastered both tongues and would only use the language peculiar to its gender when speaking with a member of the opposite sex, who would respond in his or her tongue. Such a duality is only known to exist among two or three peoples worldwide. The Yana also possessed rituals about which Ishi maintained a discreet silence. We know at most that there were ceremonies surrounding births, puberty, marriages and

Small piece of Pomo basketry. Northwestern California. Feathers and mother-of-pearl pendants are inserted between the fine plaits of vegetable fibers. The basketry of the neighboring Yana was never so sophisticated. Early 20th century. D. 4". Musée Barbier-Mueller, Geneva.

mourning. On the other hand, the Yana only practiced chanting and very little dance, which plays such an important role in other Indian rites. Besides hunting, the great numbers of salmon that came to spawn in the area's creeks were the Yana's main source of food, along with flour made from mast. Fish were dried for winter, which was as harsh as the summer was hot. It was in the summer, moreover, that the Yana would undertake their sacred pilgrimage to Lassen Peak, an ancient volcano where game and relief from the heat could be found. In winter, these Indians covered themselves in rabbit and bear skins, while deer

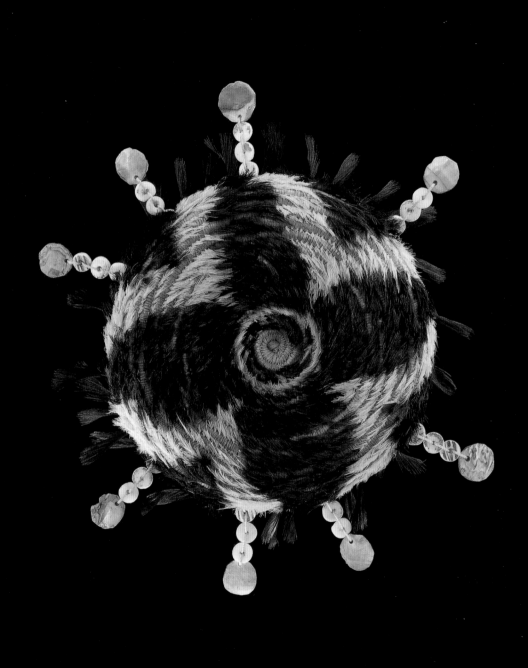

provided them with leather moccasins, capes and strips of skin to wrap around their legs. The women also wore a kind of dress made from the skins of wild cats and produced small baskets for keeping food and valuable objects. These baskets cannot bear comparison, however, with the finely woven basketry of the Pomo Indians living along San Francisco's northern coast. Superb Pomo ceremonial bowls, decorated with feathers and mother-of-pearl pendants, have come down to us. The survival of Yana subgroups therefore depended on their skill, spirit of solidarity and a perfect mastery of their sources of food, which had to be stored up in order to make it through the rigors of winter. By the late 19th century, ethnologists had begun to deplore the fact that whole peoples had disappeared without their being able to observe the natives' lifestyle.

Thus, the appearance of Ishi in 1911 seemed nothing short of a miracle to the scientific community. And for those who came to know the man, who admired his dignity, graciousness and patience, this encounter was to change their view of the Indians' world.

Gold prospectors and cattle ranchers

To appreciate Ishi's sudden appearance, however, we need to go back over a half century before this date. From Mexico, the Spanish had quickly launched the conquest of California, where today, of course, many place names recall their presence. They founded a series of missions, including Santa Barbara's, which has more or less remained the same since its construction three centuries ago. In 1844 the Mexican government awarded a number of land grants in the lower Sacramento Valley. Beneficiaries included some English-speaking settlers like Peter Lassen, who was to give his name to the Yana's sacred volcano. When California was ceded to the United States in 1848, these concessions were confirmed.

White men were now joining together to mount deadly punitive expeditions against the Yana. The Indians responded in kind by massacring here and there an isolated farmer, an unaccompanied woman. The worst, however, began in 1849 when news spread of the existence of extraordinary gold mines in California. Adventurers rushed in, blazing new trails which they then enlarged to accommodate carts and coaches (one of these crossed the Yahi's territory). Newcomers whose prospects never panned out lived by thieving and gambling. Small towns with their saloons and bordellos were founded. Thousands of Indian women were kidnapped and forced into prostitution. As Theodora Kroeber points out in a fine study of Ishi, there was nothing destructive to the earlier Spanish domination. At that time the Church had been on hand to restrain the worst excesses. Furthermore, Mexicans had been few and had not proved racist since mixed parentage had been common and no cause for scandal. All of that changed with the arrival of Anglo-American settlers. In their eyes, Indians were the serfs that Mother Nature had generously provided them with. Far outnumbering the natives, the white men also transmitted a host of diseases to the indigenous population against which their immune system was defenseless. Two decades of such treatment amounted to a true genocide. The Yana population, which had once numbered two or three thousand souls, was annihilated. By 1870 the Southern Yana had disappeared altogether and only two or three dozen Central and Northern Yana remained. As for the Yahi, also known as the Mill Creek Indians, white settlers were sure that they had been entirely exterminated. Only a few old cowhands believed that a handful of individuals were able to escape the massacres. Most people thought otherwise—incorrectly.

Ishi's story

Ishi, it seems, was born around 1860, well after the invasion of forty-niners had begun to threaten his homeland. His fellow tribesmen were still numerous and alert enough then to launch raids against herders who had settled beyond the white man's usual territory, stealing cattle and burning down barns. From the settlers' animals the Yahi dried strips of meat for the winter, just as they did with the deer they hunted.

They stole to live, not to create their own herds, for they were true survivors of a distant past, hunters and gathers, not herders and farmers. By 1860 relations between Indians and white men had become very bitter indeed. "Scouts" who were thoroughly familiar with the region were leading punitive expeditions and the Yahi were setting ambushes for the White men, killing adults and children indifferently. Troops were sent to protect both settlers and peaceful Indians, and to act against unsubdued natives and "illegal white organizations." But the soldiers also overshot the mark, rounding up Maidu and Wintun Indians. These tribes, neighboring the Yahi, were in fact altogether peaceful. Very few of these unfortunate natives survived their captivity. Meanwhile, a small number of Yana made peace with the settlers, who employed them in the fields; "militiamen" (a sorry collection of layabouts and saloon regulars) set upon these newly loyal Indians and killed them, even in the very homes of white men, where they were prized as excellent servants.

By 1864, the Yana had been wiped out and the "militiamen," and those who encouraged them, turned their attention to the Yahi. They were now blamed for every robbery, every murder committed in a region filled with cutthroats and criminals who had fled the East Coast.

The Spanish mission of Santa Barbara, founded December 4, 1786.

In 1867 and 1868 cowhands and "militiamen" discovered several shelters occupied by Yahi communities. Men, women and children were mercilessly cut down. Henceforth the survivors, who numbered two dozen individuals at most, struggled to remain out of sight. According to Ishi, who must have been less than ten years old at the time, there were no new births among his relatives and each death of course diminished the group's ability to resist. Having taken refuge mostly along the upper reaches of Mill Creek, which flows between high walls of rock, they would lower themselves to the torrent with ropes made of wild cotton to fish or wash themselves, then return to the top, climbing hand over hand. Hidden beneath trees bordering the steep cliffs, they avoided trails; ethnologists agree that this free, independent mini-nation, cut off from all contact with other Indian groups, led an exemplary "primitive" life. It's for this reason that the information later provided by Ishi, who led this life for 50 years, was so valuable.

Ishi in San Francisco

Ishi's mother probably died shortly after the four survivors' camp had been discovered in 1908. He thought his uncle and sister had been devoured by bears or pumas, if not drowned. In any case, once their hiding place had been found out, Ishi himself had lived alone, speaking to no one. He probably tried to leave his native territory in the hope of finding more readily available sources of food. Miraculously, no one ever saw him until 29 August 1911, the day he decided to join his ancestors and lay down on the ground with no hope of ever rising again.

In the account above we left Ishi in his Oroville jail cell, just as professor Waterman had convinced Ishi that he would be safe with him (a brilliant stroke when we consider that this man had been hunted all his life, could not make himself understood in his native tongue, and had every reason to fear white men). All of America by this time had heard of the "Oroville savage" and a crowd of curious onlookers followed at a respectful distance when he left for the train station.

Journalists rushed to see the "prehistoric man." They were
accompanied by circus owners who proposed enormous sums
for the chance to lodge the "savage Indian" in their traveling booths
between the bearded lady and the two-headed sheep.
Waterman and his colleague Kroeber managed though to create
an effective barrier against such intrusions and never lost sight
of their objectives. The two recorded, or rather engraved on wax
a few stories told by Ishi (these cylinders were recently
discovered and have been transferred to magnetic tape).
They filmed him constructing a summer shelter, breaking a block
of obsidian, fashioning an arrow head, shooting an arrow with a bow,
and so on. This priceless document was unfortunately stored
in an overheated area for decades and was destroyed in its canister.
Photographs, however, have come down to us, especially
those taken during an expedition to the traditional home of the
Yahi in 1914 which was put together by Waterman and Kroeber with
the assistance of Doctor Pope (who had become a great friend of Ishi).
The native American was moved by the idea of once again laying
eyes on this land, haunted by the spirits of his tribe's dead.
By an odd psychological reaction, Ishi felt quite guilty about
having robbed and even having attempted to kill these white men
who now welcomed him to their ranches.
The fact that his own people had been hunted down
and annihilated did not lessen his shame, which he conveyed
to his friends.
Following Ishi's indications, the small group visited the sites
revered by the Yahi, the villages and rocky shelters where they
had concealed themselves. He described the way he and his family
had lowered themselves along the cliffs' steep walls to the torrent
below. They fished, hunted, bathed. He candidly shared with his
friends the secrets of the life he had led. More was learned
in a few weeks about the existence of a "hunter-gatherer"
from a Neolithic society than in decades of archaeological digs.

Ishi's death

Other excursions in the field like this one could not be mounted. The following year, Ishi, who had contracted pneumonia during his early contacts with white men, began to cough ominously.

Bacteriological analyses showed the presence of tuberculosis. As soon as the illness was diagnosed, Waterman had the Oceanic objects displayed in one sunny gallery placed in cases and the room transformed into a more comfortable bedroom for the sick man. Unfortunately the best care proved useless. Tuberculosis quickly overcame Ishi's resistance. He died, surrounded by his friends from the museum, on March 25, 1916. He was cremated, according to the custom of his people. His American friends placed his ashes in a small black terracotta urn produced by the Pueblo Indians of New Mexico and on which they had these words inscribed, "Ishi, the last Yana Indian. 1916."

Doctor Pope pronounced his eulogy, solemnly affirming the following: "Stoic and fearless, America's last wild Indian has left us, writing the word END at the bottom of a chapter in history. For him, we were complicated children, intelligent but lacking wisdom, knowing many things, many of which were wrong. He knew nature which never lies... Life had frustrated him, yet he harbored no bitterness in his heart. His was the soul of a child, the mind of a philosopher."

Ishi carving a piece of juniper to make a bow. 1914.

THE NORTH AMERICAN INDIANS

As popular as comic strip and movie characters as they are ill-known in reality, the North American Indians amply deserve the kind of attention that is normally given only to the more spectacular civilizations of Mexico, Peru and Bolivia—especially in the wake of all the celebrations (and reassessments) marking the five hundredth anniversary of Columbus' historic voyage.

For such a subject, there could be no better introduction than the bitter yet dignified words of Ohiyesa, a Dakota Indian writer better known by his American name, Charles Eastman: "The first American mingled with his pride a singular humility. Spiritual arrogance was foreign to his nature and teaching. He never claimed that the power of articulate speech was proof of superiority over the dumb creation; on the other hand, it is to him a perilous gift. ... He believes profoundly in silence—the sign of a perfect equilibrium. Silence is the absolute poise or balance of body, mind, and spirit. The man who preserves his selfhood, ever calm and unshaken by the storms of existence – not a leaf, as it were, astir on the tree; not a ripple upon the surface of shining pool—his, in the mind of the unlettered sage, is the ideal attitude and conduct of life. If you ask him: 'What is silence?' he will answer: 'It is the Great Mystery!' 'The holy silence is His voice!' If you ask: 'What are the fruits of silence?' he will say: 'They are self-control, true courage or endurance, patience, dignity and reverence. Silence is the cornerstone of character.' ... Alas, into the silent life of the North American Indians we have sown the seeds

Troglodytic houses made by the ancestors of the Pueblo Indians in the 11th to 13th centuries. Anasazi culture. Canyon de Chelly National Monument.

of noise, of haste, at the same time as we introduced books, gunpowder and a thousand strange follies. In the words of Sun Chief, a Hopi born in the previous century, 'I have now learnt that a person thinks with their head instead of their heart.'"

The remarkable survival of indigenous American cultures in spite of persecution, genocide and brutal deportation bears witness to the intellectual and moral vitality of these peoples whose ancestors created superb works of art that are virtually unknown to the general public. I hope that these works, which are the heart of this chapter, will inspire due respect for these "unlettered" peoples whose harvesting of the "fruits of silence" we have cut short.

Childhoods of the fourth continent

It is now generally accepted that the peoples who came to be known as "Indians" for the simple reason that, on reaching America, Columbus believed he had found the Western route to India (an idea he clung to for the rest of his life), came over to the continent in successive waves, crossing what is now the Bering Strait between glacial periods.

In other words, the Indians came from Siberia. The pioneers reached Alaska 30,000 years ago at the earliest although, according to evidence from an archeological site in Texas, human presence on the continent goes back at least 37,000 years.

It took the migrants no more than a few millennia to work their way down to South America. The last to arrive were no doubt the Inuits (Eskimos), who have remained in the far north of the New Continent to the present day.

Equipped with tools and weapons made from wood, bone, flint or other hardstones, these nomadic hunters and gatherers of wild berries lived much as the ancestors of today's Europeans did, progressing from chipped stone to polished stone.

The "cultural revolution" that occurred in the Near East when nomads became sedentary and learned how to cultivate wild plants

Stone mask (funerary object?). Hopewell culture. 200 BC-400 AD. H. 6$^{1/4}$". Museu Barbier-Mueller Art Precolombi, Barcelona.

was paralleled in America. At around 5000 BC, Western Europeans and these future "Indians" were at comparable levels of development. But just as the Vikings never built a Parthenon or a Sistine Chapel, so the inhabitants of the deserts, plains and forests north of the Rio Grande never built any temples like those of the Maya, decorated with impressive sculptures. Nor did they develop a script to record the discoveries of their wise men. However, they did create goods and religious objects which clearly express their aesthetic concerns.

The first great religions of North America

The first hunters of the plains and forests had no bows and arrows. Instead they used flint tips on the end of short spears which they threw using a kind of launcher which they later balanced by fixing a sculpted object in a suitable position.

These early tribes consisted of only a small number of individuals, sometimes as many as several hundred of them divided up into autonomous groups.

In those days the Great Plains were covered in thick forest. The country was inhabited by animals that are now extinct: giant bears and bison, horses (which would later be reintroduced by the White Man), camels, four-horned antelopes, mastodons and mammoths. Many of these species did not survive the end of the Ice Age, some 10,000 years ago. Others were most certainly exterminated by man. The result was that there were no animals capable of pulling a cart or carrying a rider. There could be no intensive plowing.

Dwindling game made these North Americans highly receptive to lessons from Mexico, where they were trying to domesticate a wild plant that yielded an ear about as thick as a finger—corn.

This crop was cultivated and improved by hybridization, as were squashes, to varying degrees of intensiveness, but only in the central and eastern areas. Otherwise the Pacific seaboard remained home, in California, to eaters of shellfish, berries, and to the north, in Canada and Alaska, to sedentary fishermen.

This ritual object (function unknown) was made from a sheet of native copper. Caddoan culture, Mississippi period. 1200-1400 AD. H. 9¹/²". Ohio Historical Society, Columbus, US.

In this chapter, we will focus mainly on the prehistory of the forest regions of the east and desert southwest, for the civilizations of the central plains produced little in the way of noteworthy art.

The eastern plains and forests

Based as it is on Westerns and children's books and comics, our image of the "Plains Indians" (occupying the area between the Mississippi and the Great Lakes on one side and the Rocky Mountains on the other) has them galloping around on horses and hunting bison.

Before Columbus and colonization, the story was very different indeed: a tale of modest villages and farming folk. This all changed when these semi-sedentary peoples captured and started breeding the horses that escaped from Spanish stud farms.

They now became superb riders, rediscovering the ways of their nomadic ancestors.

Culturally speaking, the Plains Indians were not exactly advanced. They were influenced by the people of the Woodlands, a huge forest area to the east of the Mississippi whose several periods of development, beginning with the Archaic phase (reaching its apogee between 3000 and 1000 BC), developed traditions that would endure until the modern age – for example, the practice of making stone pipes, the forerunners of the well-known peace pipe.

The Adena-Hopewell cultures

In the past, the presence of numerous mounds gave rise to a belief in the development of a single civilization of moundbuilders. However, we now know that were several different cultural centers

a: The Archaic period of Eastern Woodlands civilization. Among the sma[ll] masterpieces it has bequeathed to us we find the pendant-like objec[t] known as bannerstones and disks, or "bow ties," with a hole throug[h] These pieces were made by abrasion using the finest and hardest stone[s] They could serve as a counterweight for the spear thrower. The birdston[e] shown here may date back to 1500 BC.

b: The culture of the Woodlands, a term commonly used to designate th[e] forest regions of the Eastern United States, came after the Archaic perio[d] The transition between the two is marked by the renowned site of Povert[y] Point in Louisiana, which has several enormous earth mounds dating ·fro[m] 500 BC—technically still in the Archaic period, but at the dawn of a ne[w] age whose most representative culture is named after the Adena site. Th[e] Adena, who lived mainly in southern Ohio, Kentucky and Pennsylvania were to create some of the finest wooden sculptures that paved the wa[y] for the Woodlands culture of the following millennium. The finest exampl[e] from this period is the so-called "goitrous" pipe.

c: The "Middle Period," beginning in the late 1st century BC, left behin[d] mounds which, at their lowest level, contain a funeral chamber made o[f] logs covered with a mound of earth about 33 feet high. There was a varian[t] of the Hopewell civilization in Illinois which may have derived from the ol[d] "Red Paint" culture. The uniformity of belief systems is attested by this cul[-] ture's stone pipes, clay figures and ritual objects cut from natural sheets o[f] mica.

d: The Mississippi culture appeared in about 700 AD on either side of th[e] great river which gave it its name. Mexican influence is clearly manifest i[n] the disk shown here (used as an ornamental breastplate), made fro[m] imported shell. This influence also inspired the construction of steppe[d] mounds as the foundations of temples and high status houses. Funerary tumuli are less frequent. Pipes and vases in the form of human heads wer[e] made from both terracotta and stone. This period ended only with the arri[-]

Opposite:
works from, a: the
Archaic period, b:
the Adena culture,
c: the "Middle
Period" of the
Woodlands culture

a

c

b

d

after the Archaic period. Among these were the Adena and Hopewell cultures, around the first century AD, whose development remains somewhat ill defined.

Hopewellian objects have for example been found in New York State. During this period the pipe bowls became miniature sculptural masterpieces, depicting figures and animals, the oldest examples being set into a kind of curved base. (In addition to having medicinal qualities, tobacco no doubt had its own special rituals.)

Finally, this period also saw the development of pottery with decorations in relief.

Hammered copper religious objects made from native minerals perpetuated an ancient tradition originating in the Great Lakes region. And it is because some of these objects found their way into tombs, where their salts preserved the fabrics from rotting, that we are aware of a highly refined textiles tradition. Copper plate was still being produced a thousand years later.

Apart from their "stone masks" (see p. 368), the most remarkable objects produced by the Hopewell culture were hands and bird talons cut from sheets of mica. Their purity is absolutely unique. These too were placed in tombs.

The Mississippi culture

In around 700 BC, after an inactive period, the Woodlands experienced a cultural revival which, it is thought, was stimulated by contact with Mexican traders. This was towards the end of the period when the civilization centered on the city of Teotihuacán dominated an extensive area that included present-day Guatemala, then occupied by the Maya.

The new civilization that grew up during the next two or three centuries takes its name from one of its great rivers.

The Mexican influence is manifest in the squared mounds on which wooden temples were built. Sometimes, as at Cahokia in Illinois, such mounds could be up to 98 feet high. The base of the biggest

"Historic" pipe in soft stone with lead inlays from the Great Lakes region. 19th century. D. 4³/₄". Musée Barbier-Mueller, Geneva.

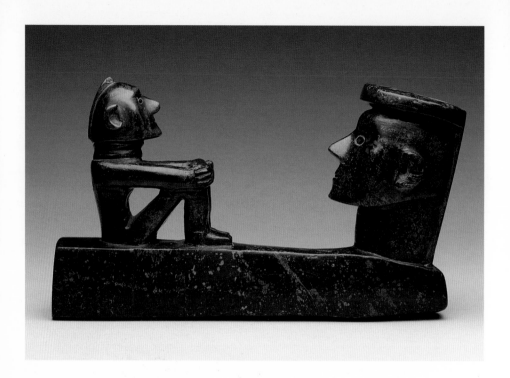

mound at Cahokia forms a rectangle measuring 656 feet by 984 feet, making it bigger than even the biggest Egyptian pyramids.

In addition to such religious edifices, funeral mounds continued to be built and the death of high-status figures always meant the sacrifice of dozens of their servants and concubines, who were expected to follow them into the afterlife. They thus extended the principle underlying the customs of the Hopewell culture, in which the rich took all their wealth with them when they died (this was confirmed by the discovery of a tomb containing huge quantities of obsidian, which was extremely rare in the Woodlands).

If Cahokia was typical of the North Mississippi era, then Moundville, in Alabama, is its southern counterpart. The remarkable polished stone objects found here include one-piece axes with sculpted handles, bowls and animal effigy pipes.

The Eastern Woodlands are known for their large production

of pottery and, above all, for the stone statues whose size, as much as 20 inches high, is very much the exception in North America, where there was a marked preference for small, refined objects.

The advent of the so-called "Southern Cult" around 1000 AD was accompanied by some fine terracotta works of art such as vases representing trophy heads or squatting or sitting figures.

Shell ornaments were common and some discs, no doubt worn as breastplates, had engraved decoration: the inset about the prehistory of the forest land (p. 374-375) shows one depicting a warrior, or perhaps priest, running, holding a severed head in his right hand and in his left head a knife or scepter of the kind found in certain Mississippian tombs. This theme, which was linked to the magic practice of headhunting, belongs to the Mexican repertoire.

In Florida, superb wooden sculptures have fortunately survived the humid climate: the feline shown here is one of the masterpieces of pre-Columbian art.

To the west of the Mississippi, a civilization influenced by that of the Woodlands was created by speakers of the Caddoan language (Sioux family).

The ancestors of the Pawnee and Wichita Indians were also participants in this tradition. At the time they were a sedentary farming people. One of their finest sites is the famous Spiro Mound, which has yielded such remarkable treasures as a human face surmounted by two antelope's horns and a stone pipe forming a highly realistic representation of a man beheading a victim.

Mississippian civilization was created by groups with widely divergent origins and languages. Among them, we could mention the ancestors of the Cherokee (related to the Iroquois of New York State) and the predecessors of the Creeks, whom Hernando de Soto encountered during his travels in 1540 and whose idiom belongs to the Muskogian family.

However, this civilization made little mark in the plains which, at the time, were covered by high grass that D. Snow has described

Sandstone figure. Late Mississippi period. 1300-1500 AD. H. 18¼". Frank H. McClung Museum, Knoxville, US.

as "merely" a marginal extension of the Eastern Woodlands.
The plains villages were protected by palisades and the houses were
heavy wood constructions built to withstand the freezing winter.
In the southern Great Plains, in Texas for example, the dwellings
were lighter. Social organization was tribal and there were no
kingdoms like those of the Natchez. Nomads continued to live
alongside the farming villages, and it was they who began buying
horses from the tribes in the western desert, who themselves had
dealings with the Spaniards starting in the early 17th century.
In a few decades they acquired a reputation as superb horsemen
and fearless warriors. This would soon be challenged by the exploits
of the Crow, whose sedentary way of life was transformed by the
acquisition of horses.
In contrast, the tribes of the Missouri valley continued to live in their
villages and practice farming.

The Southwest U.S.A.

In around 10000 BC, the region between the Rocky Mountains and
the Sierra Nevada (beyond which lies California) started to become
increasingly arid. Its inhabitants had to adapt or perish.
Thus the "desert culture" that existed in around 8000 BC was one
of berry-gathering hunters of small animals. These people already
mastered basketry but had yet to attain the refinement that came
in around 2000 BC with the technique of superimposing pieces of
wicker that were themselves bound with fine strips of fiber. The best
known site of this desert culture is Danger Cave in the Great Basin,
whose small wooden figures anticipate the amulets made in later
millennia.
It is thought that the desert culture was the cradle of the different
civilizations of the Southwest, as inflected through contact with
Mexico and the resulting introduction of corn and other plants,
such as squashes.
Between northern Utah and the Mexican border the landscape

Cliff Palace pre-
Columbian ruins,
Mesa Verde,
Colorado, US.
Anasazi culture.

varies considerably, from the winter cool of the conifer-clad mountains (Flagstaff Arizona is more than 6,500 feet above sea level) to the torrid heat of the desert lowlands with their cacti and rattlesnakes. The Southwest is the only region of the United States where stone-based architecture developed. As for ceramics, the oldest example found here, at Vakki, near the confluence of the Colorado and its tributary the Gila River, dates from 300 BC, which (as far as we know) indicates that the area was a thousand years behind the Mexican Altiplano.

Hakataya culture

Much less well known than those that followed it, this prolongation of the desert culture occupied a huge swathe of land from the Pacific coast (at the southern extremity of California) and the center of Arizona. Contemporaries of the Mogollon, Hohokam and Anasazi, the Hakataya were farmers who tried to surmount the harsh conditions of their sweeping desert homeland, but without quite managing to create the irrigation channels perfected by the Hohokam. This culture was probably a continuation of the Amargosa culture, which saw the development of the first pottery.

Mogollon culture

The first Mogollon villages appeared in around 200 BC, between southwestern Arizona and southern New Mexico. They are small and their circular houses are half-underground. Given their mountainous, forest-covered land, the Mogollon at first used agriculture occasionally as a way of supplementing their diet of berries. They never produced as much corn as their neighbors. Serious food shortages in around 500 AD were followed two centuries later by a period of expansion. Simple pottery designs were embellished. Villages retained their defensive character until around the end of the first millennium.

Also up to this time, they built kiva, those famous underground rooms for religious and other community needs. The kiva built at the turn of the second millennium were much bigger and were copied from the Anasazi, the Mogollons' northern neighbors. Also around this time a tradition of beige ceramics with black decoration developed in southern New Mexico. This famous local culture took its name from the Mimbres, the small river running through the valley at its center.

Hohokam culture

Established to the west of the Mogollon, in the desert that can still be seen around the town of Phoenix, Arizona, the Hohokam were the ancestors of the Pima and Papago Indians, who spoke Azteco-Tanoan languages. Their origins go back several centuries before the Common Era, which is when they started building villages.

This sedentary people produced pottery whose simple decoration gradually became more sophisticated as a result, especially, of mixing with Mogollon and Anasazi immigrants. This is exemplified by the "Salado culture" of around 1300 AD.

They wove cotton, as was done throughout the Southwest, and eventually began building large rectangular houses with walls in adobe (a mixture of earth and straw).

The Salado, who were related to the Hohokam, built great places with several stories, like the one at Casa Grande, south of Phoenix (not to be confused with the Mogollon Casa Grandes in Mexico).

Anasazi culture

This culture is rooted in ancient traditions. In 700 BC the south of Utah and Colorado was occupied by the "Basket Makers," a branch of the desert culture.

Up to the middle of the first millennium, they made no pottery and hunted using spears, instead of the bows and arrows of their neighbors, the Mogollon. They lived mainly in natural rock shelters and their huts were at first very crude. However, the Modified

Following pages (clockwise from top left): Mimbres-style bowl from New Mexico. Mogollon culture. Circa 1100 AD. The hole was made as part of the ritual before placing it in the tomb. D. 10". Bowl representing the Salado culture, due to an Anasazi incursion into Hohokam territory (1300 AD. D. 8¾"). Sikyatiki jar from New Mexico. Hopi people. 16th century. D. 15½". Tularosa-style jar. Anasazi culture. Circa 1100 AD. H. 7½".

Basket Maker period, beginning in around 400 AD, saw the advent of pottery and pit houses. There was also large-scale agriculture, without reliance on irrigation systems.

In the 8th century, the pit houses disappeared. Villages began to take form but they continued to dig out underground chambers as religious meeting places.

These large kivas can still be seen beside the walls of houses in such Anasazi sites as the Cliff Place at Mesa Verde, Colorado.

Chaco Canyon has the ruins of several settlements that could be described as towns. Pueblo Bonito assembles over 800 houses on a four-acre site.

Built before the Mogollon took them up, the large kivas here measured up to 65 feet across and their earth roofs supported by wooden beams (which have disappeared from the ruins open to visitors) could weigh as much as a hundred tons when the ground was waterlogged.

There was only one kiva for each town, but each clan had its own small kiva. All these dark chambers were used for practices that are still current today, including among the Hopi (whose language belongs to the Uto-Aztec family mentioned above and whose pottery comes out of a long-standing tradition including the fine Sikyatki jars of the 15th and 16th centuries.

The Northwest coast

Stylistically, this is the best-known of the North American cultural areas, its famous totem poles appearing regularly in cartoons to denote the "generic" religious art of United States Indians, whether in the plains or in the eastern forests.

In fact, though, these areas never produced any monumental art, or even anything more than a half foot high!

Totem poles on the Northwest coast. The faces related the tribe's myths. British Columbia, Canada.

Characteristic of the Northwest coast (nowadays shared between Alaska and Canada), this particular style would appear to go back many centuries.

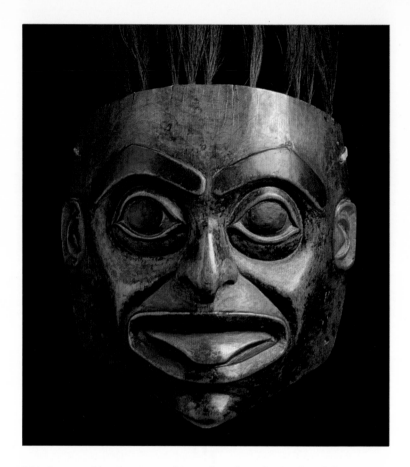

Frontlet in the form of a human face. These "masks" were worn by shamans when performing their magical and divinatory functions. Tlingit tribe, 19th century. British Columbia. Painted wood, horsehair. H. 7". Collected circa 1880 by Emmons. Formerly Museum for the American Indians, New York. Musée Barbier-Mueller, Geneva.

This is proved by the stone objects found on the banks of the Fraser River, which mark the southern limit of the expansion of the Athapaskan-speaking peoples, the ancestors of the well-known Tlingit, Haida and Tsimshian tribes.

The symbols (most often animal forms) that are such a rich presence in the art of the Northwest coast have a heraldic, totemic value. For example, when an important man died his kin would commission commemorative sculptures depicting the legendary animals emblematic of his clan either in full, by a detail or by allusions and abstract motifs intelligible only to the initiated. Witness the fine blankets made by the Chilkat, a sub-tribe of the Tlingit.

An incredible quantity of masks was also produced right into the early 20th century, until Western civilization began to pollute the Pacific coast that, hitherto, had been encroached on solely by fur buyers and gold prospectors, or a few pioneering ethnographers and collectors.

Often, these masks did not entirely cover the face but were worn on the forehead (see opposite page and p. 393).

That is why they are called *frontlets*. They were part of the equipment of the shamans, priests who, like their counterparts in Siberia, mastered the art of ecstasy. Indeed, there are many similarities between the shamanistic rites of certain Athapaskan tribes and those of their distant Siberian cousins. There is a kind of ceremonial dish that is used only by the Gilyak in Russia and the Tlingit in Alaska.

The Northwest coast was also the scene of a surprising tribal ritual, potlatch, a custom involving the organizing of ruinously extravagant feasts and offering one's guests splendid gifts.

Potlatch feasts were held with some regularity in these rich coastal societies. Hosts would even destroy valuable objects in order to enhance their prestige, and to force their guests to hold an even more ruinous feast. This system ultimately served as a kind of economic regulator, preventing certain clans from becoming too wealthy.

From the mid-19th century, white settlers' interest in local sculpture led to commercial mass production. The availability of sophisticated metal tools inspired native Indians artists to experiment with rarely used materials such as stone.

Reduced scale totem poles were made in a fairly soft, black material, argillite. The oldest examples are still of high quality because they were made by traditional sculptors.

Production of masks and other ritual objects also increased in the same proportions.

The revival being witnessed today as a result of some remarkable Indian artists has taken this productive frenzy to new heights, and stylistic traditions have inevitably suffered somewhat as a result. However gladdening in itself, this renaissance should therefore not be allowed to overshadow the antique totem poles, superb textiles, masks and paintings from old religious buildings to be seen in the museums of North America, or any of the countless objects that have made the Northwest coast one of the magical cradles of human creativity, home for many centuries to the most original forms of genius.

A Tlingit shaman with a frontlet and cape. Late 19th century.

Geography and politics

The geographical divisions shown here are necessarily schematic. In some regions the way of life remained unchanged for thousands of years while in others it was transformed by the technologies and knowledge acquired from the more developed Mexican neighbors, as with the cultivation of corn among the farmers in the forest of the East and Southwest.

The same influences also prompted the emergence of new religious rituals and prompted the construction of places of worship such as the pyramids of the eastern civilizations or the full-fledged cities whose ruins can be seen in the Southwest. These pre-Columbian cultures, which are succinctly described further on, are indicated here by letters:

An = Anasazi   A = Adena

Ho = Hohokam   H = Hopewell

Mo = Mogollon   M = Mississippi

Contact with the white man was initially a matter of chance but then occurred as rival colonial powers sought to make alliances. Some tribes sided with the English, others with the French. In the Western Plains, however, the long period of peace was brought to a brutal end by the 1849 Gold Rush.

Tribes of North America

Following Sapir's analysis, it is generally accepted that the countless languages spoken by the natives of the United States and Canada belong to five main families: Algonquin-Wakashan, Hokan-Sioux, Penute-Nadene, Aztecan-Tanoan and Eskimo. Between the Arctic and Mexico, the tribes themselves (sometimes no bigger than a few dozen members) spoke some 500 idioms.

This simplified map shows the best-known tribes. The existence of "plains regions" and "forest regions" (map p. 394) requires particular attention, for it was essentially the plains Indians, nomadic hunters and gatherers of berries who dwelled along the great rivers who later became formidable horsemen. The forest Indians were more likely to travel by canoe. It was in the eastern forests that they built the enormous pyramids copied from those in Mexico. Nothing like this existed among the plains Indians, who substituted teepees for their rustic huts.

In the Southwest, other nomads (Apache, Navajo) lived alongside the sedentary tribes who built the only cities of the pre-Columbian U.S. Their ruins are can be seen in Arizona and Colorado. Walking around here is a magical experience—if you can avoid the tourists!

The mysteries of
NIAS ISLAND

Over the last century, more than 300 books have been written about Nias, a tiny island in the Indian Ocean situated an overnight boat ride from the coast of Sumatra. And yet the strange stone monuments to be found there remain little known. It is in the hope of righting this injustice that the author has donated to France, for exhibition in the Louvre, an important stone statue representing a highly venerated village chief, dating from the end of the 18th century of the beginning of the 19th.

In fact, the people of Nias were just as skilled at portraying their great lords in wood, but this chapter does not aim to present all the art forms produced by this aristocratic society which has only recently disappeared.

The Niassians kept the spears, shields and "headhunter necklaces" that belonged to their ancestors up to 1980, but by now, at the turn of the third millennium, very nearly everything has been sold.

Austronesian expansion

Limestone gowe salawa statue from the Lasara region, probably representing an illustrious elder of the Daeli clan. 18th-19th century. Musée du Louvre, Paris. Donated by Monique and Jean Paul Barbier-Mueller.

The inhabitants of Nias speak only dialects belonging to the western branch of the Austronesian family, formerly known as Malayo-Polynesian.

The Austronesians left southern China some 5,000 years ago.

The oldest traces of their migration were found on Taiwan, where they probably stopped before reaching the northern Philippines.

It was long thought that this expansion involved only small groups of

navigators. Today, given the fact that Austronesian languages cover
a huge expanse that stretches from Madagascar in the west to Easter
Island in the east, specialists now believe they migrated in large
numbers and were thus able to impose certain techniques and beliefs,
as well as their language, on minority peoples, whom they absorbed.
This phenomenon can be compared to the Celtic expansion of the
1st millennium BC. Indo-European languages eliminated all but the
tiny preserve of Basque culture. Likewise, the Austronesian expansion
left small islets of non-Austronesian cultures.

For example, Papuan languages are spoken mainly in the highlands
of New Guinea, but also in parts of other islands such as Timor, Alor
and Solor, in Bougainville (the Solomon Islands, Melanesia).

One remarkable fact about Nias, which neighbors the Batak region
of northern Sumatra, is that no one has ever discovered any cut or
polished stone tools there. This tends to suggest that the population
of Nias arrived during the first millennium BC, during the Bronze Age,

A stone seat of honor

Stone seat called *osa osa si sara mbagi*. Central-western part of the island. 18th-20th centuries. H. 30″. Musée Barbier-Mueller, Geneva.

Throughout Nias Island there were special rituals or feasts that individuals could organize in order to climb the social ladder to a higher grade. On such occasions, members of the nobility—i.e., the family of the village chief—were carried on wooden thrones in the form of a dragon. Their triumph would be commemorated by carving a stone seat. However, this practice was limited to a small part of south-eastern Nias. With its dragon head symbolizing the god of the underworld and bird's tail symbolizing the celestial divinity, this mythological creature embodies the cosmic totality. Some thrones have two or even three heads. These monuments were placed outside the house of their owner to indicate their superior grade.

and not before. Having no copper ore (and no iron or gold either, for that matter) on their small island, the Niassians developed trading relations with other Austronesians, notably the Malays, whom we know to have been adventurous, and who sailed from island to island taking iron, bronze and gold weapons as well as fabrics to those who had none.

These precious goods were exchanged for local products. In the 18th century, women from Nias were admired for their beauty in the small sultanates dotted along the Sumatran coast, and Arab or Malay merchants paid high prices for them to village chiefs in the south of Nias. These chiefs in turn obtained these human chattels by raiding the poorer central area of the island.

Nias is usually divided into three regions: the rich South, the Center, where the "first man" came down from the skies, and the North, which includes the geographic center of the island. The far north was largely uninhabited, except by fleeing slaves.

Social and religious organization

Society throughout the island of Nias was divided up into three classes: the aristocracy, represented by the hereditary chief of the village and his kin (*siulu*), freemen (*sato*) and slaves. As with the Batak people of Sumatra, this third category comprised insolvent debtors, serious offenders against customary laws and prisoners taken in battle. Its members had no rights. The god of the upper world was Lowalangi, symbolized by a bird. The infernal divinity of the underworld was symbolized by a snake, a crocodile or

a composite monster known as the lasara. Lowalangi brought life, Lature Dano death. But, like the Indian Shiva, this terrible divinity was also the agent of renewal, thanks to whom rice germinated. This powerful dualism is expressed (albeit in a manner that has yet to be clearly explained) in certain monuments such as the wooden "seats of honor" on which certain great nobles were carried aloft. These osa osa have the head of the dragon lasara and the tail of the heavenly bird, thus illustrating the fusion of the two divinities in a cosmic totality.

Each Niassian was required to prove his courage. Headhunting was one way of demonstrating prowess, and the trophies thus accumulated brought prosperity to the entire village.

This vintage photograph, the only one we have showing a *bale* (meeting house for male villagers), was taken in the south of Nias by the Italian explorer Modigliani in around 1880. Note the skull trophies hanging from the edge of the roof. Barbier-Mueller archives, Geneva

The skulls of victims were hung along the roof of the men's meeting house and stone representations of the trophies were made to perpetuate the memory of the exploit. The chiefs' houses in the southern part of the island grew to considerable size, reflecting the wealth of their owners. This was also

demonstrated by an abundant production of gold jewelry. Monolithic monuments and gold ornaments were made during feasts held to increase the prestige of the organizer and raise their standing (or grade) in the social hierarchy.

Nobles were able to hold more feasts than commoners, and thus rise further up the social ladder. Also, gold ornaments were forbidden to commoners: hence the existence of identical finery in brass.

Stone architecture and monuments

A curious feature of the big southern villages is that they are dotted with stone monuments that are neither sculpted nor decorated, similar to megaliths elsewhere in the world. They are dolmens, stelae, pillars and giant stairways leading to the top of the hill where the village was built in an easily defendable position.

It is only in the central and lower northern parts of Nias that we find large quantities of stone statues representing either deceased chiefs or guardians watching over the peace of the village.

The stone chairs with one, two or three lasara heads are found only near the Susuwa and Gomo rivers, in the east-central area. Here the sight of villages, both deserted or still inhabited, is an astonishing one, their extravagant inventions in stone leaving visitors mute with amazement.

Modern Nias has converted to Christianity. Nevertheless there are certain surviving rites that the Muslim government of Jakarta would like to stamp out. In the Batak lands across the sea, churches have been destroyed and replaced by mosques. What with Islam on one side and torrential rains on the other, not much of Nias' extraordinary megalithic civilization is likely to be visible in a century from now.

Ama Barafe, the chief of a southern village, seen wearing his gold necklace and ancestral weapons. To his right, a stone column symbolizes his power. Ama Barafe died at the end of 1990, a few months after this photo was taken. He was over 90.

Row of mostly anthropomorphic statues
belonging to the Tohalawa clan
in the lower part of northern Nias.
This photograph dates from 1917 but
the monuments shown here were still intact
in 1990. Barbier-Mueller archives, Geneva.

EASTER ISLAND
Beyond the mystery

On Easter Day 1722, some 2,500 miles from the coast of South America and even further from the Marquesas at the center of Polynesia, the Dutch navigator Jacob Roggeveen spotted a small rocky island. It is not hard to imagine the astonishment of these Europeans when they discovered that the inhabitants of this islet, who had been isolated from the rest of the world for a thousand years or more, had, in their solitude, spent their time sculpting huge statues using only primitive stone tools, then dragging them long distances to the coast where they raised them erect. Nearly three centuries later, our sense of wonder is barely diminished by the snatches of information we have been able to acquire.

Two hundred years had gone by since Magellan had sailed around the southern tip of the Americas and entered the ocean that, no doubt in the hope of appeasing its violence, he named Pacific. Two centuries of maritime exploration and the discovery of numerous archipelagoes. And yet, people in 1722 still thought that there might be a great landmass somewhere between the New World and Asia. This assumption was all the more potent after 1687, when a freebooter named Davis spotted an unknown island off the coast of Peru. Relations were friendly, although the Europeans had as much trouble understanding the mentality of the islanders as the latter did their visitors. For the Rapanui, filching was an art form, and anything left unattended was immediately whisked away. We do not know how things suddenly turned sour. Perhaps a group of sailors were maddened by some barefaced larceny. Anyway, the fact is

Bas-relief evoking
the legendary
"bird-man." Every
year this title was
conferred on the
individual who
found the first egg
to be laid by
migrant birds
during their regular
return to the island.
The "birdman" was
sacred and lived in
isolation until his
successor was
chosen.

Preceding pages:
Dozens of stone
giants—doubtless
effigies of deified
ancestors, never
reached the shore
where they were to
be raised on plat-
forms built from big
blocks.

that the curious bystanders were mown down by musket fire and
Roggeveen's man had to dash back to their boats, taking no more than
a few provisions. They had time enough to glimpse the giant statues
that, even today, stand out against the clouds, but not to realize that
these were monoliths: they imagined them to have been modeled in raw
mud and then incrusted with stones. As Alfred Métraux later wrote,
"this was the first solution put forward for the mystery of Easter Island."
Later, the existence of these stone giants inspired all kinds of speculation.
While the navigators of the Enlightenment, such as Cook and La
Pérouse, assumed that these colossuses were raised using simple levers,
our contemporaries have been more imaginative. Among the more
far-fetched of their theories have been those of the Frenchman
Francis Mazière, for whom the statues were moved using anti-gravity

412

and electromagnetic forces, and the Swiss Erich von Däniken, who inferred extraterrestrial help.

On the edge of Polynesia

Easter Island is some 2,400 miles out to sea from the coast of Chile (to which it has been attached since 1888). It is also more than 2,500 miles from Tahiti. It thus occupies the eastern tip of the triangle formed by the Polynesian islands, whose combined landmass would (if we except New Zealand) cover about the same area as Switzerland. Roggeveen had been outrageously lucky to make landfall at this inhospitable reef measuring a mere 50 by 90 feet and bristling with rocks beyond which lay meadows and hills with no river to irrigate them. Nearly 50 years would pass before the arrival of the next visitor, the Spaniard Gonzalez, in 1770. This second exploration resulted in a topographical survey and a standard annexation. As subjects of His Majesty the King of Spain, the Rapanui were made to sign a treaty acknowledging their vassaldom. At the bottom of the document, then, they traced a few signs. One islander drew a bird-headed figure similar to the ones carved into the rocks. Was this signature the transcription of a name or a function? Should it be seen as proof of the existence of a system of writing? The more intuitive specialists continue to lose themselves in conjectures.

Like Roggeveen, Gonzalez saw the great statues and boat-shaped houses and observed that the nearly the whole island was treeless. The islanders raised chickens but also ate the large rats which abounded on the island. However, they had no pigs or cattle of any kind. Their real staples were bananas and roots: the taro, the yam, as found in other regions of Polynesia, but also the sweet potato, which occurs in this particular part of the Pacific and seems to have been imported from South America. This adds weight to the argument put forward by all those who, like the famous explorer and ethnographer Thor Heyerdahl, believe that the Rapanui were of American origin. Unfortunately for them, studies based on blood analysis and genetic indicators have

Following pages: Engraving showing 18th-century Europeans, the victims of theft on the island. Published by the navigator La Pérouse.

413

confirmed the peremptory assertions of the linguists: the population of Easter Island came from central Polynesia (no doubt the Marquesas). Archeology, oral traditions and glottochronology (which makes it possible to date the moment when two languages bifurcated) say that the population arrived during the first millennium AD—in other words, quite recently, and that this movement represented the last phase of expansion of peoples speaking the Malayo-Polynesian (Austronesian) languages, the oldest traces of which, dating back some five thousand years, have been detected in Taiwan.

We are familiar with Polynesian customs. Apart from the fact that these islanders certainly deserved to be known as the "argonauts of the Pacific," it is a proven fact that at times of tribal warfare the losers might leave their homeland with their wives, children and adequate supplies and sail in search of an uninhabited, hospitable shore where they could forget their shame.

The distances involved were enormous: Hawaii was peopled by Tahitian sailors less than a thousand years ago.

Monumental stone statues

The fleet of canoes commanded by the legendary king Hotu-Matua must have arrived on the island around about the time that Rome was falling under the onslaught of the Barbarians, near 500 AD.

This very approximate date marks the beginning of the "archaic period" for which we have located the villages and places of worship, the ahu, platforms on which, in those days, they had not begun to raise statues, and which may have been used as tombs. The stone colossuses do not appear until the "middle period," beginning some time around 1100 AD and ending in about 1680. During these centuries of prosperity the population may have risen to three or four thousand. In those days was covered with limited vegetation fed by abundant and fairly regular rain which allowed the islanders to survive there, for Rapanui (as the locals call both their island and themselves) had no springs or rivers. While there were large statues on the Marquesas, here they were

Stone tiki on the Marquesas Islands. The Rapanui came from today's French Polynesia. Their statues constitute a development of the ones here.

gigantic. Why such disproportion? Why this obsession with making things always bigger and heavier? Why this insistence on spending so much precious time (which could have been devoted to agriculture and fishing) on the Herculean task of hewing and dragging these several-ton blocks all the way to the platforms where they were raised up after yet more superhuman effort?

The answer is simple: by achieving the impossible, by surpassing themselves, they were giving their mythical ancestors, their temperamentally unpredictable gods, the most tangible proof of their respect, of the obedience and devotion of humans.

The images illustrating this short evocation and the accompanying captions give an idea of the task accomplished by this handful of islanders cut off from the rest of the world. But then is not every creator on this planet "cut off" from the rest of the world?

From this "middle period" there remain 600 statues, 150 of them unfinished and either lying around the quarries of volcanic stone or raised up on the hillsides, where they were heaved upright in order to sculpt their backs. The biggest one is 38 feet tall and weighs about a hundred tons. It has been calculated that it would have taken 30 men working full time a year to carve, then 90 men two months to transport it a distance of four miles and, finally, another three months to raise it up on its platform after adding its red stone "topknot" (*pukao*).

Wooden sculptures

A number of explanations have been offered regarding the method of transport. It is enough to recall that in those days the toromiro tree (a now extinct species of sophora) provided logs one foot and a half in diameter, although the species did not grow to much of a height. It was from toromiro that most of the statuettes and ceremonial objects made before the arrival of the Europeans were sculpted. Driftwood was rare, given the huge distances separating the island from the nearest landmasses.

The end of the heroic period. Genocide

The same questions have been asked regarding the blocks of stone in the pyramids and the Olmec statues in Mexico, which weigh over ten tons. In all these instances, the sculptors had very limited resources. It therefore seems more to the point to be amazed that the Olmecs or the Rapanui were able to conceive such monuments and then make them with their stone implements, rather than to marvel at the fact that they dragged them to their definitive emplacement.

According to one legend, the statue-making stopped when war broke out between two factions: the "long ears" and the "small ears." Specialists were soon struck by the oddness of such an explanation. In effect, all the islanders met by the first European seafarers had distended ear lobes; nobody ever saw a single representative of the "small ears." This would seem to suggest that the war mentioned here, which was highly likely, was between two tribes or confederations of tribes.

Whatever the reason, when Cook and La Pérouse visited the island in 1774 and 1786, respectively, the natives were no longer sculpting moai for the platforms shown in the 18th-century engravings. La Pérouse is clear about this: "There are no longer any chiefs important enough for a large number of men to busy themselves with preserving his memory by raising a statue to him." In 1869, what remained of Rapanui culture was tragically devastated when Peruvian traffickers captured virtually the whole population and forced them to work as slaves in the guano mines. In 1877, after this genocide, 110 Rapanui were repatriated. Ethnologists began to study their destroyed civilization. They spoke to the old men who had survived into the beginning of the 20th century. But it was not until the 1930s that a mission with considerable resources (the Lavachery-Métraux expedition) tried to gather a little information, and we are still a long way from understanding the past to which those monuments bear such striking witness—all the more striking because they speak only to our eyes.

Rapanui inscriptions

Before we leave Easter Island, there is one last, real mystery to be considered. It surrounds the score of tablets on which enigmatic signs have been engraved, like pictograms or hieroglyphs, which could be proof that this people, alone among the islanders of the Pacific, invented a system of writing. The name of these tablets, kohau rongorongo (kohau means "stick") indicates that they are a local transformation of the "minstrel's sticks" known in central Polynesia, on Mangareva and the Marquesas among other islands, where the same word is used, albeit for sticks without engravings on. Moreover, a Rapanui stick covered with signs identical to those in rows on the tablets is kept in Santiago. Most of the twenty-odd examples known to us are carved from driftwood, which tends to suggest that they do not predate the 19th century, when a fair number of European boats sailed in the waters of eastern Polynesia. One of them is indeed made from a fragment of poplar wood from an oar. The strange thing is that, all together, the tablets constitute a repertoire of nearly a thousand glyphs, or signs. A good third of these signs represent men, often carrying a stick or unknown object, and birds. They read from the bottom line, from left to right, then by turning the tablet round, from right to left, and so on. There would be no point in listing the various suppositions and theories prompted by the deciphering of these tables and of inscriptions engraved on other objects. Suffice to say here that these Rapanui glyphs have been compared to the inscriptions found during excavations of towns in the Indus region destroyed at the beginning of the 2nd millennium BC. The enigma remains and, thank God, nobody has suggested we solve it by referring to the Martian alphabet!

Opposite and following pages: A row of monumental statues that has been re-created on a restored platform. Over the centuries most of the giants near the shore were knocked down and even shattered. Their red stone "topknots" have been put back on the colossuses in this new row. We can see that the huge faces had shell eyes, a fact not suspected until recent discoveries.

Detail of one of the enigmatic "tablets" bearing an inscription which, scholars tentatively suggest, may display a pictogram-based script.

For the greater pleasure of archeologists, a certain number of giant statues remained in the quarries of volcanic stone, unfinished. This photograph gives us an idea of the way they carved out these effigies, some of which were more than 33 feet high. The front was carefully finished and the back was completed once the colossus had been moved.

Visiting Easter Island
(from the account of La Pérouse's voyage in 1786)

"Four or five hundred Indians were waiting for us on the shore: they were unarmed, a few were clad in pieces of white or yellow cloth but most of them were naked. Several of them were tattooed and their faces were painted red. Their cries and their physiognomy expressed their joy; they stepped forward to assist us and facilitate our descent ...

Soon, the soldiers were exposed to the rapacity of these islanders, whose number had by now grown. There were at least 800 of them, and in this number there were a good 150 women. The physiognomy of these women was pleasant. They offered their favors to all those who were ready to make them some gift.

The Indians entreated us to accept them. A few of them showed the pleasures that they could procure. They were separated from the onlookers by only a simple cloth blanket and, during this teasing, they removed the hats from our heads and the handkerchiefs from our pockets. They all seemed to be accomplices of the thefts that was committed ...

No one who has read the accounts of the latest travelers could take the Indians of the Southern Sea for savages; on the contrary, they have made great progress in civilization and I believe that they are as corrupt as they can be given their circumstances! The most brazen rascals of Europe are not as devious as these islanders..."

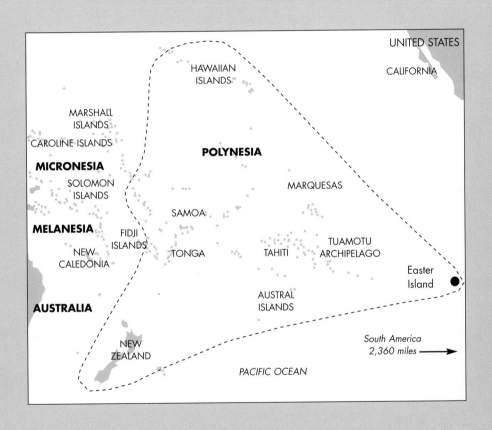

Select bibliography

THE CHILHOOD OF HUMANITY

COPPENS, Yves et al., *La plus belle histoire du monde*, Paris, Seuil, 1996.

GALLIEN, Claude-Louis, *Homo. Histoire plurielle d'un genre très singulier*, Paris, Presses universitaires de France, 1998.

LEROI-GOURHAN, André, *Préhistoire de l'art occidental*, pref. Yves Coppens, revised and enlarged by Brigitte and Gilles Delluc, Paris, Citadelles & Mazenod, 1995.

LUMLEY, Henry de, *L'Homme premier : préhistoire, évolution, culture*, Paris, Odile Jacob, 1998.

THE ART OF THE CYCLADES

The Art of the Cyclades. An Exhibition of Sculpture and Artifacts of the Early Cycladic Period : 3000-2000 B.C., New York, 1983.

GETZ-PREZIOSI, P., *Sculptors of the Cyclades. Individual and Tradition in the Third Millenium BC*, Ann Arbor, 1987.

THIMME, J., *Kunst der Kykladen*, Karlsruhe, 1976.

ZIMMERMANN, Jean-Louis, *Poèmes de marbre : sculptures cycladiques du musée Barbier-Mueller*, introd. Pat Getz-Preziosi, Geneva, 1993.

THE GREEK MIRACLE, FROM THE ORIGINS TO THE ARCHAIC PERIOD

DEMARGNE, Pierre, *Naissance de l'art grec*, revised and updated edition, Paris, Gallimard, "L'Univers des formes", 1985.

GREECE, FROM PERICLES TO ALEXANDER

PAPAIOANNOU, Kostas, BOUSQUET, Jean et al., *L'Art grec*, photos Jean Mazenod, reprint, Paris, Citadelles & Mazenod, 1975.

IN ITALY BEFORE THE ROMANS, THE ETRUSCANS

L'Art des peuples italiques 3000-300 ans av. J.-C., Hellas and Roma Association, Naples and Geneva, Electa Napoli, 1993.

CLES-REDEN, Sybille von, *Les Étrusques*, Paris, Arthaud, 1962.

THE IBERIANS

Les Ibères, (collective publication), Barcelone, AFAA, 1997.

LILLIU, Giovanni, *Civilisations anciennes du bassin méditerranéen. Corse, Sardaigne, Baléares, les Ibères*, Paris, Albin Michel, 1970.

THE ART OF THE CELTS

The Celts, (collective publication), Milan and Venice, Bompiani-Palazzo Grassi, 1991.

DUVAL, Paul-Marie, *Les Celtes*, Paris, Gallimard, "L'Univers des formes", 1985.

REPUBLICAN AND IMPERIAL ROME

ANDREAE, Bernard, *L'Art de l'ancienne Rome*, photos Jean Mazenod, Paris, Citadelles & Mazenod, 1988.

BIANCHI BANDINELLI, Ranuccio, *Rome : la fin de l'art antique : l'art de l'Empire romain de Septime Sévère à Théodose Ier*, trans. from the Italian by Jean-Charles and Evelyne Picard, Paris, Gallimard, "L'Univers des formes", 1970.

OUR ANCESTORS THE BARBARIANS

DURLIAT, Marcel, *Des Barbares à l'an mil*, Paris, Citadelles & Mazenod, 1985.

HUBERT, Jean, PORCHER, Jean and WORBACH W.F., *L'Europe des invasions*, Paris, Gallimard, "L'Univers des formes", 1967.

IMMORTAL EGYPT

MICHALOWSKI, Kazimierz, *L'Art de l'Égypte*, revised and enlarged by Jean-Pierre Corteggiani and Alessandro Roccati, trans. from the Italian by Monique Aymard, pref. Nicolas Grimal, Paris, Citadelles & Mazenod, 1994.

General Introduction Guide to the Egyptian Collection in the British Museum, Londres, British Museum, 1930.

THE ACHAEMENID EMPIRE OF PERSIA

GHIRSHMAN, Roman, *Perse : Proto-iraniens, Mèdes, Achéménides*, Paris, Gallimard, "L'Univers des formes", 1963.

THE OLMECS, THE DAWN OF MEXICAN ART

COE, Michael Douglas, *The Jaguar's children : Pre-Classic Central Mexico*, exhibition catalogue. 17 February-5 May 1965, New York, The Museum of Primitive Art, 1965.

Coe, Michael et Grove, David, *The Olmec and their Neighbors. Essays in Memory of Matthew W. Stirling,* ed. Elizabeth P. Benson, Washington, Dumbarton Oaks Research Library and Collections, trustees of Harvard University, 1981.

THE MAYA, GRANDEUR AND DECADENCE

Barbier, Jean Paul, *Guide de l'art précolombien,* pref. Carmen Fauria, Milan, Skira Editore, 1997.

Baudez, Claude François and Becquelin, Pierre, *Les Mayas,* Paris, Gallimard, "L'Univers des formes", 1984.

Benson, Elisabeth P., *The Maya World,* New York, Thomas Y. Crowell Company, 1977.

Coe, Michael, *The Maya,* Harmondsworth, 1971.

Stierlin, Henri, *Maya : Guatemala, Honduras et Yucatan,* Fribourg, Office du livre, 1964.

THE AZTECS, CHILDREN OF THE SUN

Barbier, Jean Paul, *Guide de l'art précolombien,* pref. Carmen Fauria, Milan, Skira Editore, 1997.

Matos Moctezuma, Eduardo, *Les Aztèques,* French translation by Pierre Janin, Lyon, La Manufacture, 1989.

Stierlin, Henri, *L'Art aztèque et ses origines: de Teotihuacan à Tenochtitlan,* Fribourg, Office du livre, 1982.

SPLENDORS OF PRE-HISPANIC PERU

Harcourt, R. d', *Les Textiles anciens du Pérou et leurs techniques,* Paris, Éditions d'art et d'histoire, 1934.

Lavallée, Danièle and Lumbreras, Luis Guillermo, *Les Andes : de la préhistoire aux Incas,* Paris, Gallimard, "L'Univers des formes", 1985.

Lumbreras, L.G., *The Peoples and Cultures of Ancient Peru,* Washington, Smithsonian Institution Press, 1979.

Lumbreras, L. G., *Chavin de Huantar, en el nacimiento de la civilizaciòn andina,* Lima, INDEA, 1990.

ISHI, THE CALIFORNIAN INDIAN

Kroeber, Theodora, *Ishi in two words. A Biography of the Last Wild Indian in North America,* Berkeley and Los Angeles, University of California Press, 1961.

THE NORTH AMERICAN INDIANS

Ancient Art of the American Woodland Indians, texts by David S. Brose, James A. Brown and David W. Penney, New York, Detroit Institute of Arts-Harry N. Abrams Inc. Publishers, 1985.

Frederic, Douglas H. and Arnoncourt, René d', *Indian Art of the United States,* New York, The Museum of Modern Art. 1941.

THE MYSTERIES OF NIAS ISLAND

Feldman, Jerome, *in Islands and Ancestors : Indigenous Styles of Southeast Asia,* ed. Jean Paul Barbier and Douglas Newton, New York, The Metropolitan Museum of Art/Geneva, Munich, Prestel-Verlag, 1988.

Viaro, Alain and Ziegler, Arlette, *in Messages de pierre : Statues et sculptures de l'Indonésie primitive dans les collections du musée Barbier-Mueller,* Milan, Skira Editore, 1999.

EASTER ISLAND, BEYOND THE MYSTERY

Chauvet, Stéphen, *L'Île de Pâques et ses mystères : la première étude réunissant tous les documents connus sur cette île mystérieuse,* Paris, Gallimard, 1935.

L'île de Pâques : une énigme, (collective publication), Brussels, Musées Royaux d'Art et d'Histoire, 1990.

Orliac, Catherine and Michel, *in Arts des Mers du Sud : Insulinde, Mélanésie, Polynésie, Micronésie. Collections du musée Barbier-Mueller,* edited by Douglas Newton, Paris, Adam Biro, 1998.

Acknowledgments

The publisher would like to thank all those without whom this book could not have existed: everyone at the Musée Barbier-Mueller, especially Laurence Mattet and Danièle Gardon, and Jean-François Revel for his particular interest in the book, as well as all those who helped with its production: the photographers Pierre-Alain Ferrazzini and Diane Bouchet (Studio Ferrazzini-Bouchet, Geneva), Laziz Hamani, A. and P. Mathé, Jean-Louis Sosna, Henri and Anne Stierlin, Keiichi Tahara; the agency AKG Photo, Paris; the Bibliothèque Nationale de France, Paris; the Laboratoire de Préhistoire et d'Histoire Naturelle, Paris; the photography library of the Réunion des Musées Nationaux, Paris; and all the many museums—too numerous to mention—who agreed to participate in the project.

Photography credits

Chronological table

	- 4500	- 4000	- 3500	- 3000	- 2500	- 2000	- 1500	- 1000	- 500	0	500	1000	1500	2000

The Art of the Cyclades *3200-2000 BC*

The Greek Miracle *2000-500 BC*

Greece, from Pericles to Alexander *500-323 BC*

In Italy before the Romans, the Etruscans *700-300 BC*

The Iberians *600-200 BC*

The Art of the Celts *1200-100 BC*

Republican and Imperial Rome *600 BC-476 AD*

Our Ancestors the Barbarians *300-1000 AD*

Immortal Egypt *3000-50 BC*

The Achaemenid Empire of Persia *500-250 BC*

The Olmecs, the Dawn of Mexican art *1300-200 BC*

The Maya, Grandeur and Decadence *200-900 AD*

The Aztecs, Children of the sun *1200-1500 AD*

Splendors of pre-Hispanic Peru *1500 BC-1500 AD*

Ishi, the Californian Indian *1850-1920 AD*

The North American Indians *10000 BC-1850 AD*

The Mysteries of Nias Island *1000 BC-1800 AD*

Easter Island, beyond the mystery *500-1800 AD*